LANGUAGE AND THE WORLD

LANGUAGE
AND THE WORLD

A Methodological Synthesis Within
the Writings of Martin Heidegger
and Ludwig Wittgenstein

By

GEORGE F. SEFLER

HUMANITIES PRESS
ATLANTIC HIGHLANDS, N.J.
1974

Sefler, George F.
   Language and the world.

   Bibliography: p.
   1. Languages—Philosophy. 2. Heidegger, Martin, 1889- 3. Wittgenstein,
Ludwig, 1889-1951.
   I. Title.
P106.S35   111   73-18045

ISBN 0-391-00228-7

To those who create my world . . .

Cecilia
John Francis
George Anthony

The *limits of my language* mean the limits of my world.
—Wittgenstein, *Tractatus*

Only where there is language, is there world. . . .
—Heidegger, *Hölderlin and the Essence of Poetry*

ACKNOWLEDGEMENTS

Appreciation is extended to all the publishers who granted permission to quote within this book materials from their publications.

A special acknowledgement is made to the following publishers for their kind permission to quote from the primary works of Martin Heidegger: Harper & Row and Basil Blackwell for *Being and Time;* Harper & Row for *Discourse on Thinking* and *What is Called Thinking?;* Neske and Harper & Row for *Unterwegs zur Sprache, Der Satz vom Grund, Nietzsche,* and *Vörtrage und Aufsätze;* Vittorio Klostermann for *Holzwege* and *Erläuterungen zu Hölderlins Dichtung;* Yale University Press for *An Introduction to Metaphysics,* translated by Ralph Manheim; Northwestern University Press for *Essence of Reasons;* Regnery for *What is a Thing?,* © 1967, translated by W. B. Barton, Jr. and Vera Deutsch.

Likewise, a special acknowledgement is made to the publishers of Ludwig Wittgenstein's primary works: Routledge & Kegan Paul and Humanities Press for *Tractatus Logico-Philosophicus,* translated by Pears and McGuinness; Basil Blackwell for *The Blue and Brown Books, Notebooks 1914-1916,* translated by G. E. M. Anscombe, *On Certainty,* translated by Denis Paul and G. E. M. Anscombe, *Philosophical Investigations, Remarks on the Foundations of Mathematics,* and *Zettel,* all translated by G. E. M. Anscombe.

In addition, gratitude is extended to these periodicals and publishers for permission to quote from the following articles about, commentaries on, and other works relating to writings of Heidegger and Wittgenstein: Basil Blackwell for articles in *Mind*—I. M. Copi, "Objects, Properties, and Relations in the *Tractatus,*" Vol. 67; E. Daitz, "Picture Theory of Meaning," Vol. 62; E. Evans, "*Tractatus* 3.1432," Vol. 64; G. E.

Moore, "Wittgenstein's Lectures in 1930-33," Vol. 64. The
American Catholic Philosophical Assoc.—Matthew Fairbanks'
"Wittgenstein and James," *The New Scholasticism,* Vol. 40;
R. C. Hinners' "Being and God in Heidegger's Philosophy,"
Proceedings of the ACPA, Vol. 31. *The Journal of Philosophy*
—Marjorie Glicksman, "A Note on the Philosophy of Hei-
degger," Vol. 35; J. Glenn Gray, "Heidegger's Being," Vol.
49; C. Hamburg, "Whereof One Cannot Speak," Vol. 50; A.
W. Levi, "Wittgenstein as Dialectician," Vol. 61; S. Zink,
"The Poetic Organism," Vol. 42. *The American Philosophical
Quarterly*—C. S. Chihara and J. A. Fodor, "Operationalism
and Ordinary Language," Vol. 2. *International Philosophi-
cal Quarterly*—D. O'Brien, "The Unity of Wittgenstein's
Thought," Vol. 6; A. DeWaelhens, "Reflections on the Development of Heidegger: Apropos of a Recent Book," Vol. 5.
Encounter—S. Toulmin, "Ludwig Wittgenstein," Jan., 1969.
Routledge & Kegan Paul and Macmillan—"Preface," *Essays
on Wittgenstein's 'Tractatus',* edited by I. M. Copi and Robert
Beard, © 1966. Yale University Press—Laszlo Versényi, *Hei-
degger, Being, and Truth.* Routledge & Kegan Paul—H. J.
Blackham, *Six Existentialist Thinkers.* Doubleday & Com-
pany—Frederick Copleston, *A History of Philosophy,* Vol. 8, ©
1966; J. Hartnack, *Wittgenstein and Modern Philosophy,* ©
1965. Martinus Nijhoff—E. Husserl, *Paris Lectures;* William
Richardson, *Martin Heidegger: From Phenomenology to
Thought;* V. Vycinas, *Earth and Gods.* Quadrangle Books—
Manfred S. Frings (ed.) , *Heidegger and the Quest for Truth;*
P. Thévenaz, *What is Phenomenology?* World Publishing
Company—Walter Kaufman (ed.) , *Existentialism From Dos-
toyevsky to Sartre,* © 1956; Bertrand Russell, *Bertrand Russell
Speaks His Mind,* © 1962. D. Reidel—Tullio De Mauro, *Lud-
wig Wittgenstein: His Place in and Influence on the History
of Semantics.* Duquesne University Press—Maxwell J. Charles-
worth, *Philosophy and Linguistic Analysis.* Prentice-Hall,
Inc.—Fernando Molina, *Existentialism as Philosophy,* © 1962.
Oxford University Press—Dallas High, *Language, Persons,
and Beliefs;* Norman Malcolm, *Ludwig Wittgenstein: A
Memoir,* and by permission of The Clarendon Press, Oxford,
James Griffin, *Wittgenstein's Logical Atomism,* © 1964. Lut-

terworth Press—John Macquarrie, *Martin Heidegger*. Hutchinson—G. E. M. Anscombe, *An Introduction to Wittgenstein's 'Tractatus'*. Bowes & Bowes and Humanities Press—Marjorie Grene, *Martin Heidegger*. Munksgaard—David Favrholdt, *An Interpretation and Critique of Wittgenstein's 'Tractatus'*. University of California Press—Alexander Maslow, *A Study in Wittgenstein's 'Tractatus'* reprinted by permission of the Regents of the University of California. Macmillan—M. King, *Heidegger's Philosophy*, © 1964. Basil Blackwell—Erik Stenius, *Wittgenstein's 'Tractatus'*; and Paul Engelmann, *Ludwig Wittgenstein: A Memoir and Letters*, translated by L. Furtmüller.

Finally, a thank you is extended to those publishers and individuals who granted permission to incorporate within this study various of their published quotations relevant to our basic themes: *Philosophy Today*—K. Tranoy, "Contemporary Philosophy: Analytic and Continental," Vol. 8. The Williams & Wilkins Co.—Percy Bridgman, "Operational Analysis," *Philosophy of Science*, Vol. 5. John Wild, "The Exploration of the Life-World," *Proceedings and Addresses of the APA*, Vol. 34. Cambridge University Press—Percy Bridgman, "The Nature of Some of Our Physical Concepts," *British Journal of the Philosophy of Science*, Vol. 1; René Descartes, *Philosophical Works of Descartes*, translated by Haldane and Ross; Gilbert Ryle, *Dilemmas*. Victor Gollancz Ltd.—A. J. Ayer, *Language, Truth and Logic*. The Belknap Press of Harvard University Press—Charles Sanders Peirce, *The Collected Papers of Charles Sanders Peirce*, edited by Hartshorne and Weiss. Harvard University Press—Susan K. Langer, *Philosophy in a New Key*. Routledge & Kegan Paul and University of California Press, by permission of the Regents of the University of California—Rudolf Carnap, *The Logical Structure of the World*. Macmillan—Percy Bridgman, *The Logic of Modern Physics*, © 1928. Houghton Mifflin Company—Archibald MacLeish, *Poetry and Experience*. George Allen & Unwin—Bertrand Russell, *An Inquiry Into Meaning and Truth* and "Philosophy of Logical Atomism," *Logic and Knowledge*.

PREFACE

The purpose of this book is to discern and elucidate certain features of structural congruence between the writings of Martin Heidegger and Ludwig Wittgenstein. No attempt is made herein to defend or criticize either man's writings at the respective expense or fortune of the other's. Moreover, to understand this work, the reader is expected neither to agree with nor to accept either Heidegger's position or Wittgenstein's, or both. The intent of this work is not to convert the reader toward an analytic or an existential viewpoint, but to present to him both viewpoints for a study of structural convergence. As a result, if the reader is to understand this work properly, he must approach it neither as a defense nor as a criticism of a specific philosophical perspective. Comprehension of this text requires that the reader disengage himself from his own philosophical leanings—be they existential, analytic, or whatever. Such will insure a proper methodological reading.

Comprehension of this work does, however, require a general knowledge of the works of both Heidegger and Wittgenstein. Since such a philosophical background is rare, each comparative chapter is prefaced with two expository chapters, one on Heidegger's texts germane to the comparison and one on Wittgenstein's. These chapters at best acquaint the reader with a superficial understanding of the texts crucial to the methodological investigations; in no way can they supplant the works of Heidegger and Wittgenstein. There is no substitution for a reading of the primary texts, and ideally any reader seriously interested in this study should consult the primary texts at length. No one ought to consider the expositional chapters as in-depth studies of either man's thoughts. It would be equally erroneous to view these chapters as critical commentaries of the two thinkers' ideas; they are predominantly elucidations.

I am especially indebted to Professors Wilfrid Desan and George L. Farre whose respective seminars in Heidegger and Wittgenstein, taught at Georgetown University, Washington, D.C., nurtured the original insights from which this work grew. I thank them and Professors H. D. Lewis and Thomas P. McTighe for their invaluable suggestions concerning this project. A very special gratitude is extended to my colleague, Professor Stephen H. Bickham, whose criticisms of the manuscript were quite helpful and discerning. In addition, I wish wholeheartedly to thank my wife, Cecilia, for her expert editing and typing of this work and for her much needed encouragement and consolation during those long and difficult moments of its composition. Finally, though by far not least, I want to thank my two children, John Francis and George Anthony, whose innocence and excitement for life made this work worth writing.

LIST OF ABBREVIATIONS

Martin Heidegger's Works

German Editions

EM	*Einführung in die Metaphysik*
G	*Gelassenheit*
H	*Holzwege*
HD	*Erläuterungen zu Hölderlins Dictung*
PLW	*Platons Lehre von der Wahrheit*
SZ	*Sein und Zeit*
US	*Unterwegs zur Sprache*
VA	*Vorträge und Aufsätze*
WD	*Was heisst Denken?*
WIM	*Was ist Metaphysik?*
WW	*Von Wesen der Wahrheit*

English Editions

BT	*Being and Time* [*Sein und Zeit*]
DT	*Discourse on Thinking* [*Gelassenheit*]
ET	*On the Essence of Truth* [*Vom Wesen der Wahrheit*]
IM	*Introduction to Metaphysics* [*Einführung in die Metaphysik*]
LTP	*Language, Thought, and Poetry* [anthology of various essays]
WL	*On the Way to Language* [*Unterwegs zur Sprache*]
WM	*What is Metaphysics?* [*Was ist Metaphysik?*]
WT	*What is Called Thinking?* [*Was heisst Denken?*]

Chapters and Letters, English Editions

GM	"Way Back to the Ground of Metaphysics" ["Einleitung," *Was ist Metaphysik?*, 1949]

HEP "Hölderlin and the Essence of Poetry" ["Hölderlin und das Wessen der Dichtung," *Erläuterungen zu Hölderlins Dichtung*]

LH "Letter on Humanism" ["Humanismusbrief," *Platons Lehre von der Wahrheit*]

RP "Remembrance of the Poet" ["Heimkunft! An die Verwandten," *Erläuterungen zu Hölderlins Dichtung*]

Ludwig Wittgenstein's Works

The Blue Book *The Blue Book, The Blue and Brown Books, Preliminary Studies for the "Philosophical Investigations"*

The Brown Book *The Brown Book, The Blue and Brown Books, Preliminary Studies for the "Philosophical Investigations"*

Notebooks *Notebooks, 1914-16*

PI *Philosophical Investigations* [*Philosophische Untersuchungen*]

Remarks *Remarks on the Foundations of Mathematics*

Tractatus *Tractatus Logico-Philosophicus* [*Logisch-philosophische Abhandlung*]

CONTENTS

Contemporary Philosophical Dilemma
Methodology
Elucidations and Examples in Methodology
Two Initial Difficulties

PART I. THE METHOD OF PHILOSOPHY AND ITS RELATION TO THE SCIENCES

CHAPTER

PART II. THE STRUCTURES OF LANGUAGE AND THE WORLD AND THEIR RELATIONSHIP

Heidegger's Terminology
The World of the Present-at-Hand
The World of the Ready-to-Hand
The Heideggerian World and its Worldhood
Language: A Manner of Dasein's "Being-in" the
World

The Logical Structures of the Proposition and
of the World
The Wittgensteinian Object
Representational Propositions: The Pictorial
Relation of Language to the World

INTRODUCTION

> Modern philosophers can communicate with
> each other if they care enough to do so. There
> is a deep similarity underlying their apparent
> differences, and they have much they could
> learn from each other, and we, from all of
> them.
>
> —Herbert Kohl, *Age of Complexity*

It was through the diversification of language, Genesis relates, that God punished and scattered the people at Babel. Today, it is language in the form of an interpersonal dialogue which Pope Paul VI in his encyclical *Ecclesiam Suam* encourages as the means of uniting the scattered peoples of the world. In primitive societies, it was the "word" which evoked magical powers; to know the name of a person and to be able to utilize that name in the proper incantation meant gaining control over him. Today, in his *Human Use of Human Beings,* Norbert Wiener has similarly, though in a more sophisticated manner, singled out language as a means of human control.

Language is a curious phenomenon. It has led man throughout his entire history, shaping, determining, and transforming him in a multitude of diverse and even opposing ways. Language has functioned as an inseparable facet of human existence; in fact, language has been and continues to be so intimately a part of man that most often he is not reflexively aware of its presence. Because of this, some writers would have us believe that man's reflection upon his own linguistic behavior is a relatively new experience for him.[1] Yet, to the contrary, analysis of and reflection upon language is represented throughout the very gamut of western crit-

---

1. Cf., Iris Murdoch, *Sartre* (New Haven, Conn.: Yale University Press, 1953), p. 27.

ical thought. The history of Western civilization could even be developed about the theme of language.[2]

In Greek thought, for example, Plato in the dialogue *Cratylus* devotes himself to the rightness and propriety of names; in the *Sophist,* he discusses the justification of true negative propositions. And in the *Seventh Letter,* Plato speaks of the cognitive range of language. In the early Christian era, Isidore of Seville, in the first two books of his *Etymologies,* writes on grammar, rhetoric, and dialectic, proposing the theory that knowledge of things necessitates a knowledge of their linguistic counterparts; the name is the notation whose sound makes known the thing named. Augustine of Hippo likewise propounds theories of language acquisition. Later within the medieval period, Peter of Spain in his *De Suppositionibus* makes the linguistically relevant distinction between *significatio* and *suppositio,* and William of Ockham employs it in his treatment of universals. During this same period and continuing into the Renaissance, occur the grammatical studies of Lorenzo Valla, Juan Luis Vives, and Peter Ramus.

In the period of modern philosophy, concern over language continues. Descartes singles out language as *the* distinguishing trait between man and robot, and Francis Bacon, in his exposition of the famous Four Idols, or false notions, of the human understanding, pinpoints as the most troublesome the idols of the market place; these consist in erroneous conceptions which have entered the human realm through language. Thomas Hobbes in the *Leviathan* (Chapter IV) marvels at the fabric of language, cautioning against its misuses. John Locke similarly directs attention to the significance of language. In book three of *An Essay Concerning Human Understanding* he explains that even though this work is an examination of the extent and certitude of knowledge, these studies "had so near a connection with words that unless their force and manner of signification were well understood, there could be very little said pertinently and clearly concerning knowledge, which being conversant about truth had con-

---

2. Cf., Wilbur M. Urban, *Language and Reality* (New York: Macmillan Company, 1951), p. 22.

stantly to do with propositions . . ." (III, ix, 2). Gottfried
Leibnitz devotes passages of his *New Essays on Human Understanding* to the perplexities of language, and George
Berkeley concludes his preface to *A Treatise Concerning the
Principles of Human Knowledge* by cautioning against the
deception and delusion which words can breed in scholarly
endeavors.

Interest in language is by no means new; however, the in-
creased intensity with which contemporary man reflects upon
language is a distinguishing characteristic of our age. Language is indeed one of the central preoccupations of twentieth-century man, be it studied theoretically as a means of
communication or practically in its actual usages. The scope
of disciplines interested in language ranges from sociology to
linguistics proper, from theology to cybernetics, from anthropology to the fine arts; moreover, these disciplines study
language from a multitude of perspectives, such as grammatical, syntactical, semantical, logical, phonological, mor-
phological, etc.

In contemporary philosophy a heightened intensity of
interest exists over the philosophical problems of language.
Within the empiricist-analytic movement there are the logical
atomism of Bertrand Russell, the logical positivism of Rudolf
Carnap, and the philosophy of ordinary language of Ludwig
Wittgenstein, to name but a few perspectives linguistically
oriented. Within the contemporary phenomenological-existential movement there exists a similar (though perhaps not
as widespread) interest in language. Maurice Merleau-Ponty,
a key figure in phenomenology, has seen in his later philosophical writings the critical need for a philosophy of language. Paul Ricoeur has expressed similar concern. Among
the existentialists, Martin Heidegger, again especially in his
later writings, is deeply concerned in the foundations of language and the possibility of and the presuppositions for ontology from a linguistic point of view. Philosophy of language
has become a pivotal theme for twentieth-century thinkers.

Contemporary Philosophical Dilemma

Ironically, given this intense interest in language and com-

munication theory within today's philosophical circles, philosophers from different contemporary movements are not
genuinely communicating; moreover, for the most part, they
are not interested in understanding each other. As one writer
puts it:

> British philosophers have nearly unanimously washed
> their hands of continental thought as simply impossible,
> at best some kind of metaphysical poetry, at worst pure
> nonsense. The continental philosophers repay this trib
> ute by dismissing the entire enterprise of analytic phi
> losophy . . . as trivial, philistine and infra-philosoph
> ical.[3]

Another commentator similarly observes that "the representatives of different currents of thought are not on speaking
terms. They will at best listen politely to their colleagues
from another camp, but hardly come down to a discussion. . . . There is no dialogue between them."[4] Borrowing
a term from the political vernacular, our contemporary philosophical movements merely "coexist"; a veritable communications gap exists between them.[5]

   Such a state of affairs is unfortunate, to say the least. Obviously, it is out of the question to expect today's philosophers unanimously to agree on significant issues of philosophical import; nevertheless, it would be expected of any

---

3. James M. Edie, cited in his introduction to Pierre Thévenaz, *What is Phenomenology?*, ed. James M. Edie, trans. James M. Edie, Charles Courtney, Paul Brockelman (Chicago: Quadrangle Books, Inc., 1962), p. 17.
4. I. M. Bochénski, *Phenomenology and Science in Contemporary European Thought*, ed. A. T. Tymieniecka (New York: The Noonday Press, 1962), p. viii. Cf., Peter Caws' introduction to Bochénski's work *The Method of Contemporary Thought* (Dordrecht, Holland: D. Reidel, 1965), pp. ix-x.
5. Cf., Knut Tranoy's article "Contemporary Philosophy-Analytic and Continental," *Philosophy Today*, VIII (Fall, 1964), pp. 155-68. Also cf., Herbert Kohl, *The Age of Complexity* (New York: New American Library, 1965). He relates of a very amusing yet pathetic, and perhaps even spurious, event wherein the existentialist philosopher Gabriel Marcel tried to explain his philosophy to an analytically-oriented audience, only to reach an impasse (p. 11).

respectable philosopher that he be cognizant of views different from his own for purposes at least of horizontal expansion. Perhaps, there are even worthwhile ideas in both movements, ideas which would be reciprocally beneficial and supplementary. Perhaps, at times, analysts and phenomenological-existentialists *are* attempting related solutions to problems, yet due to their different linguistic categories, they are unaware of their common interest or goal. Do not misunderstand. We are not entertaining the idea that analysts' and phenomenological-existentialists' philosophical notions are identical. Such a position is absurd, but we cannot *a priori* rule out the possibility that there exists some significant similarity or complementation between them. And, even if such complementation is not found, a genuine understanding of one's philosophical opponent remains necessary if one intends to manifest disagreement with him and perhaps show the inadequacies of, difficulties with, or inconsistencies in his opponent's position.

If philosophy in this century is to advance significantly in accordance with its potential, then it must pool its resources, which necessitates some meaningful interchange of ideas between the diverse, contemporary movements. This work is an attempt to overcome somewhat this unfortunate, prevalent communications block existent within today's philosophical realm in that we will be comparing the writings of Martin Heidegger and Ludwig Wittgenstein, respectively an existentialist and a linguistic analyst, with the primary intent of uncovering similarities between their views. It should be emphasized that our prime concern is with these writings of Heidegger and Wittgenstein. The conclusions reached in this work pertain strictly to their thoughts and only incidentally are they applicable to the camps to which these thinkers respectively belong; that is, our conclusions are relevant to the respective movements insofar as other members of the movement hold views coincidental to Heidegger's and Wittgenstein's. Any meaningful comparison of traditions or philosophical camps can be done only at the level of individuals.

Literally what I am saying is that there is no one mode of thought which is called "analytic" or "phenomenological-existential." These terms are merely linguistic conventions which for convenience are applied to thinkers insofar as various of their tenets overlap and coincide. The terms are very much what Wittgenstein would call "family resemblances"; that is, the terms do not single out one unique tenet which various philosophers share in common. Rather, they are indicative of "a complicated network of similarities overlapping and crisscrossing: sometimes overall similarities, sometimes similarities of detail."[6] I emphasize this point since in the following pages similarities found between the two men's works are in many cases based upon philosophical principles which are not held by all the men who profess to be or who are tagged by commentators to be members of a given tradition.

Yet, how can we meaningfully compare the writings of Heidegger and Wittgenstein? The two men's presuppositions, goals, linguistic categories (to name but a few factors) are so utterly dissimilar that it is difficult for the vast majority of committed Heideggerians or Wittgensteinians to communicate with their respective counterparts. After all, one cannot answer the questions of a logician from a metaphysician's viewpoint or justify the tenets of an ontologist with an empiricist's presuppositions. Wherein lies a proper technique from which to compare the language (and thus the thoughts) of a philosopher of one tradition with that of one of another tradition?

We propose *methodology* as such a proper technique.

Methodology

What does "methodology" mean? This is a most important question since methodology is the pivotal principle of our investigations; we must be careful to explicate with precision the meaning of the term so as to eliminate any possibility of confusion between our use of the term and other philosophers' uses of similar terms which likewise designate a study in method. There is always a problem in any discipline whenever a term from that discipline's already-existent vo-

---

6. Ludwig Wittgenstein, *Philosophical Investigations*, trans. G. E. M. Anscombe (New York: The Macmillan Company, 1953), Part I, 66. Hereafter this work will be cited as *PI*.

cabulary is given a technical meaning; whereas, other philosophers have already used the term within divergent contexts. Thinkers throughout the history of western philosophy have used terms such as "method," "methodic," "methodization," etc., in a number of diverse ways which *in no way* reflect our meaning of the term "methodology." Let us take an example.

One of the greatest thinkers of western philosophy for whom the question of method constituted a key issue is René Descartes. In *Rules for the Direction of the Mind*, perhaps the earliest of Descartes' mature philosophical writings, he expresses the need for founding a reliable method of discovery of certain and evident cognition. ". . . by a method," he explains, "I mean certain and simple rules, such that, if a man observes them accurately, he shall never assume what is false as true, and will never spend his mental efforts to no purpose, but will always gradually increase his knowledge and so arrive at a true understanding of all that does not surpass his powers."[7]

Such a meaning for method has prevailed to a large extent throughout the history of philosophy, and it is imperative to separate this meaning from our methodological study. Our methodological search is not for the true or the false; our study is not an examination of the works of Heidegger and Wittgenstein, either as individual men's thoughts or as representatives of a tradition, in hopes of finding that one has "the truth," while the other does not. Moreover, neither is our intent to determine which man's thought is "better" than the other's. As methodologists, we do not make value judgments concerning other philosophers' thoughts; our task is in no way to defend or justify one philosophical position at the expense of another.

Descartes proposed a *particular* method to follow in philosophizing; Heidegger and Wittgenstein similarly utilize *particular* methods in philosophizing. As methodologists, we

---

7. René Descartes, *Rules for the Direction of the Mind*, Rule IV, Haldane and Ross translation (New York: Cambridge University Press, 1931), p. 9. Descartes proceeds in *Rules*, IV, to discuss various methodic techniques for discovering the true which become systematized in *Discourse on Method*, Part II.

are not here to propose a countermethod; that is, our intent is not to present a new *particular* way of proceeding in contrast to either Heidegger's or Wittgenstein's. Rather, our function, as methodologists, is solely to examine and compare the methods utilized by Heidegger and Wittgenstein. Methodology in this context is a comparative study of method. The status of such a study is, then, purely descriptive and expository.

As methodologists, it is our contention that any facet of a philosophical perspective or position consists of a complex which can be analyzed into its elements, or content, and the structure into which these elements are related. These elements can be logical entities, linguistic categories, epistemological constructs, metaphysical principles, etc., and the structure consists in what holds between the elements in the given philosophy. This order, or structure, we define as the specific philosophy's method, or way of proceeding.

Since our study is methodological, we are not concerned chiefly with the elements of the system, but with the method by which these elements are related; moreover, the totality of relations into which the elements of the system enter (the position's overall structure) uniquely determines that system from a methodological point of view. Methodologically, the system can be completely described without any immediate mention of its contents. A methodological description of a philosophy is a description of its structural properties alone, without concern for the elements entering into these structural relations, and a methodological comparison of two philosophies consists in a comparison of their structural properties. Thus, if two philosophical systems are structured the same way, that is, if the elements of the systems enter into the same relational structures, we say that the philosophies are methodologically or structurally congruent—apart from any immediate consideration of the elements of philosophy. This will be clarified in the following section.

Elucidations and Examples in Methodology

A philosophical position, aspects of which resemble our methodological approach to philosophy, is propounded by the late Rudolf Carnap in his first major work, *The Logical Structure of the World*. In elucidating our position, it is beneficial to discuss facets of Carnap's "construction theory." It should be emphasized that the goal of Carnap's theory—the reduction of all viable concepts to sense verifiable ones—is not our own.[8] Our concern with Carnap's work revolves about the formal character of the construction theory. For both Carnap's study and our methodological investigations, the notion of structure is pivotal.

In explicating the notion of structure, Carnap first distinguishes the structure of "property descriptions" from that of "relation descriptions": "A *property description* indicates the properties which the individual objects of a given domain have, while a *relation description* indicates the relations which hold between these objects, but does not make any assertion about the objects as individuals."[9] Thus, for a given group of persons we can, utilizing property descriptions, state that one weighs 185 pounds, another 190 pounds, a third 170 pounds, etc. Utilizing relation descriptions, we can say that the first of the above three individuals is heavier than the third, or the third lighter than the first without indicating any of the specific material properties of the individuals compared. In a similar way, our methodological studies can completely describe from the methodological viewpoint a facet of a philosophical position, without explicating the specific properties which define the elements therein; at times our methodological statements even abstract from the types of objects which enter into these specific relations. Consequently, they are then properly akin to a third type of description of which Carnap speaks, a structural description. It is derivative from a relation description but differs from the

---

8. Carnap states: "Now, the fundamental thesis of construction theory, which we will attempt to demonstrate in the following investigation, asserts that fundamentally there is only one object domain and that each scientific statement is about the objects of this domain." [Rudolf Carnap, *The Logical Structure of the World, Pseudoproblems in Philosophy*, trans. Rolf A. George (Berkeley and Los Angeles: University of California Press, 1967), p. 29.]

9. *Ibid.*, p. 19. For a few critical remarks concerning Carnap's construction theory, cf., F. Waismann, *The Principles of Linguistic Philosophy* (New York: St. Martin's Press, 1965), pp. 269-79.

latter in that it makes no immediate reference to the meaning of the relation from which it is derived or to the objects for which the relation holds. Carnap states:

> Unlike property descriptions, these [structural descriptions] not only leave the properties of the individual elements of the range unmentioned, they do not even specify the relations themselves which hold between these elements. In a structural description, only the *structure* of the relation is indicated. . . . [It] can be formulated without reference to the meaning of the relation and the type of objects, between which it holds.[10]

Thus, one can meaningfully speak about the transitive relations holding between the members of our above example without mentioning the specific meanings of the relations or the objects between which the relations hold. These would be examples of structural descriptions.

Structural descriptions can be used to relate various diverse systems in which certain relations respectively hold. Carnap gives the following example. It is lengthy and complex; nevertheless, I present it here because of its relevance to our own methodological procedure.

> Let us look at a railroad map of, say, the Eurasian railroad network. We assume that this map is not a precise projection, but that it is distorted as much or more than the customary maps found in ticket offices. It does not then represent the distances, but only the connections within the network; (in the terminology of geometry) : it indicates only the topological, not the metrical, properties of the network. The example of the railroad map has previously been used to clarify the concept of topological properties. It is equally well suited to clarify the closely related, but more general, logical concept of structural properties. We assume now that all stations are marked as points, but the map is not to contain any names

---

10. *Ibid.*, p. 21.

nor any entries other than rail lines. The question now is: can we determine the names of the points on the map through an inspection of the actual railroad network? Since it is difficult to observe an actual railroad network, let us use in its stead a second map which contains all the names. Since our (first) map may be distorted more than the customary railroad maps, we will gain little by looking for characteristic shapes, for example, the long Siberian railroad. But there is a more promising way: we look up the intersections of highest order, i.e., those in which the largest number of lines meet. We will find only a small number of these. Assume that we find twenty intersections in which eight lines meet. We then count, for each such point, the number of stations between it and the next intersection on each of the eight lines, and we will hardly find two of the eight to coincide in all eight numbers. Thus, we have identified all twenty points. But if there are still two, or even all twenty, which have the same numbers, then all we have to do is to consider the connections between each of the eight neighboring intersections: whether or not they have direct connections, how many stations there are between them, how many lines meet in these neighboring intersections, etc. Given the network as it actually exists today: if we do all this, we will certainly not find any further coincidences. But if we are confronted with a network where even these characteristics do not allow us to differentiate, we would have to proceed, step by step, from the neighboring intersections to their neighbors, etc., in order to find still further characteristics for the main intersections. We proceed in this way until we find characteristics which no longer coincide, even if we have to survey our entire net. But once we have discovered the name for even one point on the map, the others are easily found, since only very few names qualify for the neighboring points.[11]

---

11. *Ibid.*, pp. 25-26.

Carnap's contention is that without ostensibly defining a system's objects, a definite description of those objects can be given merely through structure statements—assuming that the object domain of the system is stipulated. Our position is similar. Texts by Heidegger and Wittgenstein on, say, the methods of philosophy are collected, subjected to a methodological restatement, and recounted as systems of structural statements which uniquely define each man's views. And, these systems are comparable. If they coincide, the philosophical viewpoints to which they belong are said to be structurally, that is methodologically, congruent. This means that the two perspectives are structurally equivalent.

This, then, is our methodological or structural approach. Although emphasis is placed therein upon the structural, or formal, properties of a philosophical perspective, this does not allow anyone to shout in criticism unrestricted cries of "Formalism!"[12] If indeed our methodological investigations could unqualifiedly be tagged as formalistic, this would mean that we are prescinding from consideration *any* and *every* meaning of the elements utilized within a philosophical position. Certainly, one can construct a linguistic syntax without attaching any meaning to it; this situation would indeed be formalistic. Such, however, is not our intent; our purpose is to begin with the already-given works of philosophers, categorize their texts in some meaningful way, explicate these in structurally-elucidating propositions, and then examine these for methodological congruence.

For Carnap's view and ours, there must be some element of content stipulated from the beginning as a control; otherwise, one is left in a quandary. Unless in Carnap's example one knows that the topological network represented the Eurasian railroad—even in its own unconventional way—the task of interpreting it as a map of the railroad would be arbitrary. So also unless we first know that the philosophical

---

12. Cf., I. M. Bochénski, *The Methods of Contemporary Thought*, pp. 35ff, 40ff, 67, and 71 and Mikel Dufrenne, *Language and Philosophy*, trans. Henry B. Veatch (Bloomington: Indiana University Press, 1963), pp. 57-66.

propositions being structurally drafted were for both Heidegger and Wittgenstein representative of a specific domain of philosophical inquiry, our investigations would be utter fancy. If, for example, we took Carnap's topological map of the Eurasian railroad and compared it with one of the propositions of Heidegger's *Being and Time,* would we say that the two structures were congruent? To do such would be absurd.

In our methodological investigations, there cannot be a total abstraction from subject matter, unless we reduce our study to insignificance; there must be some essential content factor not bracketed from consideration so as to make the study meaningful. This factor indicates that the texts being structurally analyzed are somehow related, thus allowing for a methodological comparison of the texts. This means that there must first exist within the works of Heidegger and Wittgenstein some common themes to which a methodological comparison can be directed. It is at this point that the significance of contemporary philosophers' intense interest over problems in language becomes heightened; this interest provides that pivotal given around which our methodological studies can turn and do turn.

By now some readers may have made some correlation between the structural approach of methodology as presented herein and structuralism as proposed by Claude Lévi-Strauss in anthropology, or by N. S. Troubetzkoy and Roman Jakobson in linguistics, or by various other authors in mathematics, literary criticism, psychology, sociology, etc. Without a doubt, there exist similarities between such techniques, and they do bear some kinship with this study; nevertheless, methodology as explicated in this book must be somehow distinguished from these other methods, just as the latter have to be differentiated among themselves. Again, "family resemblance" appears to be the appropriate term to categorize such techniques. Structuralism is not a movement as such; it is not formally organized with a definitive procedure and well-defined goals, propounded by all thinkers whose methods can be called structural.

Caution must be exercised in labelling our study as one

in "structuralism." Although it fits into the family of structural approaches, it is distinct in many ways from other members of the same family. Our concern is not to find some inherited structural continuity between Heidegger's and Wittgenstein's works; we are not saying that structures are somehow self-subsisting or independent of historical events. Structure-form distinctions or reductions of all relations to some form of binary categories are of no significance to this study. Our structural approach is not a theory whereby we hope to understand the world aright, yet admittedly, there is something theoretical about this work. Our structural approach, although it does not concern itself primarily with the content of Heidegger's and Wittgenstein's thoughts, in no way suggests that such is of no or minor importance; we are simply prescinding these elements from consideration. Methodology is solely of heuristic value; it makes possible a path—one of many paths—from which contemporary thought can be approached.

Two Initial Difficulties

At this point, two difficulties arise even if our methodological approach is accepted. The first pertains to Heidegger; the second, to Wittgenstein. First, how can a methodological (structural) statement be made about Heidegger's works if their prime concern is the ground of Being—namely, Nothingness—whose defining characteristic is its pre-predicative,[13] a-structural state. To reword our difficulty: How can we structurally analyze what defies structure without falsifying it?

---

13. "Pre-predicative" is a technical term of Heidegger's philosophical writings. Predication is basically the attribution of a quality or characteristic to a subject thereby delineating and objectifying it into a thing separate and distinct, having an intelligibility in itself and apart from other things. (A more detailed elucidation of Heidegger's meaning of predication can be found in Chapter 7 of this work.) Given this meaning for predication, the "pre-predicative" refers to that ontological state of the content of the world *before* it has been fragmented into separate and distinct entities. Its ontological significance as well as its intelligibility is relationally determined. [For comments upon Heidegger's meaning of the pre-predicative, confer William Richardson, *Heidegger: Through Phenomenology to Thought* (The Hague: Martinus Nijhoff, 1967), pp. 213ff and 229.]

The second difficulty is: How can one speak of the structural properties of Wittgenstein's philosophical position, if he claims not to have one? That is, Wittgenstein claims to concern himself with philosophical problems, the dissolutions of which each require different techniques. According to Wittgenstein, there is no well-defined method via which philosophical problems are dissolved. Each problem has its own unique perplexity, which is dissolved in its own unique manner. Thus, Wittgenstein approaches each philosophical perplexity as it arises, searching out the specific linguistic confusion from which it arose. ". . . we now demonstrate a method by examples," he remarks, "and the series of examples can be broken off.—Problems are solved (difficulties eliminated) not a *single* problem. There is not *a* philosophical method, though there are indeed methods, like different therapies."[14]

Given these problems, our inquiry seems to be stymied even before we commence. Yet, these problems are not insurmountable; they are really pseudo-problems. Concerning the first, it is crucial for Heidegger that he is dealing with the pre-predicative and therefore a-structural in his analysis of Being. Yet, this does not mean, as some commentators erroneously feel, that Heidegger's approach to the pre-rational is irrational. It is an ungrounded assertion to say that because Heidegger's subject matter defies structure, his method of elucidating it is similarly unstructured—meaning haphazard and chaotic. There is a systematic structure within Heidegger's writings in his attempt to uncover Being. This will be made evident in our ensuing exposition. This structure we will discover is found in the technique by which Heidegger reveals Being and not in the content of Being itself. Moreover, is not this the precise type of structure with which we wish to concern ourselves? As methodologists, we are not interested in the status of the elements of a system, but in the way these elements are related and thus revealed in a given philosophical viewpoint. The content of Being is not our concern but rather the manner in which Heidegger

---

14. *PI* 133.

proceeds to reveal Being, the method via which he makes it manifest.

In regard to Wittgenstein's writings, we must admit it is true that in his work *The Philosophical Investigations* there is no single method utilized in dissolving the linguistic confusion which pervades philosophical discourse. This means that the approach which he therein uses in making patent disguised bits of linguistic nonsense depends upon the nonsense in question; however, this aspect of his work does not concern our present inquiry. What mainly concerns us is the structure in which Wittgenstein proposes his own philosophical doctrines and propositions in the *Tractatus Logico-Philosophicus*. At first glance, our attribution to Wittgenstein of philosophical "doctrines" and "propositions" seems to be against the very trend of his thought. For, in the *Tractatus* he explicitly states: "Philosophy is not a body of doctrine but an activity . . . Philosophy does not result in 'philosophical propositions,' but rather in the clarification of propositions."[15] Similarly, in the *Investigations* he writes that "we [as philosophers] may not advance any kind of theory."[16]

Given these texts, our remarks concerning Wittgenstein's works seem to be on a poor foundation; nevertheless, it is our contention that a definite theory, or construct, of descriptive language—the picture theory— is presented in the *Tractatus* and as such the work oversteps the descriptive bounds which Wittgenstein has set for philosophy. Wittgenstein has unwarrantedly disregarded his own concept of philosophy.[17] This notion will be discussed more fully in Chapters Two and Five.

Let us now proceed to compare methodologically the writings of Heidegger and Wittgenstein. We will first compare

---

15. Ludwig Wittgenstein, *Tractatus Logico-Philosophicus*, trans. D. F. Pears and B. F. McGuinness with an introduction by Bertrand Russell (London: Routledge & Kegan Paul Ltd., 1961), 4.112. Hereafter this work will be cited as *Tractatus*.

16. *PI* 109.

17. Tullio de Mauro, *Ludwig Wittgenstein: His Place in the Development of Semantics* (Dordrecht, Holland: D. Reidel, 1967), p. 3. Cf., David Pears, *Ludwig Wittgenstein* (New York: Viking Press, 1969), pp. 32ff and 107.

their notions of the method of philosophy and its relation to the sciences. This will lead us into a discussion of their utilization of these methods respectively on Being as manifested in man's being-in-the-world and on the logic of descriptive language. This second part of our comparison introduces us to Heidegger's conception of language and its structure as a revelation of Being, and thus it lays the way to our third and final comparison of the two men's works on the theme of ontological language.

PART I

THE METHOD OF PHILOSOPHY
AND ITS RELATION
TO THE SCIENCES

CHAPTER I

HEIDEGGER'S HERMENEUTICAL PHENOMENOLOGY

> The word "metaphysics" here ought
> to signify only that the questions dealt
> with stand at the *heart* and *middle* of
> philosophy.
>
> —Heidegger, *What is a Thing?*

Philosophy is essentially metaphysics in the Heideggerian realm, and metaphysics Heidegger identifies as a study of "Nothingness"—which is really a camouflage term for "Being." Immediately, then, we are confronted with the problematic pivotal to all of Heidegger's writings—the Being-question. To philosophize in the Heideggerian sense is to search out the meaning of Being, to become the metaphysician. Yet, a quandary evolves: If Heidegger views metaphysics as central to philosophy, why is he so critical of traditional metaphysicians, why does he want to overturn the history of metaphysics? How can he call metaphysics a decadent discipline and still pursue a metaphysical world view?

The difficulty is resolved if one admits a certain equivocation in Heidegger's use of the term "metaphysics." In a historical sense, metaphysics refers to traditional inquiries into Being, inquiries which, however, erroneously substituted something, an entity, for Nothing, Being. It is this type of metaphysics which Heidegger wishes to destroy and replace with a more primal and authentic perspective of Being. It is this latter view which Heidegger purports in *What is Metaphysics?* In this sense, Heidegger's works are metaphysical in character; his fundamental ontology in its attempt to overcome traditional metaphysics is really a renewal of meta-

1

physics (the Being-question), though in a genuine and more primordial way.

Concomitant with this twofold meaning of metaphysics is a paralleling equivocation in the term "philosophy." Traditionally, it is to be overcome, only by engaging in it at a more fundamental level.

This leads to the question of the proper technique by which Being is manifest. What is the method of authentic philosophy? In his first major work *Being and Time,* Heidegger for the first time takes this issue to task in a systematic and definitive way. He is quite emphatic that the revelation of Being cannot be prescriptive; that is, already existing categories of thought ought not to be used to make Being manifest. These classifications would only force Being into already degenerate, explanatory constructs through which it could emerge only in a falsified way.

> . . . we have no right to resort to dogmatic constructions and to apply just any idea of Being and actuality to this entity, no matter how "self-evident" that idea may be; nor may any of the "categories" which such an idea prescribes be forced upon Dasein without proper ontological consideration.[1]

Having cautioned the reader against such approaches to Being, Heidegger then proceeds in *Being and Time* to delineate in a positive manner the means he envisions which will make Being authentically manifest. What Heidegger proposes is to study Being from the perspective of phenomenology. "Phenomenology is our way of access to what is to be the theme of ontology, and it is our way of giving it demonstrative precision. *Only as phenomenology is ontology possible.*"[2] Etymologically, Heidegger explains, the word "phenomenology" is derived from the Greek words "phenome-

---

1. Martin Heidegger, *Being and Time,* trans. John Macquarrie and Edward Robinson (New York and Evanston: Harper & Row, 1962), p. 37. Hereafter this work will be cited as BT; this translation will be employed throughout except for a few variations. Abbreviated as SZ, corresponding references to the German edition, *Sein und Zeit* (Tübingen: M. Niemeyer, 1949), will appear in parentheses following the BT citation. (SZ, p. 16).
2. *Ibid.,* p. 60. (SZ, p. 35).

non" and "logos." The term "phenomenon" by itself Heidegger derives as signifying the manifest, that which shows
itself. "Logos" has as its basic meaning "discourse," and discourse etymologically means the making "manifest what one
is 'talking about'. . . . It lets us see something from the very
thing which the discourse is about."[3] Coupling the meaning
of these terms, Heidegger defines his phenomenology as "to
let that which shows itself be seen from itself in the very way
in which it shows itself from itself."[4]

This means that phenomenology for Heidegger is a
purely expository technique of manifesting and unconceal-
ing its subject matter; it does not characterize this subject
matter by subjecting it to or explaining it by any precon-
ceived categorical schemes. Phenomenology "is opposed to
all free-floating constructions."[5] Heidegger's phenomenology
purports neither to objectify nor to characterize the data to
which it is applied; the phenomenological method employed
by Heidegger neither designates the objects of its researches
nor hypothesizes about them, it merely reveals them and
makes them manifest. Phenomenology "means to grasp its
objects *in such a way* that everything about them which is up
for discussion must be treated by exhibiting it directly. . . ."[6]
The phenomenological method of Heidegger is purely
descriptive. "The expression 'descriptive phenomenology,'
which is at bottom tautological, has the same meaning."[7]

It should be noted, however, that it is a special, curious
form of description which Heidegger proposes as phenomenology—it is a hermeneutical description. Hermeneutics is
an interpretive study; consequently, an interpretive phenomenology is an interpretive description, which seems quite
an incomprehensible state of affairs.[8] We will leave this an

---

3. *Ibid.*, p. 56. (SZ, p. 32).
4. *Ibid.*, p. 58. (SZ, p. 34).
5. *Ibid.*, p. 50. (SZ, pp. 27-28).
6. *Ibid.*, p. 59. (SZ, p. 35).
7. *Ibid.* (SZ, p. 35).
8. Cf., Michael Gelven, *A Commentary on 'Being and Time'* (New York: Harper & Row, 1970), pp. 34-42, Don Ihde, "Language and Two Phe-nomenologies," *Southern Journal of Philosophy*, VIII (Winter, 1970), pp. 399-408, and Edward G. Ballard, "On the Pattern of Phenomeno-logical Method," *Southern Journal of Philosophy*, VIII (Winter, 1970), pp. 421-31.

open issue for the moment, returning to it in our "unmeth-odological remark" of Chapter 3. A much more crucial issue at this time is whether or not this method of phenomenology as proposed in *Being and Time* has application in Heidegger's later works. After *Being and Time*, he hardly uses the term; it could well be, then, that this so-called descriptive method is merely a passing fad of the early Heidegger, and does not at all reflect his later views. One commentator explicitly holds to this interpretation; he views Heidegger as completely abandoning the phenomenological method in his more mature works.[9]

There is really little evidence to support this view, however. Heidegger's philosophy is from beginning to end phenomenological—in the sense Heidegger uses the term. Admittedly, Heidegger's phenomenology is different from Husserl's. In *Being and Time* Heidegger has defined phenomenology as "to let that which shows itself be seen from itself in the very way in which it shows itself from itself."[10] And, that which shows itself is Being. "In the phenomenological conception of 'phenomenon' what one has in mind as that which shows itself is the Being of entities, its meaning, its modifications and derivatives. . . . With regard to its subject-matter, phenomenology is the science of the Being of entities —ontology."[11] Phenomenology is the revelation and unconcealment of Being, and this theme unifies the whole range of Heidegger's works.

Although it is true that an author's opinions of his own writings are not conclusive evidence, by any means, of the status of those studies, it is interesting to note that Heidegger's evaluation of his own thought indirectly supports our interpretation of the thoroughly phenomenological character of all his philosophy. Herbert Spiegelberg informs us of a personal interview which he had with Heidegger in September of 1953 in which were discussed Heidegger's attitudes toward phenomenology. In the interview, Spiegelberg relates,

9. Thévenaz, pp. 60-61.
10. BT, p. 58. (SZ, p. 34).
11. *Ibid.*, pp. 60-61. (SZ, pp. 35 and 37).

Heidegger gave no indication of wanting to be segregated from the general direction of the phenomenological movement; moreover, according to Spiegelberg, Heidegger did not hint at or mention any deviation in his later works from the techniques of *Being and Time*.[12]

In place of hermeneutical phenomenology, Heidegger uses in his later works several terms to indicate the authentic method of Being's revelation. Principal among them is "meditative thinking" [*besennliches Denken*]. In *Discourse on Thinking*, Heidegger discusses the term in some detail showing the two pivotal elements of this mode of thought to be releasement toward things and openness to the mystery.

Releasement toward things is the disengagement of the mind from the thinking of objects; as a result, it is the means of elucidating Being, which is not an object. Openness to the mystery is that receptive attitude on man's part in virtue of which Being is manifest.

To understand these terms better, let us briefly turn our attention to *On the Essence of Truth*. In the essay Heidegger centers upon the conventional concept of truth: *Veritas est adaequatio rei et intellectum.* Concerning the definition, Heidegger raises the following question: What are the presuppositions of the *adaequatio* theory? To say, for example, upon seeing a half-crown lying on the table "This coin is round," presupposes a certain relation between the half-crown and the person who made the statement. Heidegger asserts that this relation is "the letting something take up a position

---

12. Herbert Spiegelberg, *The Phenomenological Movement*, I (The Hague: Martinus Nijhoff, 1965), p. 346. This does not mean, however, that no differences exist between Heidegger's early and late writings. In fact, such differences exist that Richardson categorizes Heidegger's thought into Heidegger I (the Heidegger of *Being and Time* and other early works) and Heidegger II (the Heidegger of approximately 1929 onward). Nevertheless, these differences do not constitute a reversal or overthrow of Heidegger's earlier thought; to the contrary, they are a development of it. Basically, these differences revolve about the status of man's existential role in Being's phenomenological revelation. We will reserve, however, a discussion of this matter for Chapter 6 when we discuss in detail the "human element" of Heidegger's thought.

opposite to us, as an object."[13] To state an *object*-ive fact implies that man has taken a position opposite the object upon which he is focusing his attention and from that position exhumes the object from the matrix of environmental relations of which it is a part, thereby clearly delineating the object and causing the matrix as a totality to become a background or horizon against which the object appears.

For me to say that the half-crown is round implies that as observer I am caught up within a certain space-time relationship with the coin so that I am viewing its face in a plane precisely perpendicular to my line of sight.[14] Moreover, as observer, I am focusing my attention upon the object as apart from its surroundings. I am making the datum perceived into an object; I am *freeing* it from its surroundings. Thus, Heidegger calls the essence of truth "freedom." "Freedom reveals itself as the 'letting-be' of what-is."[15] But in this revelation, this letting-be of the object in question, the background matrix becomes cognitionally concealed. Any reference to it is only relative to objects and our representing them.[16] "What is evident of the horizon," Heidegger states, "is but the side facing us of an openness . . . which is filled with views of the appearance of what to our representing are objects."[17] Nevertheless, there exists the other side of this horizon—its unobjectified side of a pure surd-like relational matrix. This sec-

13. Martin Heidegger, *On the Essence of Truth*, trans. R. F. C. Hull and Alan Crick, *Existence and Being*, ed. with an introduction by Werner Brock (Chicago: Regnery, 1949), p. 300. Hereafter this work will be cited as ET; this translation will be employed throughout. Corresponding references to the German edition, *Vom Wesen der Wahrheit* (Frankfurt am Main: Vittorio Klostermann, 1943), will appear in parentheses as WW following the ET citation. (WW, p. 11).

14. For a somewhat related discussion on the positioning of observer to observed in relation to the assertion of propositions, see Bertrand Russell's *Our Knowledge of the External World* (New York: The New American Library, 1960), pp. 54ff, especially pp. 74ff.

15. ET, p. 305. (WW, p. 15).

16. Martin Heidegger, *Discourse on Thinking*, trans. John M. Anderson and E. Hans Freund (New York: Harper & Row, 1966), p. 64. Hereafter this work will be cited as DT; this translation will be employed throughout. Abbreviated as G, corresponding references to the German edition, *Gelassenheit* (Pfullingen: Neske, 1959), appear in parentheses following the DT citation. (G, p. 38).

17. *Ibid.*, p. 64. (G, p. 39).

ond, more fundamental aspect of horizon is so constituted that it contains no objects. This side of the horizon is the authentic source of Being's revelation, and requires a special technique on man's part to be aware of it—meditative thinking. It is a means of being aware of the undifferentiated ontological matrix which underpins the world of objects *qua* undifferentiated and non-*object*-ive. It is a way to grasp the background against which objects appear not as a background to this or that object but *qua* background. Meditative thinking is a "releasement toward things"; that is, it frees the mind from objectifying the data of the background horizon and allows the mind to "open to the mystery" of its ontological region of non-objective relatedness.

* * *

Of Heidegger's works which pertain to the relation of science to philosophy, probably the most illuminating is *What is Metaphysics?*[18] It is Heidegger's 1929 Inaugural Address at Freiburg where he assumed the chair of philosophy as successor to Edmund Husserl. The audience to whom the address was directed consisted principally of scientists, and Heidegger engaged in a topic which he thought most appropriate: the difference of metaphysics [philosophy] and science.

The sciences, unlike philosophy, deal with things, entities, that "what-is" [*Seiendes*]. "The world-relationship which runs through all the sciences as such constrains them to seek what is *in itself*, with a view to rendering it, according to

---

18. For other references concerning Heidegger's views on science and its method, see "Wissenschaft und Besinnung," *Vorträge und Aufsätze* (Pfullingen: Neske, 1954), pp. 45-70 especially pp. 56-64 and *Der Satz vom Grund* (Pfullingen: Neske, 1957), pp. 189ff.

For interesting and scholarly commentaries on Heidegger's attitude toward science in general, see William Richardson, "Heidegger's Critique of Science," *The New Scholasticism*, XLII (Autumn, 1968), pp. 511-36; Karlfried Gründer, "Heidegger's Critique of Science," *Philosophy Today*, VII (Spring, 1963), 18ff; Albert Borgmann, "Heidegger and Symbolic Logic," *Heidegger and the Quest for Truth*, ed. Manfred S. Frings (Chicago: Quadrangle, 1968), pp. 139-62; A. F. Lingis, "On the Essence of Technique," *Heidegger and the Quest for Truth*, ed. Manfred S. Frings (Chicago: Quadrangle, 1968), pp. 126-38; and Simon Moser, "Toward a Metaphysics of Technology," *Philosophy Today*, XV (Summer, 1971), pp. 129-56 especially pp. 144-53.

its quiddity— (*Wasgehalt*) . . . ."[19] Science deals with physical objects, things which are measurable and quantifiable, being caught up in a spatial frame of reference. Clearly, according to Heidegger, that which is unmeasurable and unquantifiable, as for example Being (or as Heidegger calls it in the essay, Nothingness) is not a datum of scientific investigation since it is not an object. "Nothing is neither an object nor anything that 'is' at all."[20] This does not mean that Nothing is a figment, an illusion, of man's mind; Nothing is not a physical object, but it is real. Heidegger's point is that Nothing is No-Thing and as such it cannot be studied by science since

19. Martin Heidegger, *What is Metaphysics?*, trans. R. F. C. Hull and Alan Crick, *Existence and Being*, ed. with an introduction by Werner Brock (Chicago: Regnery, 1949), p. 326. Hereafter this work will be cited as WM; this translation will be employed throughout. Abbreviated as WIM, corresponding references to the German edition, *Was ist Metaphysik?* (Frankfurt am Main: Vittorio Klostermann, 1943), appear in parentheses following the WM citation. (WIM, p. 6).

20. *Ibid.*, p. 340. (WIM, p. 16). This introduces the question of Heidegger's nihilism. His usage of the term "Nothingness" has led some critics of his thought to brand him as a nihilist. Heidegger in the Postscript to *What is Metaphysics?*, written approximately thirteen years after the initial address, alludes to these charges and dismisses the critics as "premature to . . . adopt the facile explanation that Nothing is merely the nugatory, equating it with the non-existent (*das Wesenlose*)" (*Ibid.*, p. 353). (WIM, pp. 25-26). Thomas Langan, however, takes an opposite view. In his article "Is Heidegger a Nihilist?" he describes Heidegger as, in a manner of speaking, precariously postured over the ledge of the chasm of nihilism [*Thomist*, XXI (July, 1958), pp. 316, 318-19]. It should be noted, however, that Langan in his book *The Meaning of Heidegger* reverses his stand on the matter and upholds Heidegger's defense against the charges of nihilism. Cf., Thomas Langan, *The Meaning of Heidegger* (New York: Columbia University Press, 1959), pp. 97-99.

I do not wish to engage myself in this argument since the term "nihilist" is emotionally packed; no one wants to be called such since the term has a degrading connotation to it. Yet, when asked what does the term denote, a variety of answers is given, the only common element of them being that no one wants to be called a nihilist. If, however, by calling Heidegger a nihilist one means that he denies any ontological basis to Heidegger's Nothingness, this I deny. "Nothing" is ontologically real for Heidegger. Its reality, however, is non-objective. It is no-thing. Cf., John H. Walsh, "Heidegger's Understanding of No-thingness," *Cross-Currents*, XIII (Summer, 1963), pp. 305-23. For a more detailed defense against nihilism by Heidegger himself, see his *The Question of Being*, trans. W. Kluback and J. T. Wilde (New Haven: College and University Press, 1958), pp. 33ff.

the latter concerns itself only with *what is,* that is physical entities. Thus, to ask the question *"What* is Nothing?" is a pseudo-question according to Heidegger since the "what" of the question implies that an objective character for Nothing is being sought; whereas, in fact Nothing has no objective status.

> What is Nothing? Even the initial approach to this question shows us something out of the ordinary. So questioning, we postulate Nothing as something that somehow or other "is"—as an entity *(Seiendes).* But it is nothing of the sort. . . . Accordingly, every answer to this question is impossible from the start. For it necessarily moves in the form that Nothing "is" this, that, or the other. Question and answer are equally non-sensical in themselves where Nothing is concerned.[21]

It is obvious that since the subject matters of philosophy and the sciences are then so radically different, the techniques or methods of the two disciplines are likewise diverse. Whereas the method of philosophy is hermeneutical phenomenology, that of science is calculative thinking *(rechnendes Denken).* "Calculation uses everything that 'is' as units of computation."[22] This computation, Heidegger is quick to add, ought not to be understood merely in a mathematical context. "This calculation is the mark of all thinking that plans and investigates. Such thinking remains calculation even if it neither works with numbers nor uses an adding machine or computer."[23] Calculative thinking, then, is that mode of any type of thought which deals with the quantifiable and the measurable; it is that mode of cognition which neatly categorizes all reality into thingly structures. To the scientists and their calculating methods, according to Heidegger, there "arises a completely new relation of man to the world and his place in it. The world now appears as an *object.* . . . Nature becomes a gigantic gasoline station, an energy source for mod-

---

21. WM, pp. 329-30. (WIM, p. 8).
22. *Ibid.,* p. 357. (WIM, p. 28).
23. DT, p. 46. (G, p. 14). Cf., "Wissenschaft und Besinnung," pp. 56-58.

ern technology and industry."[24] "Modern technology strives
to consummate perfection. Perfection rests in the total cal-
culability of objects. . . ."[25]

It is important to note that Heidegger in his criticism
of calculative thinking is in no way attempting to deny any
validity to it. As he states, the problem is "that the approaching tide of technological revolution in the atomic age could
so captivate, bewitch, dazzle, and beguile man that calculative
thinking may someday come to be accepted and practiced
as the only way of thinking."[26] What Heidegger fears is the
reductive viewpoint of Max Plank's dictum: "The real is
whatever can be measurable."[27] Calculative thinking, Heidegger retorts, admittedly has validity but only in its own realm,
the realm of objects. There *also* is a mode of thought which
deals with the uncalculative. It is the method of philosophy
in its quest for Being.

---

24. *Ibid.*, p. 50. Italics are mine. (G. pp. 19-20).
25. *Der Satz vom Grund*, p. 198.
26. DT, p. 56. (G, p. 27). Cf., Edward G. Ballard, "Heidegger's View and
    Evaluation of Nature and Natural Science" in *Heidegger and the Path
    of Thinking*, ed. John Sallis (Pittsburgh: Duquesne University Press,
    1970), pp. 57ff.
27. Max Plank, quoted in Heidegger's "Wissenschaft und Besinnung," p. 58.

CHAPTER II

WITTGENSTEIN'S DESCRIPTIVE ANALYSIS

> Philosophy . . . consists of logic and
> metaphysics, the former its basis.
>
> —Wittgenstein, *Notes on Logic*

Despite differences between Wittgenstein's *Tractatus* and the *Investigations,* expressed in varying degrees by Wittgenstein himself and by some of his commentators, one aspect of his thought has remained basically unchanged in the two works: It is his view on the meaning of and method for philosophy and their distinction from those of the sciences.

Throughout its history, various problems have plagued philosophy, which, according to Wittgenstein, are rooted in misconceptions of the logical structure of language. In his preface to the *Tractatus,* Wittgenstein asserts that "this book deals with the problems of philosophy, and shows, I believe, that the reason why these problems are posed is that the logic of our language is misunderstood."[1] "Most of the propositions and questions of philosophers arise from our failure to understand the logic of our language."[2] In the *Investigations* he similarly maintains: "The results of philosophy are the . . . bumps that the understanding has got by running its head up against the limits of language."[3] "A main source of our failure is to understand that we do not *command a clear view* of the use of our words."[4] To overcome this failure, Witt-

---

1. Ludwig Wittgenstein, Author's Preface to the *Tractatus,* p. 3.
2. *Tractatus* 4.003. Cf., 4.002 and 4.112. Cf., James Griffin, *Wittgenstein's Logical Atomism* (London: Oxford University Press, 1964), pp. 7ff.
3. *PI* 119.
4. *PI* 122.

genstein's philosophic goal is to make evident the logic of language, thereby disclosing those ways in which traditional philosophers have failed to understand the workings of language and dissolving the puzzlements which resulted from their misconceptions. Consequently, for Wittgenstein, "all philosophy is a 'critique of language'. . . ."[5]

Does this mean that Wittgenstein proposes a doctrine or constructs a theory concerning language? Wittgenstein unequivocally states "No." "Philosophy is not a body of doctrine but an activity."[6] Similarly, in the *Investigations* he adds: ". . . we [philosophers] may not advance any kind of theory. There must not be anything hypothetical in our consideration."[7] This, then, is the plan which Wittgenstein lays out as the method of philosophy: its method is not to advance a doctrine or propose a theory. Whether in fact this is what Wittgenstein does is mooted.[8] Be that as it may, we still must ask: If philosophy is not a doctrine, what is it and if its method does not consist in proposing hypotheses, in what does it consist? Wittgenstein answers that philosophy is an *activity*. "Philosophy does not result in 'philosophical propositions,' but rather in the clarification of propositions."[9] The method of philosophy consists in clarifications of complex propositions through a descriptive analysis of their elementary base propositions.

Philosophy begins with a problem, a perplexity, and its aim is to explicate that perplexity by describing just where it arose through a misuse of language. "A philosophic problem has the form: 'I don't know my way about.' "[10] And, Wittgenstein's aim as philosopher is to make manifest this predicament: "My aim is: to teach you to pass from a piece of disguised nonsense to something that is patent nonsense."[11]

---

5. *Tractatus* 4.0031.
6. *Ibid.*, 4.112.
7. *PI* 109.
8. In the *Tractatus*, Wittgenstein has stepped beyond his self-set limit of philosophy by proposing the picture *theory* of descriptive language. Cf., Pears, pp. 32-35.
9. *Tractatus* 4.112.
10. *PI* 123.
11. *Ibid.*, 464.

This is always done, according to Wittgenstein, descriptively, by means of a clarification of the proposition until its meaning is made evident or until it has been shown that the proposition has no meaning, the misuse of language being made patent. "I want to say here that it can never be our job [as philosophers] to reduce anything to anything, or to explain anything."[12] "Philosophy may in no way interfere with the actual use of language; it can in the end only describe it."[13] "Philosophy simply puts everything before us, and neither explains nor deduces anything.—Since everything lies open to view there is nothing to explain. For what is hidden, for example, is of no interest to us."[14] Addressing himself to philosophers, Wittgenstein dogmatically asserts that "we must do away with all *explanation,* and description alone must take its place."[15] Wittgenstein explicitly maintains: "Philosophy really *is* 'purely descriptive.' "[16]

*   *   *

Distinct from philosophy stands science. Its method is explication; this means that it proposes constructs so that one can intelligibly speak about natural phenomena. The language of science constructs models, theories, or hypotheses giving a perspective through which the physical phenomena can be explained; science's explanatory method sets up a viewpoint from which to classify and to categorize in a coherent way the phenomenon of the world. Consequently, science is radically distinct from philosophy. ". . . it was true to say that our [philosophic] considerations could not be scientific ones."[17]

In the 6.3's of the *Tractatus,* using Newtonian mechanics

---

12. Ludwig Wittgenstein, *The Blue Book, The Blue and Brown Books* (New York: Harper & Row, 1958), p. 18. Hereafter citations from *The Blue Book* will appear as *The Blue Book* and citations from *The Brown Book* will appear as *The Brown Book.*
13. *PI* 124.
14. *Ibid.,* 126.
15. *Ibid.,* 109. For an interesting and somewhat comprehensive discussion on Wittgenstein's distinction between explanation and description, see David Gruender's "Wittgenstein on Explanation and Description," *Journal of Philosophy,* LIX (September 13, 1962), pp. 523-30.
16. *Blue Book,* p. 18.
17. *PI* 109.

as an example of the sciences, Wittgenstein asserts that it tells us "something about . . . the precise *way* in which it is possible to describe it [the world] by these means."[18] He clarifies this point as follows:

> Newtonian mechanics, for example, imposes a unified form on the description of the world. Let us imagine a white surface with irregular black spots on it. We then say that whatever kind of picture these make, I can always approximate as closely as I wish to the description of it by covering the surface with a sufficiently fine square mesh, and then saying of every square whether it is black or white. In this way I shall have imposed a unified form on the description of the surface. The form is optional, since I could have achieved the same result by using a net with a triangular or hexagonal mesh. Possibly the use of a triangular mesh would have made the description simpler: that is to say, it might be that we could describe the surface more accurately with a coarse triangular mesh than a fine square mesh (or conversely), and so on. The different nets correspond to different systems for describing the world. Mechanics determines one form of description of the world by saying that all propositions used in the description of the world must be obtained in a given way from a given set of propositions —the axioms of mechanics. It thus supplies the bricks for building the edifice of science, and it says, "Any building that you want to erect, whatever it may be, must somehow be constructed with these bricks, and with these alone."[19]

Mechanics, like the other natural sciences, does not directly reveal something about the world; directly, it reveals something about the structures through which the propositions of the science organize the world. Science imposes a unified structure on the world and describes the world through that structure. And, regarding certain scientific laws, James Griffin argues "their function is not to make

18. *Tractatus* 6.342.
19. *Ibid.*, 6.341.

reports, not even very general ones, but to supply representational techniques by which reports can be made."[20] Thus Griffin concludes—and I think correctly—that "many general statements in science need not be treated as truth-functions of elementary propositions. They are not empirical so not strictly propositions. . . ."[21] In accepting this conclusion, then, there is an immediate problem revolving about *Tractatus* 4.11: The totality of true propositions is the whole of natural science (or the whole corpus of the natural sciences). Clearly, this proposition cannot be interpreted at face value, or else it would be erroneous.

We must be careful in evaluating and interpreting Wittgenstein's distinction between science and philosophy, between description and explanation; these pairs of terms are not as easily understood or as clear-cut as they may seem at first glance. By calling the method of science "explanation" and by distinguishing it from philosophy's method of description, Wittgenstein is not thereby saying that the method of science does *not* in any way utilize descriptive techniques. In 6.341 of the *Tractatus*, quoted above, Wittgenstein has explicitly referred to Newtonian mechanics as determining "one form of *description* of the world by saying that all propositions used in the description of the world must be obtained in a given way from a given set of propositions—the axioms of mechanics." The sciences indeed describe, but they do so through the specific models which they have constructed; that is, their description is really via an explanatory hypothesis. Philosophical description, however, functions without explicitly applying such constructs. Philosophy clarifies propositions of the sciences in accordance with the latter's own proposed logical structure.

Similarly, one can speak of the method of philosophy as a form of explanation—though not an explanation by hypothesis or construction. In the *PI,* for example, in an attempt to explicate what it means to know what a game is, Wittgenstein asks:

---

20. Griffin, p. 103. Cf., pp. 102-08 for a more comprehensive discussion on the language of science.
21. *Ibid.,* pp. 102-03.

> Isn't my knowledge, my concept of a game, complete-
> ly expressed in the explanations that I could give? That
> is, in my describing examples of various kinds of game;
> showing how all sorts of other games can be constructed
> on the analogy of these. . . .[22]

Here Wittgenstein is clearly speaking of an explanation
[*Erklärung*] as a description [*Beschreibung*]. The point is,
Waismann points out, that there is a variety of types of explanation.[23] There are explanations given by complete enu-
merations, by definition into *genus* and *differentia,* by describing examples, and by hypothesis. The explanation referred
to above in *PI* 75 is an explanation by describing various
examples. This is not, however, the explanation of constructing models utilized in science. Philosophical method is not
that of the sciences. Nor, is philosophy a science. "Philosophy
is not one of the natural sciences," Wittgenstein asserts, " (The
word 'philosophy' must mean something whose place is above
or below the natural sciences, not beside them.) "[24] Philosophy
does not make hypotheses or models. Rather, it is an attempt
to understand a question's problematic using basically *ordinary* language in purely descriptive and elucidating ways;
philosophy clarifies the problematic for science's constructive,
explanatory technique or reduces it to a meaningless, pseudo-
problem. "It is the business of philosophy, not to resolve a
contradiction . . . but to make it possible for us to get a clear
view of . . . the state of affairs *before* the contradiction is resolved."[25]

---

22. *PI* 75.
23. Cf., Waismann, pp. 163-93.
24. *Tractatus* 4.111.
25. *PI* 125. G. E. Moore relates how in Wittgenstein's lectures from 1930
    to 1933 "philosophy had now been 'reduced to a matter of skill,' yet
    this skill, like other skills, is very difficult to acquire. One difficulty
    was that it required a 'sort of thinking' to which we are not ac-
    customed and to which we have not been trained—a sort of thinking
    very different from what is required in the sciences." [G. E. Moore,
    "Wittgenstein's Lectures 1930-33," *Mind,* LXIV (January, 1955), p. 26.]

CHAPTER III

AN ANALYTIC PHENOMENOLOGY:
A METHODOLOGICAL COMPARISON

> The value of philosophy is, in
> fact, to be sought largely in its
> very uncertainty.
> —Bertrand Russell,
> *The Problems of Philosophy*

Now that we have presented Heidegger's and Wittgenstein's views on the method of philosophy and its relation to the sciences', someone may well insist that their perspectives are quite different and that no coincidence of ideas exists here. Indeed, dissimilarities abound between the two philosophers' thoughts. For Wittgenstein, philosophy is an analysis of linguistic expressions in an attempt to dissolve various misconceptions about language. Heidegger's main concern, on the other hand, is the pre-predicative, ontological ground of beings, namely Being. Nevertheless, if we take texts on the status of philosophy and its relation to the sciences and transform them into structural statements, we discover several significant coincidences of technique.

For both men, philosophy is not one of the natural sciences, nor can it be positioned on the same level as the sciences since it does not concern itself with what-is, i.e., physical things as such. Heidegger tells us that the subject matter of science is things; "the world-relationship which runs through all the sciences as such constrains them to seek what-is *in itself*. . . ."[1] Philosophy on the other hand "is an enquiry over and above what-is. . . ."[2]

---

1. WM, p. 326. (WIM, p. 6).
2. *Ibid.*, p. 344. (WIM, p. 19).

From the linguistic viewpoint, Wittgenstein likewise segregates philosophy from the sciences. "Philosophy is not one of the natural sciences," he asserts.[3] The language of the sciences consists of *true* propositions; its purpose is to tell, in some way, something about the world. Philosophy, however, has no doctrinal corpus; it does not concern itself with propositions of a specific type but with the elucidation or clarification of any and all types of propositions. As a result, the method of philosophy is different from the sciences'; the language of philosophy is purely descriptive whereas that of the sciences uses constructs or hypotheses. It is the method of scientific language to construct theories, hypotheses, and models to *explain* physical phenomena; whereas, philosophy using these propositions of the sciences or any other types of propositions as its subject matter elucidates any logical inconsistencies or incoherence which may have seeped into them. Thus, Wittgenstein concludes that "it was true to say that our [philosophic] considerations could not be scientific ones."[4]

Heidegger likewise segregates the method of philosophy from that of the sciences, the former being basically expository. In *Being and Time* he indicates that his phenomenological method of ontology does not construct hypotheses, but exhibits Being by revealing and elucidating it. This means that his phenomenological method is purely descriptive; as Heidegger himself states: "The expression 'descriptive phenomenology' which is at bottom tautological has the same meaning."[5]

In later works Heidegger uses the term "meditative thinking" to indicate this method of philosophy. Meditative thinking is phenomenological in that it is essentially descriptive, though by means of it, it is no longer man in his existential dimensions who reveals Being, but Being which reveals itself to man. In this self-revelation of Being, it is man's role to give an account of this revelation, i.e., to relate and recount this revelation. This means that man must *descriptively* present

3. *Tractatus* 4.111.
4. *PI* 109.
5. BT, p. 59. (SZ, p. 35).

and preserve Being's revelation. In meditative thinking, man does not construct or bring about Being's revelation: he awaits it in awareness. On man's part, there is an "openness to the mystery of Being" and a preservation of its presence. Again, Heidegger's method is characteristically narrative.

*   *   *

These above similarities might at first seem trivial and unimportant; however, when we recall that both men's radical segregation of philosophy from the sciences is to a large extent a reversal of the views of their respective teachers, Edmund Husserl and Bertrand Russell, its significance heightens. As we recall, in direct opposition to Heidegger's, it was Husserl's aim to make philosophy a rigorous science. In the *Cartesian Meditations,* for example, one of his principal aims is to search out that absolute foundation upon which philosophy would be an apodictic science.[6]

---

6. Edmund Husserl's *Cartesian Meditations,* I, Section 3-5. For interesting comments concerning Husserl's "Ideal of Rigorous Science," confer Spiegelberg, I, pp. 76-81.

It is perhaps best to indicate at this point—since we are discussing the dissimilarities between Heidegger's and Husserl's methods—that although both men call their philosophic methods phenomenological, these methods are not identical. It is true that Heidegger has dedicated *Being and Time* to Husserl "in friendship and admiration." Moreover, in footnote five of the introduction, Chapter 2 of the work, Heidegger does thank Husserl for his "own incisive personal guidance" (BT, p. 489) (SZ, p. 38) and later acknowledges that "the following investigation [*Being and Time*] would not have been possible if the ground had not been prepared by Edmund Husserl . . ." (BT, p. 62). (SZ, p. 38).

Nevertheless, we should not hastily conclude that the phenomenological method which Husserl utilized and advocated is the same as Heidegger's. Husserl's phenomenology sought out essences; concerning Being it had nothing to say. Furthermore, it had a starting point different from Heidegger's.

As Husserl states in his *Paris Lectures*:

First, anyone who seriously considers becoming a philosopher must once in his life withdraw into himself and then, from within attempt to destroy and rebuild all previous learning. . . . We thus . . . begin with the decision to disregard all our present knowledge. . . . Even the experience of the world . . . becomes an unacceptably naive belief. We can no longer accept the reality of the world as a fact to be taken for granted. . . . As radically meditating philosophers, we now have neither knowledge that is valid for us nor

Bertrand Russell's position on the relation of philosophy to the sciences—though definitely not Wittgenstein's—is not as abundantly clear as Husserl's. Throughout his philosophical career Russell propounded several points of view on the subject and, as Copleston remarks, "he has never been a man for gathering together all the threads and showing in detail how they fit together, how they form an intelligible pattern."[7] Such being the situation, let us look at Russell's most recent statement on the matter.

In the spring of 1959, interviewed for a television series, Russell was specifically questioned on the meaning of philosophy and its relation to the sciences. He replied:

> My own view would be that philosophy consists of speculations about matters where exact knowledge is not

---

a world that exists for us. [Edmund Husserl, *The Paris Lectures* (The Hague, 1964), pp. 3-7. *The Paris Lectures* consist of a pair of two-hour papers delivered at the Sorbonne on February 23 and 25, 1929. With modifications, they were later repeated in Strasbourg and eventually expanded into the *Cartesian Meditations*.]
This, then, is Husserl's initial perspective: to begin philosophizing unsuppositionally. This unsuppositional starting point is the "*a priori* of the 'I,'" the "essence of the ego qua ego." (*Ibid.*, pp. 28-29.)
In contradistinction to Husserl, Heidegger's *a priori* (his philosophical given) is the pre-predicative, pre-thematic relationship of man in his existential dimension and the world. He refers to it as the "'*a priori*' letting-something-be-involved" whereby results "the condition for the possibility of encountering anything" (BT, p. 117). (SZ, p. 85).
I am not sure whether in 1927 Heidegger was aware of this difference between his thought and his teacher's. Definitely in 1963 he was; he writes in the preface to Father Richardson's work *From Phenomenology to Thought*: "Now if in the title of your book, *From Phenomenology to Thought*, you understand 'Phenomenology' in the sense just described, as a philosophical position of Husserl, then the title is to the point, insofar as the Being-question as posed by me is something completely different from that position." [Martin Heidegger, "Preface" to William Richardson's *Heidegger: Through Phenomenology to Thought*, p. xiv. Cf., Thevénaz, pp. 37-66; Spiegelberg, I, pp. 318-26 and 346-53; and Otto Pöggeler, *La pensée de Martin Heidegger*, trans. Marianna Simon (Paris: Aubier-Montaigne, 1967), pp. 91-120, for further discussions on the usage of phenomenology by Husserl and Heidegger.]
7. Frederick Copleston, *Modern Philosophy: Bentham to Russell, A History of Philosophy*, VIII, Part II (New York: Doubleday, 1967), p. 243.

yet possible . . . science is what we know and philosophy is what we don't know. That's a simple definition and for that reason questions are perpetually passing over from philosophy into science as knowledge advances.[8]

For Russell, the problems of philosophy are the same as those of the sciences, except that philosophy approaches them first with its vague, initial hypotheses, at which time science is not in a position to confirm or refute them. When, however, the philosophical hypotheses are verified or refuted, they have become scientific, ceasing to be philosophical. Russell clearly restates this position in *Logic and Knowledge*:

> . . . I believe the only difference between science and philosophy is, that science is what you more or less know and philosophy is what you do not know. Philosophy is that part of science which at present people choose to have opinions about, but which they have no knowledge about. Therefore every advance in knowledge robs philosophy of some problems which formerly it had, and if there is any truth, . . . it will follow that a number of problems which had belonged to philosophy will have ceased to belong to philosophy and will belong to science.[9]

Russell's views as to what constitutes philosophy and the

8. Bertrand Russell, *Bertrand Russell Speaks His Mind* (Cleveland and New York: The World Publishing Company, 1960), p. 11.
9. Bertrand Russell, *Logic and Knowledge* (London: George Allen & Unwin Ltd., 1947), p. 281. ". . . Wittgenstein does not agree with Russell's view that philosophy is a science with a special nonempirical domain. Systematic search for truth in *any* domain is science for Wittgenstein, and we cannot consider philosophy as a separate science fundamentally distinct from all other sciences merely on the ground of the peculiarity of its subject matter. Thus, if philosophy is fundamentally distinct from the sciences, it must be, as we have said, because it is not a science at all, that is, it is not a pursuit of truth. Russell, according to Wittgenstein, is still guilty of confusion between science and philosophy in considering both of them as systems of true propositions. . . . Thus, our clarification ultimately does not itself consist of propositions. Philosophy is not a system of propositions, is not a science." [Alexander Maslow, *A Study in Wittgenstein's 'Tractatus'* (Berkeley and Los Angeles: University of California Press, 1961), p. 141

latter's relation to the sciences are radically different from Wittgenstein's. Russell sees the problems of philosophy as no different from those of the sciences. Wittgenstein does see a difference. Russell proposes that the methods of philosophy essentially are no different from those of the sciences: both are hypothetical. Wittgenstein views the problems of philosophy as being of a different nature and on a different level than those of the sciences. Wittgenstein never envisions the philosopher making universal hypotheses concerning the cosmos. Philosophy for Wittgenstein concerns itself with the logico-grammatical structures of language, science with existing states of affairs. The two disciplines are different both as to subject matter and method.[10]

*   *   *

At this point, our methodological study ends, yet a certain unmethodological remark remains to be made. If we step out of our role as methodologists, we observe a certain haze of ambiguity hanging over both Heidegger's and Wittgenstein's notions of "description." Both call their philosophy descriptive, yet both forms of description are puzzling. Descriptive language usage carries with it the connotation of an immediate representation of something observed or experienced;

---

10. At first glance, it may seem odd to speak of the subject matter of Wittgenstein's philosophy. After all, does he not state in *Tractatus* 4.112 that "Philosophy is not a body of doctrine but an activity. . . . Philosophy does not result in 'philosophical propositions,' but rather in the clarification of propositions."

It is true that for Wittgenstein philosophy does not have a specific subject matter as does biology, psychology, anthropology, etc. Philosophy tells nothing significant about the world. Nevertheless, one could speak of the subject matter of philosophy as language—not this specific language or that specific language but any language.

Now, in order for philosophy to clarify propositions, there must exist some propositions for it to clarify. These propositions become philosophy's subject matter. Certainly, they are the propositions of the sciences and they remain as such; nevertheless, they become the *content* which philosophy clarifies. This means that they become the subject matter for philosophical investigations. As a result, we can speak of the subject matter of philosophical clarifications without maintaining that philosophy is a doctrinal corpus. Philosophy, thus, retains its character of being solely an activity.

no interpretative, evaluative, or judgmental character enters into a purely descriptive context. Yet, Heidegger calls his descriptive phenomenology interpretive, or hermeneutical. A puzzle appears.

Wittgenstein also refers to philosophy as descriptive and definitely wants to distinguish philosophy from the sciences. But, again, such bifurcations are not as clear-cut as intended. How can philosophy be so distinct from science in both content and method when in fact the two greatest influences upon the writing of the *Tractatus* were Gottlob Frege and Heinrich Hertz, a mathematician and a physicist respectively? Hertz's *Principles of Mechanics* give the basic insights into Wittgenstein's picture theory of language. The *Tractatus* is not a purely descriptive work; even Wittgenstein's discussions on family resemblances and other minds to some extent overstep the bounds of description. Evaluative and interpretational techniques are operative in his works. Again, a puzzle appears.

In making these statements, it should not be thought that we are criticizing either thinker; rather, what has come to the surface is a certain puzzle about descriptive language—the notion of a pure description is something of an illusion. Explanation and description are not separate and distinct language activities; they blend together only to be distinguished by convention. Presented in the *Investigations*, Wittgenstein's notion of the duck-rabbit picture is quite helpful in this context; the picture is so structured that from one perspective it looks like a rabbit, from another a duck. Someone not familiar with this kind of picture, when asked what he sees, might answer "A rabbit" and proceed to describe its long ears, tiny mouth, eyes, etc. Another person, in the same situation, might view the picture as a duck and proceed to describe the duck's large bill—previously the rabbit's ears—the same small eye, and so forth. Neither person would call his description an interpretation or an explanation of what he saw; each would say he is merely *describing* what appears. Yet, both descriptions have an interpretive character about them; the two spectators have chosen different points of reference from which to view and thus interpret the picture. Neither person would say he is seeing the picture *as* a rabbit or *as* a duck;

such language would make no sense in this context. However, upon learning the situation, upon being told of the dual way of perceiving the picture, then upon viewing it for a second time, the one spectator might say "But I still see it *as* a duck" or perhaps "Oh yes! Now I see it *as* a rabbit." As Wittgenstein remarks, what seemed to be a description of something immediate, that is of some *visual* experience, turned out to be an interpretation, an indirect description.[11] Certainly, in some contexts, this interpretive element seems lacking. Take for example, eating utensils displayed upon a table in preparation for a dinner party. The cutlery in this context is simply cutlery! There really is no other way of looking at the eating utensils.[12] There is no way in this context that one could speak of seeing the utensils *as* cutlery. The reason for this, however, is that our actual language-activities—taken in a very broad sense—have not designated any other kinds of descriptions of the situation. All 'seeing" then is really a form of "seeing as." Linguistically, this means that all description is really a form of interpretation; however, in certain usages this interpretive character is so widely accepted and univocally articulated that it becomes taken for granted. "Instead of trying to define something as what is really seen," Wittgenstein maintains, "what we have rather to do is to *accept* the everyday language game. . . ."[13] Descriptive propositions, or what could be called factual, empirical propositions, are not absolutely distinct from non-descriptive ones. This does not mean that they are indistinguishable in use; rather, it means

---

11. *PI*, p. 193e. Cf., pp. 189-211.
12. *Ibid.*, p. 195e. It is interesting to note that in his *Philosophische Bemerkungen* Wittgenstein takes up the concept of phenomenology, discussing it in the context of certain of his own investigations. He speaks of it as purely descriptive technique, as a way of communicating direct experience. Spiegelberg also points out that in the last year of his life some of his studies—especially those on color-concepts—could be called by various philosophers "phenomenology." The texts are too sparse to say anything more definite or to correlate Wittgenstein's "phenomenology" with Heidegger's. Cf., Herbert Spiegelberg, "The Puzzle of Ludwig Wittgenstein's *Phänomenologie* (1929 — ?)," *American Philosophical Quarterly*, V (October, 1968), pp. 244-56. Also cf., Thomas N. Munson, "Wittgenstein's Phenomenology," *Philosophy and Phenomenological Research*, XXIII (March, 1962), pp. 37-50.
13. *Ibid.*, p. 200e.

that their uses are flexible. During the last year and a half of his life, Wittgenstein wrote some interesting remarks in this regard. They are collected in a text called *On Certainty*. Wittgenstein remarks:

> It might be imagined that some propositions, of the form of empirical propositions, were hardened and functioned as channels for such empirical propositions as were not hardened but fluid; and that this relation altered with time, in that fluid propositions hardened and hard ones became fluid.[14]

Certain linguistic uses are so rock-bottom fundamental to language activities that they have become the rules for that activity. "Isn't what I am saying: any empirical proposition can be transformed into a postulate—and then becomes a norm of description."[15] This is Wittgenstein's position.

Pure descriptions, factual utterances, are nothing more than generally accepted interpretations. I believe one could view Heidegger's concept of an "interpretive description" from the same perspective, although this cannot be positively shown through a textual analysis of Heidegger's works. In any case, both thinkers are skeptical of a pure description, as distinct from an interpretation.

Because of this basic concern of both thinkers over the term "description" and because of its equivocal character—there are many ways of describing—, we will in the following chapters speak more of a *representational* use of language, since representation is that kind of description in which we are most interested. We will use the term "description" in its general, categorical sense and "representation" as a specific kind of description, in particular that kind of description discussed in the *Tractatus*. Synonymous to "representation," we will use the terms "depiction," "depictment," and "picture." This distinction in nomenclature certainly is not un-

---

14. Ludwig Wittgenstein, *On Certainty*, edited by G. E. M. Anscombe and G. H. von Wright, translated by Denis Paul and G. E. M. Anscombe (Oxford: Basil Blackwell, 1969), 96. Cf., 94ff.

15. *Ibid.*, 321. Cf., 319-20. Wittgenstein hesitates to say *any* proposition can become solidified into a norm of description.

ambiguous and leads to various difficulties, although for our purposes the distinction is more beneficial than problematical.

In summary, we have shown that both Wittgenstein and Heidegger have radically separated philosophy from the sciences both as to subject matter and as to method. Moreover, we have shown that for both men the method of philosophy must be a simple descriptive narration. Wittgenstein's and Heidegger's respective methods of philosophy and their relations to the sciences, are methodologically congruent. This, however, is in no way indicative that the two men's philosophies are congruent *in toto*. Though both are descriptive in character, one could ask descriptive of what? It is in answer to this question—which is superfluous to methodological technique—that the convergence which we observed diverges.

For Wittgenstein, philosophy is reducible to the logical investigations of language; whereas, for Heidegger, philosophy becomes a rejuvenated metaphysics. Language is first introduced in Heidegger's early works only secondarily as part of the Being-structure by which Dasein is a being-in-the-world. Only in his later writings does Heidegger plunge with some depth into a philosophy of language. It is this later emphasis upon language in which we are primarily interested and to which our present investigations are but an introduction. Let us approach, then, Heidegger's views on language as he does—through Dasein's being-in-the-world. Thus, in the next chapter we will investigate Heidegger's ontological structure of the world of Dasein and its relation to language and Wittgenstein's logical structure of the proposition and its relation to the world and determine if any methodologic congruency exists within the two modes of thought.

PART II

THE STRUCTURES OF LANGUAGE
AND THE WORLD
AND THEIR RELATIONSHIP

CHAPTER IV

HEIDEGGER'S ONTOLOGICAL DESCRIPTION OF THE WORLD

> For it is this question—and it alone—
> that determines the way of my thought
> and its limits . . . The Being-question.
> —Heidegger, "A Letter from Hei-
> degger," *Heidegger and the Quest
> for Truth.*

The first difficulty which Heidegger confronts in his quest for Being consists in finding the proper perspective from which to reveal Being. Heidegger has already established the method of this revelation as hermeneutical phenomenology; the issue at hand is now to find that datum upon which to focus this phenomenological approach. This subject of investigation must be some entity, Heidegger reasons; since " 'Being' means the Being of entities, then entities themselves turn out to be *what is interrogated*. These are, so to speak, questioned as regards their Being. . . ."[1]

The entity appropriate for Heidegger's phenomenology we discover is man himself as the very inquirer into the Being-question; his very posing of the question, Heidegger maintains, presupposes that his Being is transparent unto himself. This inquirer—man viewed from his existential dimension—Heidegger designates by the term "Dasein."[2] An analysis of Dasein is the source of Being's disclosure.

---

1. BT, p. 26. (SZ, p. 6).
2. Literally, Dasein means "to-be-there." The translation, however, does not convey the connotations which Heidegger intends. For all practical purposes, Dasein refers to man in his concrete here and now existential life. Cf., Vincent Vycinas, *Earth and Gods* (The Hague: Martinus Nijhoff, 1961), pp. 23-28, especially 24-25.

Thus to work out the question of Being adequately, we must make an entity—the inquirer—transparent in his own Being. The very asking of this question is an entity's mode of *Being;* and as such it gets its essential character from what is inquired about—namely, Being. This entity which each of us is himself and which includes inquiring as one of the possibilities of its Being, we shall denote by the term "Dasein." If we are to formulate our question explicitly and transparently, we must first give a proper explication of an entity (Dasein), with regard to its Being.[3]

To reveal Being, Dasein must first look to its own existence. This does not mean, however, that Heidegger's philosophical starting point parallels Husserl's Transcendental Ego or Descartes' *Res Cogitans.* To the contrary, the Being of Dasein is Being-in-a-world.

. . . to Dasein, Being in a world is something that belongs essentially. Thus, Dasein's understanding of Being pertains with equal primordiality both to an understanding of something like a "world," and to the understanding of the Being of those entities which become accessible within the world.[4]

The hyphenated form of the phrase "being-in-the-world" is in no way accidental.[5] It is indicative of the primordial unity of the terms; moreover, since to-be-in-the-world is the existential character of Dasein, this structure is equally primal to Dasein itself. Thus, if we are to uncover the meaning of Being, according to Heidegger, an analysis of Dasein as being-in-the-world becomes our real point of departure. We will now discuss this phenomenon so as to disclose Heidegger's ontological structuring of the world and its relation to language. This seems, perhaps at first glance, a circuitous approach to our theme of prime interest, but it is not since language is a form of the

---

3. BT, p. 27. (SZ, p. 7).
4. *Ibid.*, p. 33. (SZ, p. 13).
5. Cf., Fernando Molina, *Existentialism as Philosophy* (Englewood Cliffs, New Jersey: Prentice-Hall Inc., 1962), pp. 58ff.

"being-in" relation between Dasein and the world; moreover, for Heidegger, any type of ontological discussion presupposes a discussion of the Being of Dasein.

Heidegger's Terminology

Before delving into Heidegger's notion of world and its relation to language, it is first necessary to elucidate some of his terminology. Heidegger's approach to philosophy does not always entail words in their ordinary senses; he is constantly coining new words or restructuring commonly used words into original combinations. It is essential to understand various of these linguistic innovations so as to grasp the meaning of the following texts. Although in the ensuing material I have attempted to keep Heidegger's technical vocabulary at a minimum and to utilize this vocabulary only in such a way that its meaning would be evident from the context, nevertheless, to insure the reader's comprehension of it, I think it necessary briefly to classify and explicate the meaning of a portion of Heidegger's technical vocabulary used in this section.

At first I envisioned at this point in the text a series of terms together with marginal definitions—Heidegger's vocabulary often defies any precise demarcation. As I scratched the surface of the task, however, I found even this procedure hopeless; Heidegger's language is too elusive. In place of these definitions, then, I have included the following table of terms categorized according to a twofold division crucial to Heidegger's thought: the existential vs the existentiell. Basic to Heidegger's scheme is the notion that any interpretation of man and his world is from one of these two perspectives. As existentiell, man is just an entity amid the multitude of other entities which populate his world. Man is interpreted as unengaged with and distinct from his fellowmen and environment; there he stands separated from and unconcerned of his world. The existential view interprets him as related to the world. Whereas, as an existentiell, man has meaning by himself; existentially, man's being becomes intelligible only in relation with that which surrounds him. Existential being is determined in and through his interaction with his environment; man's existential being transcends the discrete, isolated stature of the existentiell.[6]

One could, perhaps, in some sense make Heidegger's "existentiell-existential" distinction analogous to the "I-Thou/I-It" distinction of Martin Buber, the subjective/objective truth distinction of Soren Kierkegaard or the facticity/transcendence distinction within the *pour-soi* of J-P Sartre. Do not misunderstand. I am not in the least intimating these distinctions are all of the same kind; differences indeed abound. Yet, a loose kinship likewise abides which might be alluded to as a help in understanding the two classifications in Heidegger.

Given, then, these two dimensions or interpretive perspectives of Dasein, the following is a table of Heideggerian vocabulary used in this section. For our purposes, words under the existential or existentiell classification will be understood as being synonymous with the respective classification or as pertaining to that view. Admittedly, this is an oversimplification of Heidegger's thought.

existential	*existentiell*
ontological	ontic
authentic Dasein	inauthentic Dasein
existentiale (nominative)	categorical
form of existential)	thingly, thinghood

Keeping these distinctions in mind, let us tackle Heidegger's investigation into the world. Heidegger once again proceeds dialectically; that is, he first proposes a position which, although at first seems suitable, is really unacceptable. Consequently, he proceeds to modify, alter, and sophisticate the position till his phenomenological analysis is an accurate disclosure of the world.[7]

---

6. Cf., Richardson, pp. 49ff.
7. All of the major commentaries of Heidegger speak of Heidegger's understanding of world and its worldhood. The most comprehensive —though not the most critical—is Walter Biemel's *Le Concept de Monde chez Heidegger* (Louvain: E. Nauwelaerts, 1950).

The World of the Present-at-Hand

In his attempt to reveal the world in its ontological foundation, Heidegger first analyzes the existence of the present-at-hand as the possible authentic ground. Heidegger approaches this phenomena from a few perspectives, each a shade different; these nuances are not our concern and will thus be excluded from our discussion. Our interest in this exposition lies solely in the matter whether any approach to a world of present-at-hand-entities would be a possible avenue to Being.

"Presence-at-hand" Heidegger predicates of entities viewed within an existentiell framework. These entities have an intelligibility within themselves, separate from any environmental setting. The *world* of the present-at-hand is the totality of all entities, the sum of all houses, trees, mountains, etc., taken as an aggregation of entities side-by-side; the world of the present-at-hand is the world of things juxtaposed to each other—things solidified and unrelated. They have a positive density all their own, a substantiality by which they are categorizable. Of this approach, Heidegger concludes, "such a description is always confined to entities. . . . But what we are seeking is Being."[8]

The world of the present-at-hand can never reveal the ontological ground of entities. It is very similar in structure to the Cartesian view of the world of which Heidegger is extremely critical. Descartes has defined substance as "an entity which *is* in such a way that it needs no other entity in order to *be*."[9] Strictly speaking, by this definition only God is a substance since only He needs no other entity in order to be; however, relatively speaking Descartes allows within the realm of created entities two substances, the *res cogitans* and the *res extensa*. It is the aggregation of the *res extensa* which constitutes the Cartesian world of extended things; of such a position, Heidegger remarks: "But even if this ontology should itself succeed in explicating the Being of Nature . . . it will never reach the phenomenon that is the 'world.' "[10] "Descartes' conception of the world is ontolog-

---

8. BT, p. 91. (SZ, p. 63).
9. *Ibid.*, p. 125. (SZ, p. 92).
10. *Ibid.*, p. 92. (SZ, p. 63).

ically defective," Heidegger judges; "his Interpretation and
the foundations on which it is based have led him to *pass
over* both the phenomenon of the world and the Being of
those entities within-the-world which are proximally ready-
to-hand."[11]

With the notion of substance as primeval in Descartes'
philosophy, all entities within the world become ontologically juxtaposed in a presence-at-hand to each other; Dasein
itself becomes a substance unto itself among many. Descartes' philosophical starting point is oriented toward entities characterized by their thinghood and can never transcend this state of affairs; as a result, his analysis of the world
is doomed to fail from Heidegger's point of view. Thus,
Heidegger rejects this approach as a possible manifestation
of the ontological ground of the world, and directs his analysis upon the world of the ready-to-hand as ontologically more
primordial.

The World of the Ready-to-Hand

To understand the world, one cannot begin with entities *qua* entities or with the Being of them. The world is
known not by seeing it or its Being in itself, but by seeing
these as relative to Dasein. "Ontologically," Heidegger remarks, " 'world' is not a way of characterizing those entities
which Dasein essentially is *not;* it is rather a characteristic
of Dasein itself."[12] The authentic way of revealing the ontological ground of the world is through its relatedness to
Dasein. Before anything can be discovered as an entity of
Nature (i.e., as an entity in itself, unrelated to and apart
from its surroundings), it must already be *given* as related
to Dasein. In such a state it is ready-to-hand.

---

11. *Ibid.*, p. 128. (SZ, p. 95).
12. *Ibid.*, p. 92 (SZ, p. 64). "The *world* is *not* the world of things that are
    at hand, the things which, by virtue of their objectivity, a Person
    [Dasein] is not. . . . [O]ur tendency is to *objectify* the world, to view
    it as the spatially extended physical out-thereness. . . . What concerns
    Heidegger in this context is not the physical world, but the phenom-
    enon, the world, which gives itself to us as an immediate component
    of our basic situation being-in-the-world. The world is that in which
    the Person lives . . ." (Molina, p. 59).

This, then, is the reason why Heidegger has rejected the heretofore proposed meanings for the world: They already presuppose—though they do not admit it—the more fundamental ontological state of Dasein's relatedness to the world. They first postulate the thinghood of things and then proceed to examine their relations to Dasein. To reword this, the previously examined approaches to understand the ontological ground of the world took as their starting points the enumeration of entities and proceeded to explicate upon this basis the relations into which they enter. In Heidegger's words, this procedure erroneously views the world

> beforehand as something purely present-at-hand . . . [which] must have priority and take the lead in the sequence of those dealings with the "world" in which something is discovered and made one's own. But this already runs counter to the ontological meaning of cognition, which we have exhibited as a *founded* mode of Being-in-the-world. To lay bare what is just present-at-hand and no more, cognition must first penetrate *beyond* what is ready-to-hand in our concern.[13]

The reverse is impossible. " 'Nature,' as the categorical aggregate of those structures of Being which a definite entity encountered within-the-world may possess, can never make worldhood intelligible."[14] Traditional ontologies, Heidegger claims, detrimentally have attempted this procedure; they began with the world as apart and distinct from Dasein, and from this starting point sought to come to an understanding of Being. Such a procedure Heidegger considers a failure; it passes over Being. To overcome these difficulties, Heidegger's analysis of the world of the ready-to-hand presupposes that "in an entity which is supposedly a Thing, there is something that will not become fully intelligible through Thinghood alone,"[15] and admits of a pre-thingly encounter between Dasein and the world. In this context, then, world takes on a pre-predicative significance; the world

---

13. *Ibid.*, p. 101. SZ, p. 71).
14. *Ibid.*, p. 94. (SZ, p. 65).
15. *Ibid.*, p. 132. (SZ, p. 99).

of the ready-to-hand focuses upon entities in their relation to Dasein and establishes this relation as primal to the categorical character of the entities.

With these preliminary points set forth, Heidegger proceeds in analyzing "environmentality" as the "wherein" of Dasein's world. This analysis introduces to the reader two new words of Heidegger's technical vocabulary: "dealings" and "concern." Although Heidegger does not go into a detailed discussion of "dealings," for all practical purposes it can be equated with "concern," which Heidegger has previously defined as "an ontological term for an *existentiale*, and [it] will designate the Being of a possible way of Being-in-the-world."[16] In simpler terms, concern is the relational character of Dasein by which it refers itself toward things proximate to itself. Concern is that "which manipulates things and puts them to use."[17] It is the Being of these various entities of which man is concerned that Heidegger will use as his phenomenological starting point. "Such entities [of concern] . . . shall be taken as our preliminary theme and established as the pre-phenomenal basis for our study."[18] The generic term which Heidegger gives to these entities with which Dasein concerns itself is "equipment"; it is a collective term which applies to no specific item, but to all of Dasein's items of concern in general.

Entities of equipment cannot be such unless they are usable by Dasein; it is such a relation which constitutes the readiness-to-hand of these items and consequently precedes Dasein's awareness of the thingly character of the entities. It is the referential relation of, for example, hammering which is ontologically primordial to Dasein's understanding of a hammer as a thing.

> In dealings . . . our concern subordinates itself to the "in-order-to" which is constitutive for the equipment we are employing at the time; the less we just stare at the hammer-Thing, and the more we seize hold of it and use

---

16. *Ibid.*, p. 83. (SZ, p. 57).
17. *Ibid.*, p. 95. (SZ, p. 67).
18. *Ibid.*, pp. 95-96. (SZ, p. 67).

it, the more primordial does our relationship to it become, and the more unveiledly is it encountered as that
which it is—as equipment.[19]

The practical activity of hammering is antecedent to the
possibility of understanding the ontological meaning of
a hammer. And when the meaning of the entity "hammer" is grasped in and through the activity, it is done as something "ready-to-hand." The ready-to-hand, then, is constituted in a relation to Dasein—a relation which Heidegger
here designates as "activity." Heidegger illustrates this point
by the example of cobblery. To summarize the example:
In making a shoe, as cobbler, Dasein's chief concern is
the activity; however, this activity is itself referential in two
directions. It refers (has recourse) in retrospect to the
tools and materials used in making it; moreover, these
tools and materials refer back to Nature—to animals from
which comes the shoe's leather and to the wood and steel
which compose the hammer. Likewise, the activity has a for-
ward referentiality: The making of the shoe can only be
comprehended in relation to for whomever the shoe is
made. It is a *totality* of interconnected relationships bound
to a single activity which defines the shoe which underpins
the activity. In the making of a shoe there exists through the
shoe a chain of relationships linking Dasein to the shoe, to
the equipment used in making the shoe, and even to Nature
itself which composes the various pieces of equipment. Thus,
Heidegger concludes that "when we deal with them [entities]
by using them and manipulating them, this activity is not a
blind one; it has its own kind of sight, by which our manipulation is guided and from which it acquires its specific Thingly character."[20] Notice here Heidegger is stating that the use
of an entity gives that entity *only* its "specific Thingly character." Does this use also make Dasein aware of the entity's
"specific Thingly character"? Here the answer must be "no."

Equipment can genuinely show itself only in dealings
cut to its own measure (hammering with a hammer,

---

19. *Ibid.*, p. 98. (SZ, p. 69).
20. *Ibid.* (SZ, p. 69).

for example) ; but in such dealings an entity of this kind is not *grasped* thematically as an occurring Thing, nor is the equipment-structure known as such even in the using. The hammering does not simply have knowledge about the hammer's character as equipment . . . .[21]

Activity (being-related-to-Dasein) only primordially structures and shapes an entity as such; this activity alone and in itself does not *reveal* the entity's thinghood to Dasein. Such a *revelation,* as Heidegger points out, occurs through a deficiency in activity; it occurs through some form of blocking activity between Dasein and the entity to which it is related.

> When we concern ourselves with something, the entities . . . may be met as something unusable . . . . The tool turns out to be damaged, or the material unsuitable. . . . When its unusability is thus discovered, equipment becomes conspicuous. This *conspicuousness* presents the ready-to-hand equipment as in a certain unreadiness-to-hand.[22]

Things ready-at-hand can be encountered only as "unready-to-hand." This consists in a disruption of the referentiation between an entity which is ready-to-hand and Dasein itself. Such a disruption, Heidegger explains, can come about in three ways: the entity which should be ready-to-hand is in itself unready-to-hand because either the entity itself to which Dasein is related becomes unusable in the sense of being damaged or mutilated, or the entity itself to which Dasein is to be related is missing, or another entity's presence or absence disrupts the relation between the ready-to-hand entity and Dasein.[23] At this point within the text Heidegger introduces three new terms—conspicuousness, obtrusiveness, and obstinacy—and respectively correlates one to each mode of un-readiness-to-hand.

When an entity which is ready-to-hand is unusable, it becomes conspicuous; that is to say, it has existentially lost its

---

21. *Ibid.* (SZ, p. 69).
22. *Ibid.,* pp. 102-03. (SZ, p. 73).
23. *Ibid.,* p. 103. (SZ, p. 73).

usable referentiality to Dasein. Dasein is suddenly disrupted from the activity with which it was concerned and its attention is *drawn* toward the item of equipment not as something to which it is related but as something there, within itself, apart from all else. ". . . that what cannot be used just lies there . . . ."[24] Its concrete, existential readiness-to-hand fades and all that Dasein encounters is the entity's thinghood. This entity's readiness-to-hand has not *completely* vanished from the latter's constitution; its concrete, existential relationship to Dasein has only been radically subdued. "This presence-at-hand of something that cannot be used is still not devoid of all readiness-to-hand whatsoever; equipment which is present-at-hand *in this way* is still not just a Thing which occurs somewhere."[25] If it were, then it could not be differentiated *in any way* from something which is merely present-at-hand.

When an item of equipment which is ready-to-hand is missing, it becomes obtrusive. The item which should have been "ready-to-hand" is no longer present to Dasein. Its absence has, so to speak, created a "hole" in a matrix of relationships directed towards Dasein. In doing such, the missing entity has "frozen" this matrix's concrete, workable relatedness and has called Dasein's attention (again, note Dasein's passivity) to this structure as such and most especially to its "hole" due to the absence of the ready-to-hand entity. This "hole" (silhouetted in the matrix of relations) is seen by Dasein precisely as bounded by the other items of equipment in the matrix; it is seen as precisely outlined and apart from these items; it is seen in its thinghood. Its existential relatedness to Dasein has become subdued.

When an entity blocks an item of equipment from Dasein's view—thereby "standing in Dasein's way" of concern for the latter—it becomes obstinate. This blocking entity confronts Dasein as the unwanted or unusable; and, as such, it becomes unrelatable to Dasein. The unusable entity presents itself to Dasein as some-*thing,* an *object* in its presence-at-hand, and the existential relatedness to Dasein of the item of equipment has become subdued.

---

24. *Ibid.* (SZ, p. 73).
25. *Ibid.* (SZ, p. 73).

These above three deficient modes of Being—conspicuous-ness, obtrusiveness, and obstinacy—are the three ways in which an entity ready-to-hand manifests itself to Dasein. "But," Heidegger asks, "how far does this clarify the *phenomenon of the world?*"[26] This is the key question. Heidegger's main theme is to uncover the phenomenon of the world and its worldhood; in what way has his analysis thus far accomplished this? Heidegger's answer to this question lies in the fact that his analysis thus far has "brought ourselves to a point where we can bring it [the world and its worldhood] into view."[27] The ready-to-hand is encountered within-the-world. The Being of the entity which is ready-to-hand thus stands in some ontological relationship towards the world and towards worldhood. In anything ready-to-hand, the world is already there. "Whenever we encounter anything, the world has already been previously discovered . . . . The world is that in terms of which the ready-to-hand is ready-to-hand."[28]

The Heideggerian World and its Worldhood

Thus far in his investigations, Heidegger has focused upon the entity ready-to-hand and has disregarded the system of relations which holds between the entity ready-to-hand, its surroundings, and Dasein. It is precisely this "lifting out" of the ready-to-hand from this totality-matrix of environmental relationships that has caused Heidegger to pass over the world and its worldhood. Both have been peripherally present throughout Heidegger's exposition; now, however, Heidegger intends to bring them to the foreground by re-examining the ready-to-hand in its *integral relatedness* with surrounding referents of the totality-matrix from the viewpoint of their referential and assigning character. The assigning character and reference, however, should not be interpreted as properties which the ready-at-hand possesses. They are rather the ontological conditions by which an entity can eventually be defined within the context of the ready-to-hand.

26. *Ibid.*, p. 104. (SZ, p. 74).
27. *Ibid.* (SZ, p. 74).
28. *Ibid.*, p. 114. (SZ, p. 83).

But what, then, is "reference" or "assignment" to mean? To say that the Being of the ready-to-hand has the structure of assignment or reference means that it has in itself the character of *having been assigned or referred*. An entity is discovered when it has been assigned or referred to something, and referred as that entity which it is.[29]

It is this referential involvement which "is the condition for the possibility of encountering anything ready-to-hand. . . ."[30] To encounter some-*thing* as ready-to-hand consists in a freeing of it from a totality of involvements and centering upon its most primary employment. Utilizing the example of the hammer, Heidegger relates that, when a cobbler uses the instrument to repair a shoe, the hammer's *immediate involvements* constitute its readiness-to-hand: The hammering unites the cobbler, the shoe, and the nail being hammered into the shoe. Yet, an even greater totality-matrix of involvements is ontologically contributive to this event: the owner of the shoe, the event by which his shoe became unusable, the raw materials which went into making the nail, the shoe, and even the hammer, etc. Ontologically, all these events contributed to the cobbler's sitting down to his bench and repairing the shoe in question, though only the most proximate are what constitute the hammer as an instrument ready-to-hand in repairing the shoe.

As the Being of something ready-to-hand, an involvement is itself discovered only on the basis of the prior discovery of a totality of involvements. . . . In this totality of involvements which has been discovered beforehand, there lurks an ontological relationship to the world.[31]

This totality-matrix of relationships wherein Dasein directs itself to a specific relational involvement of an entity ready-at-hand is the world. The "wherein" by which Dasein

---

29. *Ibid.*, p. 115. (SZ, pp. 83-84).
30. *Ibid.*, p. 117. (SZ, p. 85).
31. *Ibid.*, p. 118. (SZ, p. 85).

"assigns or refers itself, is that for which one lets entities be encountered in the kind of Being that belongs to involvements; and this 'wherein' is the phenomenon of the world."[32] The Heideggerian world is Dasein's "wherein"; it is the overall context of relations into which Dasein can enter. And, the character of this context constitutes the worldly character of the world—or as Heidegger refers to it, the world's "worldhood." "And the structure of that to which Dasein assigns itself is what makes up the *worldhood* of the world."[33] The relations, assignments, and references which constitute the totality-matrix of the world "are bound up with one another as a primordial totality. . . . This is what makes up the structure of the world—the structure of that wherein Dasein as such already is."[34] The world is a surd-like system of relations relative to Dasein, and its worldly dimension is its relational framework. "The context of assignments or references, which, as significance, is constitutive for worldhood, can be taken formally in the sense of a system of Relations."[35] The world is neither a spatial container nor an aggregation of things—but an existential state of Dasein. As Magda King sums up Heidegger's position:

> The world is not a thing, but man himself is world-ish: he is, at the bottom of his being, world-disclosing, world-forming. Man alone is so, that he fore-goingly, a priori, understands his own being in a relation-whole, in which and from which he can meet other beings and understand them in *their* being.[36]

Language: A Manner of Dasein's "Being-in" the World

On hearing the phrase "being-in," we of the twentieth century, so conditioned by mathematical calculation and geometrico-physical constructions, immediately think of a spatially-containing relationship like "The broom is *in* the clos-

---

32. *Ibid.*, p. 119. (SZ, p. 86).
33. *Ibid.* (SZ, p. 86).
34. *Ibid.*, p. 120. (SZ, p. 87).
35. *Ibid.*, p. 121. (SZ, p. 88).
36. Magda King, *Heidegger's Philosophy: A Guide to His Basic Thought* (New York: The Macmillan Company, 1964), p. 73.

et" or "The car is *in* the garage." "By this 'in' we mean the
relationship of Being which two entities extended 'in' space
have to each other with regard to their location in that
space."[37] This notion of "in" refers to things, entities which
are present-at-hand and thus always related by juxtaposition.
This, however, is not the relation which Dasein has to the
world.

> Being-in . . . is a state of Dasein's Being; it is an
> existentiale. So one cannot think of it as the Being-
> present-at-hand of some corporeal Thing (such as a hu-
> man body) "in" an entity which is present-at-hand. Nor
> does the term "being-in" mean a spatial "in-one-another-
> ness" of things present-at-hand, any more than the word
> "in" primordially signifies a spatial relationship of this
> kind.[38]

Dasein's "being-in" the world is not a spatial enclosure of
Dasein by the world's extensional boundaries. Being-in is
instead Dasein's circumspective concern toward equipmental
entities. Equipment, as we recall, has a readiness-to-hand;
each item of equipment has a specific relation to the totality
of equipment of which it is a part and to Dasein to which it
is ready-to-hand. It is this relation which constitutes the *place*
of the ready-to-hand piece of equipment. Its spatiality is not
a physical position but a relational location to Dasein. Dasein's "'spatiality' cannot signify anything like occurrence at
a position 'world-space,' nor can it signify Being-ready-to-
hand at some place."[39] This means that the spatiality of Dasein makes entities potentially ready-to-hand; it structures
and organizes them in a specific matrix of relations so that
they can become "explicit and easily manipulable."[40] Heidegger's ontological world-space is a referential matrix to which

---

37. BT, p. 79. (SZ, p. 54).
38. *Ibid.*, pp. 79-80. (SZ, p. 54). This does not mean that Dasein cannot
    enter into spatial relations or that it never assumes the character of
    an object present-at-hand; Dasein can indeed take on the character of
    thinghood. However, such a character is not part of its authentic way
    of being.
39. *Ibid.*, p. 138. (SZ, p. 104).
40. *Ibid.*, p. 143. (SZ, p. 108).

Dasein involves itself with its circumspective concern.

Dasein is a being-in-the-world, not as an entity inside of it, but as that which relates itself and projects itself into worldly involvements. This projectivity, moreover, is not limited to one specific and determined way of being-present to the world; rather, it is constituted by the multitude of ways by which Dasein can relate itself to the world. This multitude of undifferentiated possibilities—in order to be significant—is to be mapped out into certain definite paths and intelligibly demarcated within the totality-matrix which it constitutes. This is done through language; it is "the articulation of intelligibility."[41] Language, then—in conjunction with understanding and states of mind—, constitutes Dasein's mode of being-in-the-world.[42]

Language is the way of articulating and laying bare the ontological structure of the world onto a level of intelligibility, which it shares in common with the latter insofar as both are projections of Dasein. "What the discourse is about is a structural item that it necessarily possesses; for discourse helps to constitute the disclosedness of Being-in-the-world, and in its own structure it is modelled upon this basic state of Dasein."[43]

The numerous ways by which Dasein can engage itself to the world is the totality-region through which meaning is made possible. Heidegger refers to this region as the "totality-of-significations."[44] Dasein's everyday activities, however, are always contingent and merely fragmentary paths within

---

41. *Ibid.*, p. 204. (SZ, p. 161).
42. Given these modes of Dasein as that by which the worldly character of the world is constituted, it would seem that Heidegger's ontological status of the world is reduced to a psychological state of Dasein. Heidegger is very much aware of such a criticism and vehemently denies it ". . . if we raise the question of the 'world,' *what* world do we have in view? . . . not the subjective world (i.e., Dasein's psyche), but *the worldhood of the world as such*" [*Ibid.*, p. 92. (SZ, p. 64). Cf., p. 121. (SZ, pp. 87-88).] This is certainly Heidegger's contention. Yet, it is one thing to deny charges of psychologism and another thing to prove this denial. This issue is discussed again in Chapter 6. Cf., King, p. 71.
43. *Ibid.*, p. 205. (SZ, p. 162).
44. *Ibid.*, p. 204. (SZ, p. 161).

this totality-matrix. Language through Dasein's projective relation to the world disengages specific relational paths from the totality-matrix and solidifies them with specific meanings. The question thus arises: "... what kind of Being goes with language in general. Is it a kind of equipment ready-to-hand within-the-world, or has it Dasein's kind of Being, or is it neither of these?"[45] Heidegger never really answers this question in *Being and Time;* it is not until the later Heidegger emerges that a firm answer is given. Nevertheless, he does point out in *Being and Time* that the logical approach of the present-day philosopher of language is not equipped to answer this question. "Philosophical research will have to dispense with the 'philosophy of language' if it is to inquire into the ... fundamental kind of Being belonging to discourse...."[46] According to Heidegger, the problem with the logical approach toward language and its relation to the world is that it takes as its starting point entities present-at-hand and thus passes over their ontological foundation; consequently, Heidegger maintains that there exists "the necessity of re-establishing the science of language on foundations which are ontologically more primordial."[47]

45. *Ibid.*, p. 209. (SZ, p. 166).
46. *Ibid.*, pp. 209-10. (SZ, p. 166).
47. *Ibid.*, p. 209. (SZ, p. 165). Cf., Borgmann, p. 141.

CHAPTER V

WITTGENSTEIN'S LOGICAL DESCRIPTION
OF LANGUAGE

> My *whole* task consists in explaining the nature of the proposition.
>
> —Wittgenstein, *Notebooks.*

Heidegger had proclaimed that every philosopher centers his writings upon a single thought. For Heidegger himself this thought is Being; for Wittgenstein, it is the proposition. The same intense concentration with which we observed Heidegger analyze the world in an attempt to elucidate Being, we now find within Wittgenstein's analysis of elementary propositions in an attempt to elucidate the logical structure of representational language. Let us follow Wittgenstein in his attempt to lay bare this structure and observe how he relates it to the world. We will begin with an analysis of texts found in the *Tractatus.*

> The whole sense of the book might be summed up in the following words: what can be said at all can be said clearly, and what we cannot talk about we must pass over in silence.

With these words Wittgenstein prefaces his *Tractatus Logico-Philosophicus.* From such introductory remarks, one would think that the work is written in flowing prose, lucid in style to any and every reader. Yet, this is hardly the case; Wittgenstein's terse, extremely compact, aphoristic style creates an enigmatic aura. Rudolf Metz writes of the *Tractatus*: "It is for the ordinary reader a book sealed with seven seals, of which the significance is only to be revealed to the

most esoteric devotees . . . ."[1] Brand Blanshard remarks in a
similar vein that "Wittgenstein . . . has the strange distinction
of having produced a work on logic beside which the *Logic* of
Hegel is luminously intelligible."[2] The *Tractatus* has indeed
not been accepted as *the* most translucent philosophical work
of this century; nevertheless, it is already a classic.

The Logical Structures of the Proposition and of the World

Within the *Tractatus*, Wittgenstein distinguishes between
a proposition [*Satz*] and an elementary proposition [*Elemen-
tarsatz*]. The proposition is the result of operations applied
to elementary propositions, and is thus reducible to them by
analysis. "It is obvious that the analysis of propositions must
bring us to elementary propositions."[3] Ultimately, then, the
goal of Wittgenstein's quest as expressed above in *Notebooks*
22.1.15 lies in the elementary propositional structure. It is
here then that our investigations must begin.

The elementary proposition, Wittgenstein states, is the
simplest kind of proposition and it consists of names in immediate combination. "An elementary proposition consists
of names. It is a nexus, a concatenation, of names."[4] These
names, furthermore, have a specific relational structure as a
result of their concatenation; they are determined as names
in their relation to each other. The concatenation is not a
mere gathering together of names. "A proposition is not a
medley of words.— (Just as a theme in music is not a medley
of notes.) A proposition is articulated."[5] The sum total of
propositions is not the sum total aggregation of names in combination. It is rather the sum total of the specific sensical relations wherein names are determined.

These relations, however, are nothing over and above the

1. Rudolf Metz, quoted in the introduction to *Essays on Wittgenstein's
   'Tractatus,'* ed. Irving M. Copi and Robert W. Beard (New York:
   Macmillan Company, 1966), pp. ix-x.
2. Brand Blanshard, quoted in the introduction to *Essays on Wittgenstein's 'Tractatus,'* p. x.
3. *Tractatus* 4.221. Cf., 5.22, 5.23, and 2.0201.
4. *Ibid.,* 4.22.
5. *Ibid.,* 3.141. Cf., 2.141, 3.14, 3.141.2, 3.1431 and 4.0311.

names themselves in concatenation. The relations are the ways names are situated to one another, logically speaking. As Wittgenstein states in gloss 3.1432 of the *Tractatus:* Instead of, 'The complex sign "aRb" says that a stands to b in the relation R,' we ought to put, '*That* "a" stands to "b" in a certain relation says *that aRb.*' By this is meant that the relation symbolized by R of *aRb* has no isolated, substantive—as Wittgenstein uses the term[6]—logical role. It is not an argument place as are a and b. Wittgenstein confirms our interpretation in his *Notes on Logic.* Here he explicitly states: "Symbols are not what they seem to be. In 'aRb,' 'R' looks like a substantive but it is not one. . . . Hence 'R' is *not* the indefinable [object] in 'aRb.' "[7]

Correlative to the logical structure of the proposition, Wittgenstein describes the logical structure of the facts of the world. In fact, the structures are coincidental, with merely a change in terminology. Whereas language consists in the totality of propositions, "the world is the totality of facts. . . ."[8] "The world divides into facts."[9] And, the fact—what is the case—"is the existence of states of affairs."[10] The world and representational language are like two sides of one and the same reality, sharing in common a specific form. Just as the elementary proposition is a concatenation of names, its worldly counterpart, the fact, or existing state of affairs, is a concatenation of objects [*Gegenstand*]. It is their configurations which form states of affairs. "In a state of affairs objects stand in a determinate relation to one another."[11] And, it is this "determinate way in which objects are connected in a state of affairs [which] is the structure of the state of affairs."[12] The question is, then, how are the objects connected in a state of affairs? Is there something in the state of affairs over and above it, structuring it in a determinate way? The answer is in the negative. "In a state of affairs objects fit into

6. *Ibid.,* 2.021 and 2.0211.
7. *Notebooks,* p. 99.
8. *Tractatus* 1.1.
9. *Ibid.,* 1.2.
10. *Ibid.,* 2.
11. *Ibid.,* 2.031.
12. *Ibid.* 2.032.

one another like the links of a chain."[13] The structure of the
fact is the way the objects are concatenated; it is internal to
the objects as related and not some substantive relation apart
from them.

The Wittgensteinian Object

What is a Wittgensteinian object [*Gegenstand*]? In the
Notebooks, Wittgenstein reflects that "the particular object is
a very remarkable phenomenon."[14] How true this is! Its re-
markability is evidenced by commentators' widely divergent
interpretations of it. Griffin, for example, refers to its being
analogous to a material point.[15] Alexander Maslow refers to it
as constituted by sense data, in accordance with his positivistic
interpretation of the *Tractatus,* though he also admits as other
viable interpretations: Plato's universals, Whitehead's objects, and Santayana's essences.[16] Copi maintains that an object
is a bare particular, that is, a particular "having no material properties whatever," but merely formal ones. Accordingly, he concludes that neither relations nor properties are
objects.[17] Stenius takes a somewhat different view; he includes predicates (properties) as examples of objects. ". . . an
elementary sentence 'consists of names in immediate connection' (4.221) —and here not only names of individual objects
must be meant, but also 'names' of predicates."[18]

13. *Ibid.,* 2.03.
14. *Notebooks* 11.7.16.
15. Griffin, p. 47ff.
16. Maslow, pp. 9-12.
17. Irving Copi, "Objects, Properties, and Relations in the *Tractatus,*"
    Mind, LXVII (April, 1958), p. 163. Cf.,, *Essays on Wittgenstein's
    'Tractatus,'* Richard J. Bernstein's "Wittgenstein's Three Languages,"
    pp. 231-48, especially pp. 237-42, and Wilfrid Sellars' "Naming and
    Saying," pp. 249-70. David Keyt argues that Copi's error in bluntly
    asserting that Wittgenstein's objects have "no material properties what-
    ever" (p. 163) results from his failure to notice the broad sense in
    which "property" is used in the *Tractatus.* Copi's conclusion, accord-
    ing to Keyt, would be sound if the word "quality" is substituted for
    "property." Cf. Keyt's article: "Wittgenstein's Notion of an Object,"
    Essays on Wittgenstein's 'Tractatus,' pp. 289-304, especially pp. 291ff.
    In answer to Keyt's accusation, it should be noted that Copi does
    acknowledge Wittgenstein's "certain looseness" in employing the key
    term "property." Cf., Copi, pp. 160ff.
18. Erik Stenius, *Wittgenstein's 'Tractatus'* (Oxford: Basil Blackwell,
    1964), p. 68. Cf., pp. 25 and 97.

Which commentator is correct in his interpretation? If we look to the pre-*Tractatus* writings, we find that they all can substantiate their interpretations to varying degrees. In the *Notebooks,* Wittgenstein proposes a multitude of possible objects including "points in the visual field,"[19] "patches in the visual field,"[20] "the visual appearance of stars,"[21] "material points of physics,"[22] and "relations and properties"[23] in general. Yet—and this is the crucial point of this discussion—having proposed these as possible examples of objects, he concludes: "Our difficulty was that we kept on speaking of simple objects and were unable to mention a single one."[24] Therefore, one cannot utilize these texts as bases for a coherent theory as to what constitutes a Wittgensteinian object. As Favrholdt states of these and similar pre-*Tractatus* passages:

> It is impossible to find out from them what Wittgenstein himself regarded as an example of an object, and the text of the *Tractatus* is no more helpful as it does not contain any examples, which are given as examples, but only a few hints which cannot support an argumentation.[25]

This point is well taken. The Wittgenstein of the *Tractatus* certainly does not explicitly offer an example of an object. As a result, Maslow interprets those parts of the *Tractatus* dealing with objects as being among the most abstruse.[26] Admittedly, certain of the *Tractatus* texts on this theme are difficult to comprehend; nevertheless, we should not be misled into thinking that the glosses are so obscure that arbitrarily any and every interpretation of an object is acceptable. Certain definitive points can be made in this regard and certain commentators' remarks are misdirected.

---

19. *Notebooks* 18.6.15.
20. *Ibid.*
21. *Ibid.*
22. *Ibid.*, 21.6.15.
23. *Ibid.*, 16.6.15.
24. *Ibid.* 21.6.15.
25. David Favrholdt, *An Interpretation and Critique of Wittgenstein's 'Tractatus'* (Copenhagen, Denmark: Munksgaard, 1964), p. 56.
26. Maslow, p. 4.

Norman Malcolm relates how he once asked Wittgenstein whether he had solidified his thoughts upon the matter during the writing of the *Tractatus* and had finally decided upon an example of a simple object. Wittgenstein is to have replied that "at that time his thought had been that he was a *logician*; and that it was not his business, as a logician, to try to decide whether this thing or that was a simple thing or a complex thing, that being a purely *empirical* matter!"[27] At first, I concluded that this response was an evasion of the question; however, since then having reflected upon it in conjunction with gloss 4.1272 of the *Tractatus*, I retract my conclusion. In gloss 4.1272, Wittgenstein indicates that "object" is a *logical* term within the *Tractatus* and functions as such. Its *logical* role is to act as a place marker for the arguments within any given proposition; thus, its content is always dependent upon specific contextual instantiations of propositional values and is determined by an "empirical" investigation of propositions. The Wittgensteinian object in its logical role has no content apart from the contextual content of the arguments which saturate it in *de facto* propositions.

Leading to gloss 4.1272, Wittgenstein distinguishes between formal concepts and concepts proper. The former are expressed as propositional variables, the latter as the instantiations of those variables. Thus, "The book is on the table," configures a proposition since it consists in a concatenation of concepts proper; no variables appear within the sentence. But to say "The object is on the table" or "There are 100 objects"—intending by this a genuine sensical proposition—results in a pseudo-proposition, since "object" is a variable concept and not a concept proper. This is the importance of gloss 4.1272: it makes explicit that the Wittgensteinian "object" is a variable, a place marker having no content apart from given instantiations. Thus, to ask for an example of an object, without having given a specific propositional context, results in a pseudo-question. For it to be a meaningful question, an elementary propositional context must be given, and

27. Norman Malcolm, *Ludwig Wittgenstein: A Memoir* (London: Oxford University Press, 1958), p. 86.

from it the instantiations of the formal concept (the object) can be determined. But this is an empirical matter. Maslow summarizes the situation rather well as follows:

> There are no entities in the world for which the term "object" stands as a proper or general name. "Object" does not indicate anything in the world, but is a linguistic device for speaking about genuine or generic concepts like "table" or "red," or proper names, which when in use do stand for something in reality. "Object" is a variable standing in an incomplete expression; it is but a blank in a propositional schema or propositional function which is to be filled before this schema acquires definite sense, becomes a significant proposition. It is, for example, the "x" of $f(x)$.[28]

In the *Tractatus,* Wittgenstein is seeking out the *logic* of descriptive language. To ask for an example of an "object" is not a logical question and superfluous to the trend of thought found in the *Tractatus.*[29] Furthermore, such a question is meaningless insofar as the instantiations of and, therefore, the exemplification of the variable "object" cannot logically occur in isolation, but only in a given propositional context.[30]

From Wittgenstein's presentation of "object" as a logical entity, it becomes clear that objects do not have an ontological status. Thus, when in 2.021 of the *Tractatus* it is stated that "objects" make up the substance of the world," it is readily seen that the term "substance" has no metaphysical connotations,[31] although some commentators attribute such an ontological interpretation to the text. For example, Maslow states:

---

28. Maslow, p. 8.
29. It is true, however, that in the *Notebooks* Wittgenstein does concern himself with examples of objects. Cf., 18.6.15 and 16.6.15.
30. Cf., Robert Sokolowski, "Ludwig Wittgenstein: Philosophy as Linguistic Analysis," *Twentieth-Century Thinkers,* ed. with an introduction by John K. Ryan (Staten Island, New York: Abba House, 1964), pp. 178-79.
31. Cf., Griffin, pp. 70-71, for a discussion on the difference between Aristotelian and Wittgensteinian usages of the term "substance."

. . . occasionally he [Wittgenstein] succumbs to the
temptation and talks metaphysical nonsense; his treatment of "object" is an example. It seems that at times he
means by "object" the ultimate ontological simple entities out of which the real world "in itself" is made. . . .[32]

The "substantiality" of the Wittgensteinian object does not
refer to an unchanging or immutable metaphysical essence
or nature. "Substance is what subsists independently of what
is the case."[33] To exist independently of what is the case is
indicative of a logical, not an ontological, status. Ultimately,
logical substantiality means that objects lack internal composition: "Objects make up the substance of the world. That
is why they cannot be composite."[34] Substantiality is objects'
non-composite, undefinable "rock-bottom" logical foundation
of states of affairs. The substantiality of objects means that
they are the *logically* indivisible constituents of a fact.

Representational Propositions: The Pictorial
Relation of Language to the World

Elementary propositions are names in immediate concatenation. To say that they picture facts, or existing states
of affairs, means two things: first, that the names in the proposition stand for the objects in the state of affairs and second, that the structural configuration of concatenated names
in the proposition mirror the concatenation of objects in the
state of affairs. Wittgenstein states in the *Tractatus:*

> A name means an object. The object is its mean-
> ing.[35]
> In a picture the elements of the picture are the
> representatives of objects.[36]
> The fact that the elements of a picture are related
> to one another in a determinate way represents that
> things are related to one another in the same
> way.[37]

32. Maslow, p. 11. Cf., Griffin, pp. 153ff.
33. *Tractatus* 2.024.
34. *Ibid.,* 2.021.
35. *Ibid.,* 3.203.
36. *Ibid.,* 2.131.
37. *Ibid.,* 2.15.

The configuration of objects in a situation corresponds to the configuration of simple signs in the propositional sign.[38]

Each name in a proposition is correlated with an object. "*That* is how a picture attaches to reality; it reaches right out to it."[39] This correlation of the picture's elements with the objects of the state of affairs, Wittgenstein refers to as the pictorial relationship. The picture's elements are like feelers projecting upon the objects. Insofar as the objects are determined by their specific relationship to each other, the picture's elements' projective relation to them manifests an equivalent relationship. The picture's (proposition's) elements are related to one another in the same determinate way as are the objects of the state of affairs. The one configuration mirrors the other.[40]

The picture "is laid against reality like a measure,"[41] so that the picture's (proposition's) elements are correlated with the fact's. The result of this correlation is that what the proposition "must have in common with reality, in order to be able to depict it—correctly or incorrectly—in the way it does, is its pictorial form."[42] This pictorial form is its logical form. This is evident from the following glosses: "A picture whose pictorial form is logical form is called a logical picture" (2.181). "Every picture is *at the same* time a logical one" (2.182). This logical form which the proposition as picture and its depicted fact have in common is the same type of internal relation as holds between a musical theme, the grooves of a phonograph record of the theme, the theme as it appears upon sheet music, and the theme as performed by an or-

---

38. *Ibid.*, 3.21.
39. *Ibid.*, 2.1511.
40. Anscombe calls our attention to an excellent point made by Giancarlo Colombo, the Italian translator of the *Tractatus.* He observes that given the isomorphic relation between the internal feature of the world and language, why is an existing state of affairs always the described and language the mode of description? Why could it not be held that the described state of affairs be regarded as a description of the proposition which would normally be said to describe it? Cf., G. E. M. Anscombe, *An Introduction to Wittgenstein's 'Tractatus'* (New York: Harper & Row, 1965), p. 67.
41. *Tractatus* 2.1512.
42. *Ibid.*, 2.17.

chestra. "They are all constructed according to a common logical pattern."[43]

In order for it to be judged that the proposition and existing state of affairs do in fact have the same logical form, it is essential to be able to translate the concatenation of names in the proposition into the concatenation of objects in the state of affairs. This requires a "translation key," so to speak, similar to the legend of a map by which one can judge whether or not the map is accurate. Wittgenstein refers to this "key" as representational form. "A picture represents its subject from a position outside it. (Its standpoint is its representational form.) That is why a picture represents its subject correctly or incorrectly."[44] If the picture is accurate, that is, if given a representational form it correctly maps the existing state of affairs, it is true; if not, it is false. "A picture agrees with reality or fails to agree; it is correct or incorrect, true or false."[45]

Commentators' Dilemmas

A firm grasp of Wittgenstein's picture theory is crucial for an understanding of his views on the logic of depictional language. Yet, its meaning has been a much debated issue among commentators of the *Tractatus*. To date more commentaries and articles—each assuming a divergent viewpoint—have been written upon the picture theory than upon any other phase of Wittgenstein's philosophy. In this literature we find some of the greatest essays written about the *Tractatus* and also some of the worst. To borrow a phrase from Gustav Bergmann, we could say that here exists "the glory and misery" of Wittgensteinian commentaries.[46] "A Wittgenstein picture is not the kind of thing which is put into a frame and hung upon the wall," David Shwayder wittily comments.[47]

43. *Ibid.*, 4.014. Cf., 4.0141.
44. *Ibid.*, 2.173. Cf., Griffin, pp. 95-97.
45. *Ibid.*, 2.21. Cf., *Notebooks* 26.11.14.
46. For a comprehensive anthology of essays covering the "glory to misery" gamut of picture theory commentaries, see *Essays on Wittgenstein's 'Tractatus.'*
47. David S. Shwayder, "On the Picture Theory of Language: Excerpts of a Review," *Essays on Wittgenstein's 'Tractatus,'* p. 305.

Yet, it might be advantageous to image some of the commentators' remarks upon the picture theory and hang them upon
the wall in effigy. Judith Jarvis is right in proclaiming that
the literature written on the *Tractatus* is beginning to resemble a description of the real meaning of the great White
Whale.[48]

It is not our intention to review *all* or the majority of
articles written on the topic since that would only obscure
our goal of elucidating the texts of the *Tractatus*. We will
discuss only a few articles—representative of the more interesting interpretations—as means of positively (and negatively)
revealing Wittgenstein's position.

The gloss in the *Tractatus* around which commentators'
dilemmas pivot is 3.1432. The gloss reads: Instead of, 'The
complex sign *"aRb"* says that *a* stands to *b* in the relation R,'
we ought to put, *'That "a"* stands to *"b"* in a certain relation
says *that aRb.'* We have already discussed this text and we
did not find it to be unduly cryptic, especially in light of other
texts taken from the *Tractatus* and the *Notebooks*. Yet, commentators with various misconceptions have made the text
complex and paradoxical. Edna Daitz, for example, in her article "The Picture Theory of Meaning" remarks of the gloss:

> This way of converting sentences into facts creates
> a difficulty: in conversion, an n-termed sentence becomes
> an n+1-termed fact. Consider "Sophia hates Amos." This
> becomes the fact *"Hates" is between "Sophia" and
> "Amos,"* which has the consequence that it is impossible
> to gear the form of a sentence to the form of the fact.
> The sentence "Sophia hates Amos" is not identical in
> form with, *i.e.,* has not the same number of elements as,
> the fact *Sophia hates Amos.* For the sentence is the fact
> *"Hates" is between "Sophia" and "Amos,"* i.e., it has
> four elements while *Sophia hates Amos* has only three.
> This view brings with it the consequence that all ordin-
> ary sentences have, for fact-stating purposes, one word
> too many![49]

48. Judith Jarvis, "Professor Stenius on the *Tractatus*," *Essays on Wittgenstein's 'Tractatus,'* p. 217.
49. Edna Daitz, "The Picture Theory of Meaning," *Mind*, LXII (April,
1953), p. 189. For the novice of Wittgenstein's philosophy who wishes

Ms. Daitz has analyzed the sentence "Sophia hates Amos" into four elements: the words "Sophia," "hates," and "Amos" and the specific grammatical arrangement of these words in the sentence. The fact mirrored by the proposition she has analyzed into three elements: Sophia, the hating, and Amos.

---

to deepen his understanding of the picture theory of language, I wholeheartedly dissuade him from Ms. Daitz's article. She proposes to elucidate the picture theory by drawing upon Wittgenstein's *Tractatus* in conjunction with works by Russell. The problem is, however, that at times one is not sure from which source she is drawing upon. Moreover, at times she discusses themes quite reminiscent of *Tractatus* thoughts, yet the conclusions she draws and the interpretational paths she takes are quite foreign to the specific details of Wittgenstein's texts. I am referring to Wittgenstein's texts regarding the saying/showing distinction, the naming/describing traits of language respectively characteristic of simple signs and propositions, and the notion that propositions are pictures. Ms. Daitz's statements on these Wittgensteinian themes are quite un-Wittgensteinian. To be more specific, let us review the following:

> Not only must both picture and pictured be entities, but they must also be entities in what—for want of a better word—I call the same *genre*. A picture is a visual pattern and can picture only what is visually accessible. A still-life of a duck cannot show the taste of the bird as it may show its markings. The sense in which a picture shows a tasty bird is the sense in which I see a tasty bird, that is, I see a bird which looks as if it would be succulent to the taste. I cannot *see* the taste of a bird any more than a picture can show it. As Wittgenstein says: "2.171 The picture can represent every reality whose form it has. The spatial picture, everything spatial, the colored, everything colored, etc." Of course, picture and pictured cannot be in the identical *genre*. If they were, the one would be a replica, a duplicate, or a model of the other and not a picture of it. (Daitz, p. 185.)

Ms. Daitz tells us that the picture and the pictured must be first of all entities. Wittgenstein never said this nor is it true. Recall in *Tractatus* 4.014 and 4.0141 Wittgenstein's example of the musical score of a symphony and the actual performance of the symphony. The former is a picture of the latter—the situation could also be reversed. Yet, do we call the performance of the symphony an entity? Not at all.

Furthermore, Daitz tells us that the picture and pictured must be of the same *genre;* then she remarks that they cannot be of identical *genres*. "If they were," she states, "the one would be a replica, a duplicate, or a model of the other and not a picture of it" (*Ibid.*, p. 185). But, is not this precisely what a picture is—a replica of the pictured? Furthermore, the distinction between "the same *genre*" and "identical *genres*" is not at all clear, if not blatantly a pseudo-distinction.

Daitz has substituted the term "genre" as her own translation of Wittgenstein's "logical form," i.e., as meaning that the possibility that the elements in the picture can be related to those in that which it pictures. However, the term "genre" does not convey this meaning. For

Based upon this analysis, she concludes that Wittgenstein's picture theory is untenable because a one-to-one correspondence between the sentence's and the fact's respective elements is impossible.

Ellis Evans, in an attempt to harmonize Wittgenstein's texts with Daitz's position, postulates that according to Wittgenstein there are really *four* elements in aRb. Utilizing Daitz's example of "Sophia hates Amos," Evans points out that over and above Sophia, the hating, and Amos, there is the *order*: Sophia hates Amos as opposed to Amos hating Sophia.

If, in describing how the symbolism of *"aRb"* works, we say merely that *"aRb"* says *"a* stands in R to *b,"* we have not shown what it is about the sign *"aRb"* that indicates how, in the fact that aRb, the three elements

---

Ms. Daitz, then, to conclude that "the *Tractatus* also satisfies the model's demand that sign and signified be in the same *genre*" (*Ibid.*, p. 186), is completely to misrepresent the work.

The *Tractatus* achieves this, she remarks, "by equating the sign (the proposition) to the signified (the fact)" (*Ibid.*). Wittgenstein never *equated* the propositional sign and its signified fact; his position is that they share in common the same logical form. Furthermore, for Wittgenstein, the propositional sign alone does not constitute the proposition as Ms. Daitz's use of parentheses would indicate. The proposition consists in the propositional sign together with the latter's projected sense; the proposition is constituted by its logico-syntactical employment.

In addition, Daitz would have us believe that the Wittgensteinian picture and that which it pictures must share in common some *tangible* physical property. "A picture is a visual pattern and can picture only what is visually accessible," she states. Returning to gloss 4.014, we ask: Is a symphony as played visually accessible? Is its audibility a visual pattern? Are there not audible pictures and temporal ones as Griffin holds (Griffin, pp. 60-61, 80, 152-53)? These certainly are not visible.

Daitz continues by quoting 2.171 of the *Tractatus:* "The picture can represent every reality whose form it has, the spatial picture everything spatial, the colored everything colored, etc." She interprets this text as bolstering her claim that the picture and pictured must be of the same *genre*—the spatial picture depicts spatial data, both belonging to the *genre* of spatiality; the colored picture depicts colored data, both belonging to the *genre* of color. It is true that spatial pictures can depict spatial data, colored pictures, colored data. However, this does not mean that colored data are depicted only by colored pictures or that spatial data are depictable *only* by spatial pictures, as Daitz would lead us to believe. The musical score is a spatial picture of the notes of the musical composition. Yet, is the actual playing of the notes of the composition a spatial event? Hardly.

corresponding to "*a*," "R," and "*b*" are combined. In our statement of what "*a*R*b*" says, namely "*a* stands in R to *b*," we have reproduced the order of the signs in "*a*R*b*." But that order is symbolic: thus we have reproduced a covert symbolic element in "*a* stands in R to *b*," and thus "*a*R*b*" has not been completely analyzed. We have said that "*a*" means *a*, that "R" means R, and that "*b*" means *b*, and we have said it in that order: but we have not shown that it is the fact that those signs are in that order that allows us to say that "*a*R*b*" says "*a* stands in R to *b*" and not "*b* stands in R to *a*." Consequently, the complete analysis should show that it is the order of the terms in "*a*R*b*" that determines that "*a*R*b*" says that *a*R*b* and not that *b*R*a* or some other structure of the elements corresponding to "*a*," "R" and "*b*" (if such be possible).

. . . .

To the individual elements of the sign, correspond the elements of the fact: but it is the *order* of the elements of the sign that corresponds to the *structure* of the elements of the fact. To take Mrs. Daitz's example, "Sophia hates Amos" indicates that Sophia hates Amos rather than that Amos hates Sophia in virtue of the order of the words concerned. Wittgenstein would have said, I think, that the fact that Sophia hates Amos contained four elements: the two people, the hating, and the structure of these, i.e., that it is Sophia and not Amos that is doing the hating and Amos and not Sophia that is receiving it. The individual words correspond to those first three elements, and the order of the words to the fourth.[50]

The two major mistakes of Evans' and Daitz's interpretations of Wittgenstein's thought consist in their confusion of the logical form of a proposition with its grammatical arrangement of words and in their treatment of "R" in "*a*R*b*" as a substantive. Let us briefly examine these errors.

50. Ellis Evans, "*Tractatus* 3.1432," in *Mind*, LXIV (April, 1955), pp. 259-60. Cf., David Keyt, "Wittgenstein's Picture Theory of Language," *Essays on Wittgenstein's 'Tractatus*,' pp. 377-92 for his penetrating criticisms of Evans' views.

It is true that in some languages (such as English) a specific word-order helps convey the structure of a sentence; in other languages, however, it is not essential. In Latin, for example, it is the declension of words which conveys the structure of the sentence. Even though a specific word-order is recommended, the words of a Latin sentence can be arranged in any jumble, and its sense is still ascertainable in most cases. Such being the case, this word-order of which Evans and Daitz speak pertains to a superficial level of grammar and not to the logical form of the proposition, lying beneath this grammatical structure. In the *Tractatus* Wittgenstein states:

> Language disguises thought. So much so, that from the outward form of the clothing it is impossible to infer the form of the thought beneath it, because the outward form of the clothing is not designed to reveal the form of the body, but for entirely different purposes.[51]

The logical form of the proposition is clearly not the surface, outer grammatical form of the sentence. Wittgenstein explicitly continues this line of thought in the *Philosophical Investigations,* his second major work, when he refers to the logical form of the proposition as depth grammar and distinguishes it from the proposition's superficial grammatical structure which he calls surface grammar.

> In the use of words one might distinguish "surface grammar" from "depth grammar." What immediately impresses itself upon us about the use of a word is the way it is used in the construction of the sentence, the part of its use—one might say—that can be taken in by the ear.——And now compare the depth grammar, say of the word "to mean," with what its surface grammar would lead us to suspect. No wonder we find it difficult to know our way about.[52]

The surface grammar consists in the mere words of the proposition; as aptly stated in the *Notebooks,* "words are like

51. *Tractatus* 4.002.
52. *PI* 664.

the film on deep water."[53] It is into the watery depths beneath this filmy surface that Wittgenstein's logical investigations plunge.

The point which must be kept in mind is Russell's distinction between the grammatical and logical forms of a proposition. Wittgenstein acknowledges it as Russell's contribution to linguistic philosophy in gloss 4.0031 of the *Tractatus,* and now in the *PI* he utilizes this distinction under the terminology of surface and depth grammar respectively. Surface grammar is the mere string of words in the sentence, depth grammar is its logical structure. It is at this depth level that a sentence's logical form is revealed; the word-order of the proposition does not constitute an element of its logical form. Copi concurs with our interpretation, though he maintains that "R" in "*aRb*" is an element of the proposition.

> For Wittgenstein the elements of an elementary proposition are the words (names or simple signs) occurring in it; their order or arrangement is not regarded by him [Wittgenstein] as an additional element. Hence, for Wittgenstein the elementary proposition "*aRb*" contains *three* elements, not four.[54]

To say that the proposition "*aRb*" contains *three elements* is quite misleading. It could be inferred that these elements are all of the same constitution; consequently, "R" would take on a naming function, which evidently is not Wittgenstein's view. Relations are not names; "R" has no substantive status. Wittgenstein explicitly states in *Notes on Logic*: "In '*aRb*' 'R' looks like a substantive but it is not one."[55] Certainly, given the logical notation of the *Principia Mathematica* of which "*aRb*" is a part, "R" has a specific role, the function of conveying the propositional form of the dyadic relation. The point is, however, within a Wittgensteinian context, this role of "R" is of a type different from that of "*a*" and "*b*." One could say that "R" is an element of the *Principia Mathematica* notation, but for Wittgenstein it is an unfortunate, mislead-

---

53. *Notebooks* 30.5.15.
54. Copi, p. 155.
55. *Notebooks,* p. 99.

ing element, an element which is dispensable. In *aRb*, one really is portraying a concatenation of two names; R indicates only how they are related. Ideally, logical notation should elucidate the logical structure of a statement rather than conceal it. A better notation would include only *a* and *b* as elements of the proposition; the positionings of the two—given the framework of meaning operative—would manifest their related structure. It should be noted that the gloss immediately preceding 3.1432, the infamous *aRb* gloss, suggests that a proper, clear way of understanding a propositional sign would be to imagine it as a composite of spatial objects such as tables, chairs, books, etc.; in this case "the spatial arrangement of these things will express the sense of the proposition."[56] In such a context, the relations between the objects are immediately evident from the way the objects appear. No explicit notational element as such would be required to express the relation between the objects. In accordance with this point of view, Anscombe and Copi have each suggested a non-linear positioning of names as the proper Wittgensteinian symbolism of a propositional sign.[57] Assuming a specific frame of meaning reference, with a, b, c, d, and e designating names, such a sign might look like

$$a \quad b \quad c$$
$$d \qquad\qquad e$$

In this ideal symbolism, names and only names appear. All other signs, being irrelevant, are deleted. Relations and orders are shown by the specific concatenation of objects rather than being designated by special symbols or letters of the alphabet. Consequently, the formal, relational aspects of the proposition do not appear as something substantial. "In order to avoid such errors [namely, to give relations substantive status]," Wittgenstein relates, "we must make use of a sign-language that excludes them . . . that is to say, a sign-language that is governed by *logical* grammar—by logical syn-

---

56. *Tractatus* 3.1431.
57. Cf., Copi, pp. 156-60 and G. E. M. Anscombe, "Mr. Copi on Objects, Properties, and Relations in the *Tractatus*," *Essays on Wittgenstein's 'Tractatus*,' pp. 187-88. Cf., Maslow, p. 91 and Wilfrid Sellars, "Naming and Saying," p. 250.

tax."[58] As has been shown above, what this means for Wittgenstein consists in taking the logical symbolism of propositions found in the *Principia Mathematica* and purifying it of
symbolic errors and misconceptions (as Wittgenstein sees
them). Even though Wittgenstein has greatest respect for
Russell and the notation found in the *Principia Mathematica,*
he maintains that it fails to exclude all mistakes.[59]

Some commentators construe this position, held by Wittgenstein, as a rejection by him of the validity of ordinary language in favor of an artificial language. Copi, for example, although admitting weighty arguments for both sides of the
issue, nevertheless concludes that in the *Tractatus* "the tendency to reject ordinary language seems to me to predominate
. . . . I understand Wittgenstein to be primarily concerned
with specifications for an artificial symbolic language."[60] This
is certainly the viewpoint of Maslow; Bertrand Russell also
maintains this in his Introduction to the *Tractatus.*[61] Obviously, such a position was not taken in the *Investigations.* In section 132 of the work, Wittgenstein states that "a
reform of ordinary language . . . is perfectly possible. But
these are not the cases we have to do with . . . ." Still the question remains: Was the Wittgenstein of the *Tractatus* interested in constructing an ideally perfect language? Russell and
Copi indeed think such to be the case; Frank P. Ramsey, on
the other hand, is critical of Russell's position.[62] Max Black
expresses similar discontent.[63]

To be sure, in the *Tractatus* Wittgenstein does make reference to "a sign-language that is governed by *logical* grammar—by logical syntax."[64] But the goal of this sign-language
is to elucidate the logic already present in ordinary language.

---

58. *Tractatus* 3.325.
59. *Ibid.,* 5.452 and 5.5351.
60. Copi, pp. 146-47.
61. Cf. Maslow, p. xv and Bertrand Russell, "Introduction," *Tractatus,* p. 7.
62. Frank P. Ramsey, "Review of the *Tractatus,*" *Essays on Wittgenstein's
    'Tractatus,'* p. 9.
63. Max Black, *Language and Philosophy: Studies in Method* (Ithaca, New
    York: Cornell University Press, 1949), p. 143. Cf., Max Black, *A Com-
    panion to Wittgenstein's 'Tractatus'* (Ithaca, New York: Cornell Uni-
    versity Press, 1964), pp. 6ff.
64. *Tractatus* 3.325. Cf., 5.53, 5.534 and 6.122.

"In fact, all the propositions of our everyday language, just as they stand, are in perfect logical order."[65] ". . . any possible proposition is legitimately constructed. . . ."[66] The purpose of the Tractatus is to elucidate the logic of ordinary language and not to replace it. In the *Notebooks,* Wittgenstein explicitly states: "I only want to justify the vagueness of ordinary sentences, for it can be justified."[67] The *Tractatus* is an attempt at such a justification.

Negation, Logical Space, and Negative Facts

Like relations, logical operators such as "or," "and," "not," etc., do not function as argument places in propositions. This must be kept in mind or various mistaken notions about the picture theory of the *Tractatus* will result. Let us take an example. Copi maintains: "Since '$\sim \sim p$' contains more elements than 'p,' they do not have the same multiplicity. . . . The present argument is in effect a *reductio ad absurdum* proof that the picture theory of meaning is intended for elementary propositions only."[68]

Copi has misinterpreted Wittgenstein on two points in this text, and both misrepresentations are reducible to the erroneous presupposition that operations function as argument places. First, Copi mistakenly views the picture theory as restricted to elementary propositions, having no connections with non-elementary ones. "Intended for propositions only," he states, "it applies not to *all* propositions, but to elementary propositions alone."[69]

It is true that only elementary propositions directly are pictures; this does not mean that the picture theory does not entail all propositions, since all propositions (with the exception of universal propositions) [70] are—or are reducible to—elementary propositions without residue. Non-elementary pro-

---

65. *Ibid.,* 5.5563. Cf., 4.002ff.
66. *Ibid.,* 5.4733.
67. *Notebooks* 25.10.14.
68. Copi, p. 151.
69. *Ibid.,* p. 149.
70. This exception is made because of gloss 5.521 of the *Tractatus:* "I dissociate the concept *all* from truth-functions." The problem with "all" statements is that they are not reducible without residue to ele-

positions are the result of truth-operations upon elementary propositions.[71] And, these operations have no constitutive status within the proposition.[72] The non-elementary proposition contains no more than its constitutive elementary propositions and is reducible to them without remainder.[73] As a result, Wittgenstein's picture theory is equally applicable to elementary and non-elementary propositions.

This leads, then, to Copi's second mistake: the postulation of negation as an argument place from which follows the conclusion that "~ ~p" has more elements than "p." For Wittgenstein, however, the multiplicity of argument places is the same for both "p" and "~ ~p." Negation is not a substantive. Wittgenstein in 5.24 and 5.41 of the *Tractatus* emphasizes his disagreement with Russell and Frege for giving "~" a logically substantive role.

> The proposition "~ p" is not about negation, as if negation were an object. . . . And if there were an *object* called "~," it would follow that "~ ~ p" said something different from what "p" said, just because the one proposition would then be about ~ and the other would not.[74]

But this is obviously not the case. Both "p" and "~ ~ p" say the same thing in that they both point to the same state

---

mentary propositions. If one said "All men are mortal," this is reducible to a conjunction of "a is mortal" and "b is mortal" and "c is mortal" until the entire supply of *all* men is enumerated, but this analysis is not accomplished unless the individuals listed are somehow shown to be *all* men. Thus, we have come full circle. A complete analysis of an "all" proposition includes some statement that the individuals listed are *all* the individuals of the class, which statement is not that of a state of affairs. One cannot overcome the difficulty by analyzing the proposition "all men are mortal" into "a is mortal" and "b is mortal" and "c is mortal," etc. The *etcetera* sign subliminally includes the "all" concept within it; again the "all" proposition is analyzed into a complex which itself is not reducible into a series of states of affairs. Cf., William Kneale, "Is Existence a Predicate?," *Readings in Philosophical Analysis*, ed. H. Feigl and W. Sellars (New York: Appleton-Century-Crofts, Inc., 1949), pp. 33-34.

71. *Tractatus* 5.3.
72. *Ibid.*, 4.441 and 5.4.
73. *Ibid.*, 5.24 and 5.41.
74. *Ibid.*, 5.44. Italics are mine.

of affairs; both manifest the same concatenation of objects. The difference between "p" and "~ ~ p," however, is that whereas "p's" sense directly points to the logical place occupied by "p," "~ ~ p" does the same task through a logically more circuitous manner. To make this position explicit, we must first briefly examine what Wittgenstein means by logical space. Although in the *Notebooks* he expresses concern over being unable to reveal the meaning of logical space and its constituent places,[75] certain definite statements can be made in this regard.

Logical space is a metaphorical device indicative of the totality of possible structural combinations of objects by which propositions map out reality.[76] Thus, if one asks "What ontological status does logical space have?," the answer is that it has none. Logical space is a purely procedural construction by which Wittgenstein attempts to explicate the logical structure of depictional propositions. Rudolf Carnap makes a crucial distinction which is helpful in elucidating the issue at hand. He distinguishes between two ways of questioning about the existence of something: the first pertains to the existence of an entity within the framework of a specific system and the second pertains to the existence of the framework itself. These two ways Carnap refers to as internal and external questioning respectively. To ask the internal question concerning the existence of logical space, is to ask if within the framework of Wittgenstein's logic of descriptive language "logical space" has a specific, coherent function. Thus, this question of existence is really a question of operational meaning. To it, an answer must be given in the affirmative: logical space together with its counterparts logical object and logical place do indeed make sense within the *Tractatus*. They indicate a coherent way of using language in the work. However, as to the external question of existence, it must be made known that logical space again with its counterparts do

---

75. *Notebooks* 18.11.14.
76. Arthur Danto in his book *What Philosophy Is: A Guide to the Elements* (New York: Harper & Row, 1968) makes some interesting remarks about the "interspace" between language and the world. It is not a term equivalent to Wittgenstein's logical space, but certain intriguing similarities exist. Cf., pp. 9-10.

not exist in the real world. In Wittgenstein's terminology, these are not the case.[77]

Now the question at hand is: What is the structure of logical space? From all indications, it is a matrix, patterned after analytical symbolism. Similar to such structures, this logical space can be portrayed as intersecting geometric axes, whose resulting coordinates constitute the total possible concatenations of objects, that is, the total number of *positive* possible states of affairs. Wittgenstein states in the *Tractatus:*

> 3.411   In geometry and logic alike a place is a possibility: something can exist in it.
>
> 2.202   A picture represents a possible situation in logical space.
>
> 3.41   The propositional sign with logical coordinates— that is the logical place.

Again Wittgenstein remarks: "A proposition can determine only one place in logical space: nevertheless, the whole of logical space must already be given by it. . . . (The logical scaffolding surrounding a picture determines logical space. The force of a proposition reaches through the whole of logical space.) "[78] Since logical space is the matrix of all possible states of affairs, *given* a state of affairs it necessarily has a specific place in logical space and from its specific coordinates the whole of the matrix is related to it. The whole of logical space is related to the state of affairs as the latter's logical relational surroundings. A given state of affairs presupposes the whole of logical space as the *a priori* logical apparatus surrounding the proposition in question. As a result, Wittgenstein states of a space of possible states of affairs that "this space I can imagine empty, but I cannot imagine the thing without the space."[79] This notion becomes clear if we once again look at the system of Cartesian coordinates. Each pair

77. Cf., Rudolf Carnap, "Empiricism, Semantics, and Ontology," *Semantics and the Philosophy of Language*, ed. L. Linsky (Urbana: University of Illinois Press, 1952), pp. 208-30.

78. *Tractatus* 3.42. Cf., 3.4.

79. *Ibid.*, 2.013. Since non-elementary propositions are the result of operations performed upon elementary propositions adding nothing to them, but merely relating them in various ways, the points of logical space are then points for elementary propositions.

of coordinates has a sense only in reference to the whole system. One could not, for example, pluck out the (2, 2) pair or the (−3, 4) pair for examination. Once these points are exhumed from their relational matrix, their determinate character loses all significance; apart from the coordinates' framework, the coordinates are meaningless. Thus any pair, to be meaningful, already presupposes the entire system; (2, 2) makes sense only in reference to (1, 1), (−3, −3), (−3, 4), (8, −4), etc. Furthermore, each place is a *possible* space in reference to the others; a figure or curve does not have to go through each point for it to exist as a possible place.

Now we must turn to the question of the logical status of false propositions. Do they plot onto logical space negative facts? What sense does it make (if any) to say that a false proposition pictures a negative fact? To answer this question, a new dimension of logical space must be examined—the dimension of sense, or more properly, that of negation-affirmation. The sense of the proposition singles out a specific place in logical space by pointing to it in agreement or disagreement. Note the following texts:

> Just as one arrow behaves to another arrow by being in the same sense or the opposite, so a fact behaves to a proposition; it is thus bi-polarity and sense come in.[80]
> Every proposition is essentially true-false. Thus a proposition has two poles (corresponding to case of its truth and case of its falsity). We call this the *sense* of a proposition.[81]
> Negation reverses the sense of a proposition.[82]
> Names are like points; propositions like arrows—they have sense.[83]

Both a proposition, say "p," and its negation point to the same state of affairs in logical space but in opposite ways. As

80. "Notes on Logic," *Notebooks*, p. 97.
81. *Ibid.*, p. 94.
82. *Tractatus* 5.2341.
83. *Ibid.*, 3.144. This gloss is somewhat misleading; it could be interpreted from it that since objects are points, they occupy individual logical places in logical space, but this is clearly not Wittgenstein's intent. The whole trend of the *Notebooks* and the *Tractatus*, as our above discussion has indicated, is that states of affairs occupy places in logical space.

Wittgenstein words it, "the propositions 'p' and '~ p' have opposite sense, but there corresponds to them one and the same reality."[84] He then goes on to say: "The negating proposition determines a logical place *different* from that of the negated proposition."[85] At first it would seem that we have a contradiction. Wittgenstein has stated that "p" and "~ p" have corresponding to them one and the same reality, yet they determine different logical places. This, however, is not a contradiction.

Both "p" and "~ p" focus upon the same reality—state of affairs. However, since they focus with opposing senses, the former proposition, let us assume, points to the state of affairs as being the case, the latter as not being the case. As not being the case, the proposition "~ p" uses the state of affairs mirrored in "p" as a referential point for saying that whatever is the case it is not "p." To reword this, given a proposition, its negation assumes, obviously, the original proposition, and in projecting itself away from the logical place of this original proposition, it says that the truth-argument for its negating sense lies somewhere outside the place of the original proposition. At what particular place, though, we are not told. Wittgenstein words the matter thus: "The negating proposition determines a logical place with the help of the logical place of the negated proposition. For it describes it as lying outside the latter's logical place."[86]

The negating proposition does not point toward a specific place in logical space; it points away from one. As a consequent, there is no such thing as a negative state of affairs having definite coordinates in logical space and furthermore, there is no such fact as a negative fact.[87] "It is the *dualism,* positive and negative facts," Wittgenstein tells us in *Note-*

---

84. *Ibid.,* 4.0621.
85. *Ibid.,* 4.0641.
86. *Ibid.*
87. In his "Notes on Logic," Wittgenstein's thought tends in an opposite direction. He states: "There are positive and negative facts. . . . Negative facts only justify the negations of atomic propositions. Positive and negative facts there are, but not true and false facts" (*Notebooks,* p. 94). I must admit that this quotation leaves me stymied. In my judgment, it is a contradiction in terms. There are positive and negative propositions; this makes sense. But, it makes no sense to say that there are negative facts. A fact is what is the case—an *existing* state of affairs. As such, it is a positive state.

books 25.11.14, "that gives me no peace. For such a dualism can't exist." Indeed it cannot. A non-existent state of affairs (a negative fact) is not a fact at all since a fact is to be the case and to speak of a non-existent state of affairs is to speak of a state of affairs which is not the case, that is, not a fact.

Of course, one could retort by saying that the negative proposition, for example "∼ p," asserts: It is a fact that "p" is not a fact. But this is not an assertion of a negative fact—a negative fact makes no sense. It is an assertion of the *positive* fact that whatever is the case it is *not* "p." Thus, as Wittgenstein states: "But really even in this case the negative proposition is constructed by an indirect use of the positive."[88] The negative proposition presupposes the positive proposition which it negates. "*Must* the sign of the negative proposition be constructed by means of the sign of the positive one? (I believe so.) "[89]

Thus ends our commentary on Wittgenstein's *Tractatus;* we now have examined the way in which Wittgenstein logically structures depictional language and concomitantly the world. Methodologically, we are in a position to reconstruct these texts and compare them to Heidegger's. An important question, though, remains before we set upon this task, namely: To what extent do the above texts and viewpoint coincide with the notions of the later Wittgenstein? It is certainly important to our studies to determine whether the view we are methodologically going to study reflects only the early thoughts of a man who later supposedly sidestepped them.

Meaning is Use: An Essay on Wittgenstein's TRACTATUS

To the person familiar with Wittgenstein's works, the title of this section perhaps appears incongruous. After all, the "meaning is use" dictum is one of the pivotal themes of Wittgenstein's *Philosophical Investigations, not* of the *Tractatus Logico-Philosophicus.* In section 43 of the *Investigations,* Wittgenstein explicitly maintains that "the meaning of a word is its use in the language"; whereas at gloss 3.203 of the *Tractatus* he maintains: "A name means an object. The object is its meaning."

---

88. *Tractatus* 5.5151.
89. *Notebooks* 24.11.14.

The *PI* text indicates that words (names) have meaning through their specific contextual employment; whereas, the gloss from the *Tractatus* would seem to indicate that names have meaning apart from actual use. Accordingly, a primordial ostensible definition of the name would give it meaning, and this meaning is retained by the name throughout its various uses, the latter being accidental to the determination of the name as such.

It is the goal of this section, however, to show that such an interpretation is not founded and that the meaning of *Tractatus* 3.203 and the gist of the *Tractatus* are in harmony with *Investigations* 43. To accomplish this, let us begin by briefly reviewing several texts of the *Investigations* wherein the "meaning is use" dictum is explicitly applied to the logic of naming.

It is maintained at *PI* 43 that names signify simples. Yet, what are simples? To take Wittgenstein's example, let us ask: What are the *simple* constituent parts of a chair?[90] Bits of wood? Molecules? Atoms? To answer this question, one must first know what the usage, that is meaning, of the term "simple" is in this context. "It makes no sense at all to speak absolutely of the 'simple parts of a chair.' "[91] To ask for such parts without somehow explicating the specific employment of the term "simple" is to pose a meaningless question.

Is a "book" a simple? It is one thing; nevertheless, it is a compilation of many different pages. Is a "chessboard" simple? It is *one* entity; nevertheless, it is composed of a pattern of separate and distinct colored squares. If we designated the chessboard by the sign "R," is "R" an example of a name (the sign for a simple) or of a descriptive proposition (the sign for a nexus of names) ? "But whether it is a word or a proposition," Wittgenstein answers, "depends on the situation in which it is uttered or written."[92]

According to the *Investigations*, the appropriate answers to the above questions, then, depend upon the use of the term "simple" in each context. The meaning of a term is its

90. *PI* 47. Italics are mine.
91. *Ibid.*
92. *Ibid.*, 49.

use in the language; as a result, names are contextually determined.

> We may say: *nothing* has so far been done, when a thing has been named. It has not even *got* a name except in the language-game. This is what Frege meant too, when he said that a word had meaning only as part of a sentence.[93]

The problem is, Wittgenstein maintains:

> We are inclined to forget that it is the particular use of a word only which gives the word its meaning. . . . The use of the word *in practice* is its meaning. . . . That is to say, a label [name] would only have a meaning to us in so far as we made a particular use of it. Now we could easily imagine ourselves to be impressed by merely seeing a label on a thing, and to forget that what makes these labels important is their use.[94]

Names do not exist in isolation; it makes no sense to speak of names "by themselves." Alone, names have neither being nor non-being. Names are words and thus name only in and through the logico-semantical structure of a proposition.

> What does it mean to say that we can attribute neither being nor non-being to elements?—One might say: if everything that we call "being" and "non-being" consists in the existence and non-existence of connexions between elements, it makes no sense to speak of an element's being (non-being) ; just as when everything that we call "destruction" lies in the separation of elements, it makes no sense to speak of the destruction of an element.[95]

Given this, Wittgenstein's application in the *Investigations* of the "meaning is use" dictum to the logic of naming, our task is to determine the relationship of this viewpoint to that expressed in *Tractatus* glosses:

> 3.203 A name means an object. The object is its meaning.

---

93. *Ibid.*
94. *The Brown Book*, p. 69.
95. *PI* 50.

3.22 In a proposition a name is the representation of an object.

At first glance, it would seem that the above glosses do not reflect the position maintained in the *Investigations;* they would seem to be akin to the position maintained in Bertrand Russell's logical atomism. After all, Russell does maintain that the ideas of his atomism "are very largely concerned with explaining certain ideas which I learnt from my friend and former pupil Ludwig Wittgenstein."[96]

According to Russell, names are "object-words." ". . . 'object-words' are defined, logically as words having meaning in isolation. . . ."[97] Names mean objects apart from any specific linguistic employments. The meanings of names are given "absolutely"; as a result, names, or object-words, are explicitly distinguished from words whose meanings are contextually determined.

> Many words only have meaning in a suitable verbal context—such words as "than," "or," "however," cannot stand alone. . . . There are words, however—including all those that a child learns first—that can be used in isolation. . . . These are what I call "object-words," and they compose the "object-language." . . . These words have various peculiarities. First: their meaning is learnt (or can be learnt) by confrontation with objects which are what they mean, or instances of what they mean. Second: they do not presuppose other words.[98]

Object-words do not presuppose other words in order to be meaningful; as a result, elementary (atomic) propositions derive their meanings from the already established meanings of the names contained therein. Representational propositions, or propositions which state facts, "are composed of words, and have meaning derivative from that of the words

96. Bertrand Russell, "The Philosophy of Logical Atomism," *Logic and Knowledge,* edited by R. C. Marsh (London: George Allen & Unwin Ltd., 1956), p. 177.
97. Bertrand Russell, *An Inquiry into Meaning and Truth* (Baltimore: Penguin, 1962), p. 62.
98. *Ibid.,* p. 23.

that they contain. . . ."[99] For propositions to have meaning, their names must *first* have meanings; the propositions' meanings are dependent upon and derivative of these names.

If Russell's above position is indeed the viewpoint utilized by Wittgenstein in the *Tractatus,* then the Wittgensteinian object is that to which a name refers and that reference is permanently established apart from any linguistic context. The meaning of a name is logically prior to the proposition in which it appears; the meaning of the proposition is derived from those of its constituent names. Upon close examination, however, Russell's viewpoint is radically different from that expressed by Wittgenstein in the *Tractatus.* Recall our explanation of the Wittgensteinian object. It is a formal, or variable, concept; its role is to act as a *logical* place marker for the arguments within any given proposition; thus, its content is always dependent upon the specific contextual instantiation of propositional values. The Wittgensteinian object, then, has no content apart from the contextual content of the arguments which saturate it in propositions. For the objects of the *Tractatus* to be the meaningful counterparts of names, they must be instantiated in states of affairs. Objects have no isolated, absolute meanings. Note *Tractatus* 2.0123:

> If I know an object I also know all its possible occurrences in states of affairs.

It is the life of an object to be in such possible combinations. "Every one of these possibilities must be part of the nature of the object."[100] An object cannot logically exist apart from a state of affairs; it is just that type of logical entity which appears only in and can only appear in states of affairs.

Names are likewise contextually determined; there are no names apart from propositional contexts. Wittgenstein unequivocally remarks at *Tractatus* 3.3 that "*only* in the nexus of a proposition does a name have meaning." In isolation from such a context, names have no function and as a result no meaning. "It is impossible," Wittgenstein states, "for

---

99. *Ibid.,* p. 28.
100. *Tractatus* 2.0123.

words to appear in two different roles: by themselves and in propositions."[101] "If a sign is useless, it is meaningless."[102]

Wittgenstein's position in the *Tractatus*, then, is radically different from Russell's. Russell maintains that the meaning of a proposition is derivative of the meanings of the words contained therein; the meanings of names in isolation are logically prior to the meaning of the proposition as a whole. The juxtaposition of names in their isolated referential functions constitutes the proposition.

In the *Tractatus*, propositions do not derive their meanings from those of the contained names; to the contrary, names become such and function as such only in and through their specific concatenations. The Wittgensteinian elementary proposition is a functional unity, not a series of juxtaposed names, each having an already determined meaning. Such a juxtaposition, Wittgenstein maintains, would never be able to show the sense of a descriptive proposition. "Only facts can express a sense, a set of names cannot. A proposition is not a medley of words— (Just as a theme in music is not a medley of notes.) ."[103] As a result, the "meaning is use" dictum of the *Investigations* is not an element of *only* the later Wittgenstein; the meaning of the dictum is already present in the *Tractatus*. There exists, then, at least this continuity between the two works: In both works, meaning is determined in and through linguistic usage; apart from such usage, names have no meanings and objects no content. Russell's theory of "object words" is quite foreign to the Wittgensteinian object of the *Tractatus*.[104]

---

101. *Ibid.*, 2.0122.
102. *Ibid.*, 3.328.
103. *Ibid.*, 3.141 and 3.142.
104. An excellent essay dealing with the kinds of questions we have just been discussing, only dealing with them at a much more complex level, is Hidé Ishiguro's "Use and Reference of Names," *Studies in the Philosophy of Wittgenstein*, ed. Peter Winch (London: Routledge & Kegan Paul, 1969), pp. 20-50.

Chapter VI

LOGIC, DESCRIPTION, AND THE WORLD: A METHODOLOGICAL COMPARISON

Syllables govern the world.
—John Selden, *Table-Talk:*
Power, State

We have worked through those texts of Heidegger and Wittgenstein which explicate their respective views of the structures of language and the world and their relationship. Now, as methodologists, we are to compare these viewpoints for structural congruence and divergence. We will divide this task into two parts. First, we will methodologically discuss the common characteristics of technique employed by both thinkers in their expositions on the structures of language and the world. These characteristics we have categorized as: operational, pragmatic, relational, and human. In the first two instances, where the characteristic in question is relative to the primary notion of an already existing philosophical movement, we have prefaced our methodological comparison with a few words on the movement itself. In doing this, we are not in any way suggesting some direct influence of operationalism or pragmatism upon either Wittgenstein or Heidegger. Rather, we are asserting that their thoughts fit within the broad framework of such kinds of inquiry. The second part of this chapter will consist in a methodological study of the manner by which both men relate language and the world.

An Operational Character

Ever since Einstein's theory of relativity, modern physics has undergone a tremendous upheaval in procedural alteration. Traditional models of space and time, along with other absolutes, were abandoned in view of their inadequate explanations of newly found data. In their place, newer models and methods were proposed.

One such method is Operationalism. It appeared upon the scientific scene in 1927 with the publication of a work entitled *Logic of Modern Physics* by Percy Bridgman. The method consists in defining physicists' concepts in terms of performable operations.[1] As Bridgman states: "In general, we mean by any concept nothing more than a set of operations; *the concept is synonymous with the corresponding set of operations.*"[2] Operations are not merely necessary for the determination of meaning. They *constitute* it. Operational definitions not only specify that which is to be defined but also generate it. The meaning of a concept is, then, a function of activities. ". . . analysis of the conditions attendant on the use of the term is an analysis of activity of one sort or another, or in other words, an analysis of operations. From this point of view, *meanings are operational.*"[3] "The fundamental idea back of an operational analysis is simple enough; namely, that we do not know the meaning of a concept unless we can specify the operations which were used by us or our neighbor in applying the concept in any concrete situation."[4]

Let us take an example. Bridgman defines length as follows:

> We evidently know what we mean by length if we can tell what the length of any and every object is. . . . To find the length of an object, we have to perform certain physical operations. The concept of length is therefore

---

1. A. C. Benjamin relates that while "there was some criticism of Bridgman's formulation of the method, his general proposal was accepted by most physicists as the procedure most likely to contribute to the advancement of physics and, in particular, most likely to avoid future difficulties of the kind created by the theory of relativity." [A. Cornelius Benjamin, *Operationalism* (Springfield, Illinois: Charles C. Thomas, 1955), p. 3.]
2. Percy Bridgman, *Logic of Modern Physics* (New York: Macmillan Company, 1927), p. 5.
3. Percy Bridgman, "Operational Analysis," *Philosophy of Science*, V (April, 1938), p. 116.
4. Percy Bridgman, "The Nature of Some of Our Physical Concepts," *British Journal of the Philosophy of Science*, I (February, 1951), p. 257.

fixed . . . : that is, the concept of length involves as much as and nothing more than the set of operations by which length is determined.[5]

To say that "the table is three feet in length" does not mean, according to Bridgman, that there is an inherent property in the table called "length," and with the aid of a ruler one can uncover that specific property; property analysis is not utilized by Bridgman. He explicitly maintains that "the proper definition of a concept is not in terms of its properties but in terms of actual operations. . . ."[6] The length of the above table consists in the fact that a three-foot measuring stick, placed along the edge of the table, coincided end for end with the table. In another example, Bridgman defines operationally the liquid in a given container as being acid to mean that the insertion of a strip of blue litmus paper into the liquid turned the former red. The meaning of the concept is equal to an operation.

In later works, Bridgman's formulation of operationalism is somewhat modified; in them operations are indeed defined as necessary conditions of meaning, but not as *the only* conditions. Referring to the above text from *Logic of Modern Physics* which states that the "concept is synonymous with the corresponding set of operations," Bridgman admits that such a position "was obviously going too far . . ."[7] although, in reference to the examples of length and time which immediately follow the above statement of the operational method presented in *Logic of Modern Physics,* Bridgman still maintains that such an equation is justified. Nevertheless, he does modify his original position. As early as 1938, Bridgman professes this modified operationalism. In "Operational Analysis" he asserts that he does "not maintain that meanings involve nothing more than operations. . . . It is perhaps possible to see other elements in the complex covered by meaning."[8] In an essay entitled "The Nature of Some of Our Physical Con-

5. Bridgman, *Logic of Modern Physics*, p. 5.
6. *Ibid.*, p. 6.
7. Bridgman, "The Nature of Some of Our Physical Concepts," p. 257.
8. Bridgman, "Operational Analysis," p. 116.

cepts" published in 1951, Bridgman reaffirms that the "operational aspect is not by any means the only aspect of meaning, but it is often *the most important single aspect.* . . ."[9] Commentators have differentiated this modified operationalism from Bridgman's earlier theory by referring to the two as the broad and narrow theories of operationalism respectively.[10]

From the above, brief exposition, we observe that, methodologically speaking, operationalism as a way of thought is primarily one of functional activities. Meaning is either totally or partially determined by and equated to operational techniques. Within this same basic structure of ideas abide Heidegger's and Wittgenstein's methods. Both can be called operational in that for both thinkers operations are pivotal to meaning-determination. Once again this should not be interpreted to mean that either man's thoughts are equivalent to Bridgman's, nor should it be inferred that our exposition of Bridgman's operationalism is meant to be comprehensive. There are many important elements of his thoughts which we have left unmentioned. For example, the only kinds of operations Bridgman will consider are actual physical ones; as a result, any concept not explainable in such terms he deems as meaningless. ". . . concepts can be defined only in the range of actual experiment, and are undefined and meaningless in regions as yet untouched by experiment."[11] Heidegger would certainly not agree with such a position. There are then obvious differences among the three thinkers. Yet, the ideas of all three do gravitate about the notion of operations as designatory of meaning.

*   *   *

Heidegger locates the meaning of the worldhood of the world and that of the ready-to-hand—both crucial notions in *Being and Time*—in operational structures. In the realm of the ready-to-hand he refers to entities encountered in concern by Dasein as "equipment," indicating that "there '*is*' no such thing as *an* equipment. . . . Equipment is essentially 'something in-order-to . . .' such as serviceability, conduciveness,

9. Bridgman, "The Nature of Some of Our Physical Concepts," p. 257.
10. Cf., Benjamin, pp. 4ff and pp. 64ff.
11. Bridgman, *Logic of Modern Physics*, p. 7. Cf., p. 28.

usability, manipulation."[12] The worldly character of the
ready-to-hand is not defined by Heidegger in terms of substance and accident, but in terms of operations. Things are
defined in their operational utilization called "dealings."

> Equipment can genuinely show itself only in dealings cut
> to its own measure (hammering with a hammer, for ex-
> ample) ; but in such dealings, an entity of this kind is
> not *grasped* thematically as an occurring thing [sub-
> stance]. . . . The hammering . . . has appropriated this
> equipment in a way which could not possibly be more
> suitable. In dealings such as this, where something is put
> to use, our concern subordinates itself to the "in-order-
> to" which is constitutive for the equipment we are em-
> ploying at the time.[13]

The "in order to," that is, the operation, of the equipment
is constitutive of it. What made a hammer to be such is its
hammering; a needle, its sewing; a pin, its pinning—all operations. Only operationally, can the worldly character of Heidegger's universe be revealed; given something ready-to-hand,
"the more we seize hold of it and use it, the more primordial
does our relationship to it become, and the more unveiled
is it encountered as that which it is—as equipment."[14] The
operational manipulation of equipment reveals its character
and constitutes it ontologically. The ontological foundation
of equipment—and ultimately of the world as the totality of
equipment—consists in the *operations* with which Dasein can
utilize it. Its Being transcends brute facticity;[15] its Being is

12. BT, p. 97. (SZ, p. 68). Cf., Richardson, pp. 54-58.
13. *Ibid.*, p. 98. (SZ, p. 69).
14. *Ibid.* (SZ, p. 69).
15. For Heidegger the "*being* of a utensil goes on beyond the mere fact
that it *is*, to include the totality of uses by means of which the utensil
in question can manifest its character" (Molina, p. 60). Richard
Schmitt in an attempt to explicate this utensility of Heidegger, distinguishes between that for which a tool, i.e. utensil, is and that for
which it is used. Cf., "Heidegger's Analysis of 'Tool,'" *The Monist*,
XLIX (January, 1965), pp. 70-86, especially pp. 75ff. Cf., also Schmitt's
chapter on "things" (Chapter II, pp. 31-54) in his excellent commentary of *Being and Time, Martin Heidegger on Being Human* (New
York: Random House, 1969).

determined in the totality of ways it can function. The ontological structure of equipment is characterized by its operational activities centering around Dasein. This is the operational element of *Being and Time*.

*   *   *

Looking at the *Tractatus* methodologically, we find a moderate *logical* operationalism similar to that professed by the later Bridgman. For both men, operations are essential for, though not totally explanatory of, the generation and meaning of concepts. Wittgenstein's statements in the *Tractatus* dealing with the logic of language as a formal series of propositions likewise place an emphasis upon operations. All significant propositions for Wittgenstein are truth-functions of elementary propositions. As such, these truth-functions can be ordered in a series, and this series can be generated by a given operation—the operation consisting in the internal relatedness of the series. Wittgenstein states:

5   A proposition is a truth-function of elementary propositions.

5.3   All propositions are results of truth-operations on elementary propositions.
         A truth-operation is the way in which a truth-function is produced out of elementary propositions.

5.1   Truth-functions can be arranged in series.

5.232   The internal relation by which a series is ordered is equivalent to the operation that produces one term from another.

Truth-functions of elementary propositions are the results of operations performed upon those propositions. Even though these operations are not constitutive of the propositions as argument places, they are still compulsory to the formulation of propositional series. Thus, in order that a specific proposition in this formal series be specified, a term in the series must be given *and also* the operation by which the series is generated. In fact, as Wittgenstein points out, the general member of a formal series is determined by giving the first member of the series and the general form of the generating operation.[16] The operation is essential toward the generative constitution of the series. This, then, is Wittgenstein's logical operationalism of the *Tractatus*.

In the later writings of Wittgenstein, this logical operationalism gives way to an operationalism of actual semantical usage. C. S. Chihara and J. A. Fodor "hold that the later writings of Wittgenstein express a coherent doctrine in which [functions] an *operationalistic* analysis of confirmation and language. . . ."[17] Wittgenstein clearly states in *The Blue Book* that one should "think of words as instruments characterized by their use. . . ."[18] It is their specific use, or operation, which determines the meaning of words. "Look at the sentence as an instrument," Wittgenstein reasserts in the *PI*, "and at its sense as its employment."[19] Commenting on texts like these, Chihara and Fodor remark: "This notion of analysis leads rather naturally to an operationalistic view. . . ."[20] This seems to be accurate.

Recall the example with which Bridgman first introduces his operationalism in *Logic of Modern Physics* (the example which he has most often repeated), that of length. Length consists for Bridgman in the performance of various operations which determine "length." Wittgenstein, who uses the same example, professes a similar operational technique in his linguistic analysis. Wittgenstein states:

The question "What is length?" . . . produce[s] in us a mental cramp. We feel that we can't point to anything

---

16. "We can determine the general term of a series of forms by giving its first term and the general form of the operation that produces the next term out of the proposition that precedes it" (*Tractatus* 4.1273).
17. C. S. Chihara and J. A. Fodor, "Operationalism and Ordinary Language: A Critique of Wittgenstein," *Wittgenstein, the Philosophical Investigations: A Collection of Critical Essays*, ed. George Pitcher (Garden City, New York: Anchor, Doubleday, 1966), pp. 384-85. Italics are mine. This work contains the most positive statement of Wittgenstein's operational views on language. For a general statement of operationalism in the philosophy of language, see Ernest Nagel, "Operational Analysis as an Instrument for the Critique of Linguistic Signs," *Journal of Philosophy*, XXXIX (March 26, 1942), pp. 177-88.
18. *The Blue Book*, p. 67.
19. *PI* 421.
20. Chihara and Fodor, p. 388.

in reply to them and yet ought to point to something. (We are against one of the great sources of philosophical bewilderment: a substantive makes us look for a thing that corresponds to it.) [21]

Length does not have a substantive meaning; it has an *operational* one. "The meaning of the word 'length' is learnt among other things, by learning what it is to determine length."[22]

One judges the length of a rod and can look for and find some method of judging it more exactly or more reliably. So—you say—*what* is judged here is independent of the method of judging it. What length *is* cannot be defined by the method of determining length.—To think like this is to make a mistake.[23]

Using this example as a stepping-stone to a full-scale operational theory of linguistics, Wittgenstein generalizes: "To understand a language means to be master of a technique."[24] Meaning is use for Wittgenstein. The meanings of all linguistic terms are determined by how they operate within a given language system.

A Pragmatic Character

Pragmatism has been almost universally tagged as *the American* philosophy. It reflects a temperament among philosophers that was produced to a certain extent by the cultural milieu in which it matured, the USA. Unfortunately, however, among its many advocates, the term "pragmatism" has taken on a multitude of meanings. Arthur O. Lovejoy has pointed out at least thirteen different meanings of the term utilized before 1908.[25] True, some of these differences are trivial, but they do point out a divergency of philosophical at-

---

21. *The Blue Book*, p. 1.
22. *PI*, p. 225e.
23. *Ibid*.
24. *Ibid*., 199.
25. Arthur O. Lovejoy, quoted by Joseph L. Blau, *Men and Movements in American Philosophy* (Englewood Cliffs, New Jersey: Prentice-Hall, 1952). On the origination of pragmatism, confer C. S. Peirce, *Chance, Love, and Logic: Philosophical Essays*, ed. M. R. Cohen (New York: Harcourt, Brace and Company, 1923), p. xix.

titudes within a single movement. Of these divergent interpretations, we have selected the writings of Charles Sanders
Peirce as the source of our brief description of pragmatism
since he is generally recognized as its American founder. Once
again it must be emphasized that the purpose of discussing his
writings is not to make either Wittgenstein or Heidegger a
disciple of Peirce. We are using the latter's ideas to illustrate
briefly a *kind* of philosophizing, a *broad*, functional framework wherein Heidegger's and Wittgenstein's philosophical
notions can reside.

Peirce's pragmatism was first formulated through discussions of, as Peirce referred to it, the "metaphysical club," a
group of intellectuals who met informally in Boston and
Cambridge about 1870. Peirce's main philosophical contention of pragmatism is to present "a method of reflection having for its purpose to render ideas clear."[26] It is a theory of
conceptual meaning; it is "a method of determining the
meaning of intellectual concepts."[27] The most well-known
formulation of this method of pragmatism occurs in an essay
"How to Make our Ideas Clear." Peirce states: "Consider
what effects, that might conceivably have practical bearing,
we conceive the object of our conception to have. Then, our
conception of these effects is the whole of our conception of
the object."[28]

Another formulation of the maxim reads:

In order to ascertain the meaning of an intellectual con-

---

26. C. S. Peirce, *Collected Papers of Charles Sanders Peirce* (Cambridge,
Mass.: Harvard University Press, 1935), 5.13, note 1.
27. *Ibid.*, 5.8. It is upon this pivotal point that we see Peirce's pragmatism
differing from James'.
    James unequivocally states in the preface to *The Meaning of Truth*
that "the pivotal part of my book named *Pragmatism* is its account
of the relation called 'Truth' which may obtain between our idea
(opinion, belief, statement, or what not) and its object." [William
James, *Pragmatism, and Four Essays from the Meaning of Truth*
(Cleveland: World Publishing Company, 1955), p. 195.] It was pro-
nouncements such as these which led Peirce to rename his philosophy
"pragmaticism" and to disassociate his thought from James'. The version of pragmatism popularized by William James is associated primarily with a theory of truth. Peirce's, on the other hand, is basically
a theory of meaning.
28. *Ibid.*, 5.402.

ception, one should consider what practical consequences might conceivably result by necessity from the truth of that conception; and the sum of these consequences will constitute the entire meaning of the conception.[29]

Let us examine some of Peirce's applications of the pragmatic maxim to understand it better. Peirce proposes to explain what the maxim means by examining the proposition "the diamond is hard." The whole conception of "being hard," as with every other concept, Peirce discloses "in conceived practical effects." Pragmatically, then, to say that "the diamond is hard" means that when pressure is exerted upon it, it resists, that when a sharp object comes in contact with it, it is difficult to scratch, that when weight is placed upon it, it does not crush, etc. It is the sum total of these *practical* consequences which constitutes the meaning of the concept. Concepts have their meanings constituted in *practical* conduct.

> We say that a diamond is hard. And in what does this hardness consist? It consists merely in the fact that nothing will scratch it; therefore its hardness is entirely constituted by the fact of something rubbing against it with force without scratching it.[30]

From texts like the above, Peirce concludes that "there is absolutely no difference between a hard thing and a soft thing so long as they are not brought to the test."[31] Modifying his position somewhat, he continues:

> We may . . . ask what prevents us from saying that all hard bodies remain perfectly soft, until they are touched, when their hardness increases with the pressure until they are scratched. Reflection will show that the reply is this: there would be no *falsity* in such modes of speech.[32]

There is indeed falsity in such modes of speech! If the meaning of a concept consists in the practical consequences

---

29. *Ibid.*, 5.9. For other formulations and related texts, confer 5.18, 5.467, 5.412, and 5.438.
30. *Ibid.*, 7.340.
31. *Ibid.*, 5.403.
32. *Ibid.*

which constitute it, the fact no experimentation was performed upon the entity in the above example does not mean that it "remains perfectly soft, until it is touched." To predicate softness of it means that it had been examined and touched, and, as a consequence, it was easily reshaped, it did not resist pressure, it was easily scratched, etc. These practical consequences constitute the meaning of saying it is soft. But the very example which Peirce gives is that the body in question has not been touched. No practical consequences have occurred since no experiments have been performed. Thus, it is fallacious to say of it, as does Peirce, that "it remains perfectly soft, until touched." Rather, the pragmatic maxim forces one to say that it is meaningless to predicate hardness or softness to it until it is touched and examined. In later writings, Peirce did acknowledge the error of his former position:

> I myself went too far in the direction of nominalism when I said that it was a mere question of convenience of speech whether we say that a diamond is hard when it is not pressed upon, or whether we say that it is soft until it is pressed upon. I *now* say that experiment will prove that the diamond is hard, as a positive fact. That is, it is a real fact that it *would* resist pressure, which amounts to extreme scholastic realism.[33]

Despite this change from nominalism to scholastic realism,

---

33. *Ibid.*, 8.208. It could be argued that Peirce has not contradicted himself by saying that there is no *falsity* in maintaining that all hard bodies remain perfectly soft until they are touched because of the rather unique way in which Peirce has defined falsity.

Peirce postulates a variety of different kinds of falsity; the type in question here is logical falsity. Peirce states:

When we speak of truth and falsity, we refer to the possibility of the proposition being refuted; and this refutation (roughly speaking) takes place in but one way. Namely, an interpretant of the proposition would, if believed, produce the expectation of a certain description of percept on a certain occasion. The occasion arrives: the percept forced upon us is different. This constitutes the falsity of every proposition of which the disappointing prediction was the interpretant.

Thus, a false proposition is a proposition of which some interpretant represents that, on an occasion which it indicates, a percept will have a certain character, while the immediate perceptual one factor remains the same throughout all his works: the role of *practical* activities in the determination of meaning. Action in the form of practical activity is the source of pragmatic meaning. Pragmatic meaning centers around not theoretical activity but *practical* activity. Once again, this concept although pivotal to pragmatism should not be seen as *the only* character of Peirce's pragmatism, since it is the only character of his pragmatism which we have discussed. Once again our immediate discussion is not aimed at giving a complete picture of Peirce's philosophy, but of providing ourselves with a general frame of reference which could be called "pragmatic philosophy," a framework in which Heidegger and Wittgenstein function. If we reflect upon Heidegger's analysis of the world and of the "ready-to-hand" and Wittgenstein's, of language-games as a "form of life" and meaning's equation with actual use, we will see this same emphasis upon *practical* significance in its constituent aspect of meaning—be it ontological or linguistic.

*   *   *

In Heidegger's analysis, as Richard C. Hinners remarks, the "basic constitution of existence is being-in-the-world. But this 'world' is not simply the sum total of entities within it. It is rather a relational structure of *practical* significance. . . ."[34] This constitutes the pragmatic element in Heidegger. In his analysis of the "ready-to-hand" we recall that

judgment on that occasion is that the percept has not that character. (*Ibid.*, 5.569).

Falsity consists, then, in the actual occurrence of an event, the outcome of which is different from that expected. As a result, one cannot speak of the *falsity* of the proposition "All hard bodies remain perfectly soft until touched," precisely because the proposition has not been brought to the test. Nevertheless, the question remains: By what criterion or habit of action has the body been predicated with the term "soft" in the first place? That is, in the context of gloss 5.403, meaning is determinable by actual practical consequences; and if the body in question had not been examined in some way, then no qualities whatsoever could be predicated of it. "And were it impossible that anything should rub against it in this way, it would be quite without meaning, to say that it is hard, just as it is entirely without meaning to say that virtue or any other abstraction is hard" (*Ibid.*, 7.340).

34. Richard C. Hinners, "Being and God in Heidegger's Philosophy," *Proceedings of the American Catholic Philosophical Association*, XXXI, ed. Charles A. Hart (Washington, D.C.: The Catholic University of America, 1957), p. 158. Italics are mine.

Heidegger introduces the subject with the notions of practical "dealings" or "concern." These terms are not mere conceptual categorizations. "The kind of dealing which is closest to us is . . . not a bare perceptual cognition, but rather that kind of concern which *manipulates* things and puts them to use. . . ."[35] "The ready-to-hand is not grasped theoretically at all. . . ."[36] The encounter with the ready-to-hand by which the world is revealed is not noetic, but one of *practical* utilization. "Such entities [ready-to-hand] are not thereby objects for knowing the 'world' theoretically; they are simply what gets *used,* what gets *produced,* and so forth, etc."[37] They are constituted by their practical applicability; they have an "in-order-to" reference or assignment such as serviceability, usability and manipulability.[38] These terms Heidegger refers to as "practical behavior."[39] He clearly distinguishes theoretical observational studies from them. Recall Heidegger's discussion of the hammer as an item of equipment. "As equipment, a 'hammer' too is constituted by a serviceability. . . ."[40] This serviceability is its *practical* application in reference to Dasein. The hammer as equipment ready-to-hand is analyzed into a set of actual activities. The hammer's meaning is its practical utilization by the cobbler as he mends a worn shoe, by the carpenter as he builds a table, by the blacksmith as he pounds out a horseshoe, etc. The ontological being of equipment is the totality of ways it can be set into a context of practical activities or uses by which its character is manifest.

Dasein as being-in-the-world always projects itself into the world. It actively relates itself to the world with *concernful practical circumspection.* Dasein does not relate itself to the world by standing back from objects. It does not know the hammer by taking a position opposite it and staring at it. The kind of concern by which Dasein acquaints himself with the hammer is "rather that kind of concern which manipulates things and puts them to use."[41] Heidegger avers "the

35. BT, p. 95. Italics are mine. (SZ, p. 67).
36. *Ibid.,* p. 99. (SZ, p. 69).
37. *Ibid.* p. 95. Italics are mine. (SZ, p. 67).
38. *Ibid.,* p. 97. (SZ, p. 68).
39. *Ibid.,* p. 99. (SZ, p. 69).
40. *Ibid.,* p. 109. (SZ, p. 78).
41. *Ibid.,* p. 95. (SZ, p. 67). Cf., Richardson, pp. 54-58.

less we just stare at the hammer-Thing, and the more we seize hold of it and use it, the more primordial does our relationship to it become, and the more unveiledly is it encountered as that which it is—as equipment."[42] The real ontological significance of the world is predicated upon Dasein's practical engagement therein. It is for this reason that Marjorie Grene characterizes the Heideggerian man as *homo faber:* "For Heidegger man is *homo faber* before he is *homo sapiens:* it is materials, tools, opportunities by which he finds himself surrounded."[43] They are "stuff for use," she continues, which use constitutes their ontological significance.[44]

De Waelhens emphasizes this same point. He points out within Heidegger's writings "the primacy of the *pragma,* this ontological preeminence of a relationship of activity. . . . [I]ts instrumentality resides in this network of relations, developed not by thought but by *praxis.*"[45] The lived Heideggerian world is not an entity or an aggregation of entities, but the totality of practical activities within which Dasein can relate itself with entities; the world is the equipmental totality with which Dasein engages itself.

*   *   *

---

42. *Ibid.,* p. 98. (SZ, p. 69).
43. Marjorie Grene, *Martin Heidegger* (London: Bowes & Bowes, 1957), p. 22. Cf., H. J. Blackham, *Six Existentialist Thinkers* (New York: Harper & Row, 1959), pp. 89-90.
44. *Ibid.* Laszlo Versényi similarly remarks: "In fact, not only are utensils not discovered as mere things first, and then employed for our purposes, but nothing ever is discovered as 'merely there' (*vorhanden*), because Dasein's discovery of ontic beings is always guided by a practical intent or purpose. Originally, Dasein views ontic beings exclusively as *pragmata* or *chremata* in the literal sense, or something belonging to our *praxis,* defined by our *chresis* (service, need, want, etc.)." [Laszlo Versényi, *Heidegger, Being, and Truth* (New Haven and London: Yale University Press, 1965), p. 12.]
45. Alphonse de Waelhens, "Reflections on the Development of Heidegger: Apropos of a Recent Book," *International Philosophical Quarterly,* V (September, 1965), p. 482. De Waelhens warns, however, that we should not interpret this *praxis* in a Marxian sense.
    . . . certain authors have believed that they saw in this assertion and in the descriptions which support it a recollection of Marx or an affinity with Lukacs. This is wrong; *praxis* for Heidegger is totally different from that of the Marxists, were it only for the fact (in its own way decisive) that Heidegger's is before all else a *praxis* that is comprehensive of Being. (*Ibid.,* p. 486).

The pragmatic element of Wittgenstein's work is found primarily in two aspects of his thought. First, it is found in the "meaning is use" maxim whereby linguistic meaning is constituted by the *actual* usages of language. And, second, it is found in the related theme of language-games as practical linguistic activities. Though both themes are primarily developed in the *Investigations,* one should not limit Wittgenstein's pragmatism to his later thought. Indications of his pragmatism are already found in the *Tractatus,* though to a limited degree.

Recall that in gloss 3.328 of the *Tractatus* Wittgenstein states: "If a sign is *useless,* it is meaningless." Again at 3.3 he says: "Only propositions have sense; only in the nexus of a proposition does a name have meaning." This means, as one Wittgensteinian words it, that "names have no private life of their own." The meanings of names, although constituted by reference to objects, always occur in and can occur only in *actual* specific usage. To know the meaning of the object is to know the ways in which it can be used, and the ways it can sensically be used are determined by the ways it *actually* is used. It is true, as Wittgenstein remarks at 5.4733, any possible proposition is legitimately constructed; this, however, does not mean that all possible propositions have meaning in our *de facto* system of representational language. Thus, the proposition "Socrates is identical" is a possible proposition; the symbol itself is not of itself illegitimate. Rather, the statement is nonsensical because in fact our *actual* language system does not include an adjectival meaning for "identical." If our language did include such a use, then the proposition would be meaningful. Already in the *Tractatus* meaning is dependent upon how language *actually* functions.

In the *Investigations* this idea of actual usage as the determination of meaning is enlarged upon in the notion of language-games. ". . . the term 'language-*game*' is meant to bring into prominence the fact that the *speaking* of language is part of an activity, or of a form of life."[46] Language's constituents become that which are actually utilized in the activity. In *The Blue Book,* Wittgenstein insists that one should

---

46. *PI* 23.

"think of words as instruments characterized by their use, and then think of the use of a hammer, the use of a chisel, the use of a square, of a glue pot, and of the glue."[47] Language is an instrument. "Look at the sentence as an instrument, and at its sense as its employment."[48] Instruments are defined by their utilizations, i.e., how they work. The structure of ordinary language is determined through actual usage. "Every sign *by itself* seems dead. *What* gives it life?—In use it is *alive*. Is life breathed into it there?—Or is the *use* its life?"[49]

> If I have exhausted the justifications [of linguistic activity], I have reached bedrock, and my spade is turned. Then I am inclined to say "This is simply what I do."[50]

According to Wittgenstein, it is the practical consequence of the actual use of ordinary language which in the vast majority of cases establishes and founds its own "rules." As a result, these rules are not strict definitions; they, to the contrary, are a maze of integrated relationships criss-crossing, intertwining, and overlapping. They are generalizations which admit of as many exceptions to the rule as instances of it. In a word, the definite, well-defined, prescriptive use of words is only a small segment of the uses of ordinary language. In most instances, rules for linguistic usage do not precede actual use; it is practical usage which formulates these rules. To illustrate his position, Wittgenstein gives the example of the term "number" in the ordinary usage of language. "Why do we call something a 'number'?" he asks.

> ... because it has a direct relationship with several things that have hitherto been called number; and this can be said to give it an indirect relationship to other things we call by the same name. And we extend our concept of number as in spinning a thread we twist fibre on fibre.[51]

47. *The Blue Book*, p. 67.
48. *PI* 421. Cf., 291. Cf. also Stephen Toulmin, "Ludwig Wittgenstein," *Encounter*, XXXII (January, 1969), pp. 67ff.
49. *Ibid.*, 432.
50. *Ibid.*, 217.
51. *Ibid.*, 67.

In the ordinary use of language, the term "number" is not first given specific boundaries in which instances of it are subsumed. The process is much freer, much looser. Certainly, Wittgenstein admits, "I *can* give the concept 'number' rigid limits in this way, that is, use the word 'number' for a rigidly limited concept, but I can also use it so that the extension of the concept is *not* closed by a frontier."[52] It is this second sense which makes languages game-like. We do not know the rules until we have played the game; the actual activity of playing is the ultimate justification of language's regulative patterns.

Wittgenstein uses the term "sign-post" to convey this meaning of the rules of ordinary language. Sign-posts are indicators of ways of doing things, and these ways are determined by custom. It is not the contrary, that these sign-posts determine custom; custom determines sign-posts.[53] So also with language, usage of words determines the "rules" of usage; rules of usage do not determine the usage itself.[54] Summing up, we can indeed state that the later works of Wittgenstein are heavily imbued with a pragmatic element. Language is seen as an activity whose meaning consists in its practical significance. Language is "doing"; its meaning is derived from its actual linguistic manipulation.[55]

A Relational Character

Thus far we have manifested certain methodological similarities between the writings of Heidegger and Wittgenstein by revealing common notions of technique in their philosophy and indicating how these fit within a broad contextual framework of an already existing philosophical movement. In this

---

52. *Ibid.*, 68.
53. *Ibid.*, 198-201.
54. *Ibid.*, 217-25.
55. Von Wright points out that not only Wittgenstein's philosophy, but also his personal and intellectual life were pragmatically oriented:
    Knowledge, for Wittgenstein, was intimately connected with doing. It is significant that his first studies were in the technical sciences. He had a knowledge of mathematics and physics not derived from extensive reading, but from a working familiarity with mathematical and experimental techniques. His many artistic interests had the same active and living character. (Von Wright, quoted in Malcolm, p. 20).

section, however, we will show a character common to both men's thoughts which has not, to the best of my knowledge, been utilized as the name of a specific philosophical movement, though its connotations have been previously used to characterize philosophies throughout western history. For want of a better word, we call this element "relational."

If we reflect upon this term, we will find it to suit both men's thought rather aptly. For both philosophers, "to be" is "to be in a relation," whether we are speaking about the facts of logic or of the world. For both men, meaning is in terms of relations rather than through predicates—though the latter are ultimately explicated within these relations. Nevertheless, the meanings of these predicates do not pertain to or inhere in objects as such, but to objects as they function within the whole relational complex in which they are enveloped. It is not the object standing alone and in isolation from its surroundings which has significance; it is the combinational whole which has significance.

Furthermore, for both Heidegger and Wittgenstein this combinational whole has a specific structure. The proposition is not a mere medley of words for Wittgenstein nor is the world a juxtaposition of physical present-at-hand entities for Heidegger. The elements of each are in a definite relational structure and it is precisely because of that structure that they have meaning. The result is that there are no "absolute" units of significance; significance is relationally determined. An analysis or breakdown of the world for Heidegger and of the proposition for Wittgenstein end up ultimately in relational structures; resolve those structures into their components and meaning has been dissolved out of the complex.

Recall that Heidegger refers to the totality-matrix of Dasein's projective relationships as the world. With qualifications, the Cartesian " 'substantial Being' of entities within-the-world [has] been volatilized into a system of Relations. . . ."[56] ". . . one lets entities be encountered in the kind of Being that belongs to involvements; and this 'wherein' is the phenomenon of the world."[57] To be worldly is to be in

56. BT, p. 121. (SZ, p. 87).
57. Ibid., p. 119. (SZ, p. 86).

a relation. The world is neither a spatial container nor a physical location; instead, it is a contextual region of relations; it is Dasein's projective "in-order-to" assignment of relations. ". . . the structure of that to which Dasein assigns itself is what makes up the *worldhood* of the world."[58] Blackham summarizes Heidegger's position by saying:

> This is the primitive meaning of objects or things, and remains their fundamental concrete meaning; like *Dasein* they are constituted by their relations to other things in the world and to an existent of the nature of *Dasein:* the needle implies the thread, the garment, the sewer, and the wearer. That is to say, the object as tool is constituted by the system of relations in which it exists, and refers to and ends in *Dasein,* which is itself constituted by its relations to the system. . . . *Dasein* as possibility (the source of possibilities) and constituted by relations with objects as tools in a serviceable system (enabling possibilities to be realized) gives intelligibility to the world as the realization of projects.[59]

In a word, relationality is Heidegger's ontological ground within which things appear.

Similarly, for Wittgenstein, a proposition is not analyzed into isolated objects in an attempt to explicate it; rather, it is analyzed into other propositions whose *relational* complex describes the proposition in question. Observe how Wittgenstein describes analysis: "Every statement about complexes can be resolved into a statement about their constituents and into the propositions that describe the complexes completely."[60] Even if a primitive sign within a propositional context is obscure as to its meaning, this meaning is given relative to a context of known signs. This Wittgenstein calls elucidation.

> The meanings of primitive signs can be explained by means of elucidations. Elucidations are propositions that

---

58. *Ibid.* (SZ, p. 86).
59. Blackham, p. 89.
60. *Tractatus* 2.0201.

contain the primitive signs . . . only in the nexus of a proposition does a name have meaning.[61]

The meaning of a name consists in an object, and objects are constituted by the total number of relations into which they can enter. This is the relational logic of the *Tractatus*. The actual application of such a logic appears in the *Investigations;* here the relationalism is practically expressed in the "meaning is use" dictum which we have already discusssed.

Another avenue of approach to the methodological congruency that can be discovered in Heidegger's and Wittgenstein's relationalism is to discern that for both philosophers the term "property" loses its traditional status of meaningfulness, or more properly takes on a different meaning. The meaning of something is no longer its properties but the relations into which it enters; attributes of an entity are not properties of it, but the relations into which it enters. Recall Heidegger's example of the hammer. Its ontological significance is not analyzed into a conglomeration of property-like attributes; instead, its serviceability or utilizationality is its ontological meaning. "As equipment, a 'hammer' too is constituted by a serviceability. . . ."[62] And this serviceability is a relation, not an inherent property. Heidegger states:

> But the "indicating" of the sign and the "hammering" of the hammer are not properties of entities. Indeed, they are not properties at all, if the ontological structure designated by the term "property" is that of some definite character which it is possible for Things to possess.[63]

Wittgenstein is also very critical of property analysis, principally because of its inability to explicate the logic of all forms of propositions. All propositions cannot be analyzed into a subject and a predicate. The point is, states Wittgenstein, that "the existence of the subject-predicate sentence does not show everything needful. . . ."[64] Some propositions can fit into such a framework, but not all. Therefore, Witt-

---

61. *Ibid.*, 3.263 and 3.3.
62. BT, p. 109. (SZ, p. 78).
63. *Ibid.*, pp. 114–15. (SZ, p. 83).
64. *Notebooks* 4.9.14.

genstein structures his propositions differently. No longer is it a subject-predicate combination, but a concatenation of objects which is constitutive of the proposition. The property theory of analysis dissolves for Wittgenstein into one of a nexus of objects. "So, for example, [given Wittgensteinian analysis] the question, 'Are there unanalyzable subject-predicate propositions?' cannot be asked."[65] Why? Because it is a meaningless question for Wittgenstein. His analysis reduces propositions to objects in concatenation and not to subjects and predicates.

* * *

One major difference, however, exists between the relationalism of Heidegger and of Wittgenstein, and this difference must be brought into sharp focus. For Heidegger the meaning of a thing ready-to-hand is its use, i.e., its utensility by Dasein and its relation to its immediate environment. For Wittgenstein the meaning of a name in a proposition is its use in a proposition. This has indeed already been established. However, for Heidegger the use of a thing ready-to-hand does not imply only its use by Dasein and its immediate relation to its environment; underpinning this specific relational matrix is the totality-matrix called the world. This totality-matrix is always implied in any specific matrix as that background, or region, against which the specific matrix appears; and the latter's meaning is determined ontologically by the former.

For Wittgenstein such an out-and-out relationality is not expressed. Objects have meaning only in states of affairs and names only in propositions, but once a state of affairs is given or a proposition is articulated, it stands alone, having a determinate sense of its own. "States of affairs are independent of one another," Wittgenstein asserts; "from the existence or non-existence of one state of affairs it is impossible to infer the existence or non-existence of another."[66] The Wittgensteinian world consists of *independent* facts; there is no integral totality-matrix of relationship among facts and propositions which gives them their individual significance as occurs

---

65. *Tractatus* 4.1274.
66. *Ibid.*, 2.061 and 2.062.

in Heidegger's philosophy. Max Black refers to the Wittgensteinian world as "a mosaic of independent items."[67] The world, like the proposition, is indeed a network, but one of *independent* items. Let us take an example to explicate Wittgenstein's position.

Given a pair of geometrical axes, all the possible coordinates in that geometrical space are presupposed before any combination is actually mapped out in it. The space consists in a network of points. In this sense any given, mapped-out pair of coordinates logically presupposes the *possible* mappings of all coordinates in that space. However, the *actual* mapping of *one* pair of coordinates in the space in no way implies the *actual* mapping of another, different one. Just as in a mosaic each tile is separate and discrete, so also each point of the geometrical space is separate and discrete. Yet, the location of one pair of coordinates presupposes the locations of all the others.

Take another example. Let us utilize Wittgenstein's suggestion that a state of affairs or a proposition can be portrayed by a concatenation of spatial objects such as tables, chairs, books, etc.;[68] the spatial objects we will employ, however, are germane to Heidegger's philosophy. Assume that a cobbler, his bench, his tools and other materials, a box of tacks, a worn-out shoe, etc., are the objects situated in the logical space delimited by the cobbler's one-room shop. The total possible combinations of the above entities are the positions within the logical space—states of affairs such as the cobbler is sewing a sole to the shoe, the cobbler is hammering a tack into the shoe, the cobbler's hammer is to the cobbler's right, the hammer is to the left of his tacks as he looks upon them, etc. All these states of affairs are logically prior to actual states of affairs, each of which is factually independent in the Wittgensteinian system. For example, the fact "the cobbler is sitting at his bench and mending the shoe" is independent of the fact "the box of tacks is to the cobbler's left" and of the fact "the hammer is to his right." Each fact is independent of the others.

67. Max Black, *A Companion to Wittgenstein's 'Tractatus'* (Ithaca, New York: Cornell University Press, 1964), p. 3.
68. *Tractatus* 3.1431.

For Heidegger, however, the ontological significance of the above fact that the cobbler is sitting at his bench mending the worn shoe ontologically implies the totality of factual surroundings—the facts that the tacks are to the cobbler's left, that the hammer is to his right, that his other tools are all laid out in front of him, etc. These constitute the ontological region in which the original fact, the mending, occurs. In a Heideggerian world the cobbler's activities do not occur in some ontological void, but rather in a determining concrete situation which *de facto* includes a total complex of surrounding relations.

*　　*　　*

A grave difficulty is generated in this context of relationalism. There is something quite misleading, if not wrong, in saying that something is determined by relations. If anything, being in a relation first necessitates something substantive to be in that relation. H. D. Lewis has made this point quite cogently.[69] Wittgenstein likewise argues in this direction; he introduces into the *Tractatus* the notion of a primordial logical substance; objects are the substantive in his system of representative language.[70] Otherwise, there would be an infinite relational regress in the determination of meaning.[71] Similarly, in explicating the generation of complex propositions, Wittgenstein does not reduce this process to a system of pure relations—but to a relational system generated by a specific operation *and* the sum total of elementary propositions functioning within the system.[72] The latter become the logical substance of the system of complex propositions. No out and out relationalism exists within a Wittgensteinian framework.

The situation is the same, I maintain, in Heidegger's philosophy, although admittedly his view is not quite as clear-cut. Heidegger's criticisms of Descartes cannot be taken to mean that Descartes was in error for speaking of things substantial; this is not Heidegger's intent. Heidegger is not denying the

---

69. Cf., H. D. Lewis, *The Elusive Mind* (London: Allen & Unwin, 1969), chapter 9.
70. *Tractatus* 2.027.
71. *Ibid.*, 2.0211.
72. *Ibid.*, 5.5 and 6.

notion of substantiality. Rather, he is arguing that intelligibility is generated only contextually, that is, by entities in relation to Dasein. Heidegger's discourse on hammers in *Being and Time* does not reduce the equipmental entity to pure operations. Such entities are *things,* Heidegger would never deny this. But they are more precisely *things-to-be-used.* It is their use which determines their significance to man. Heidegger's point is that they are more than just things lying about without any immediate purpose to man; they are things invested with an immediate *value* for him. This item's earthly status is fixed by its being a thing and its significance by its use to man. "Therefore, equipment is half a thing, since it is determined through thinghood and yet [it is] more. . . ."[73] In his more recent works, Heidegger speaks of earth [*die Erde*] as distinct from the world [*die Welt*] and as more primordial.[74] Earth is the basic indeterminant stuff out of which the world is structured. It could be argued that this stuff constitutes the Heideggerian notion of substance; it certainly functions as that basic substratum of articulated reality.

In *The Origin of the Art Work* [*Der Ursprung des Kunstwerkes*] Heidegger explicates the notion of "earth" by directing our attention to a Greek temple situated in the midst of a rocky enclosed valley. The temple stands with the rocky earth as a foundation to its structure; the temple "discloses as being there a world and at the same time it places the world back upon the earth, which only now finds itself as the world's native ground."[75] The temple's smooth columns reflect the gleaming character of the sun, the raging torrents of the rain,

73. Martin Heidegger, *Holzwege* (Frankfurt am Main: V. Klostermann, 1950), p. 18. My own translation. *Der Ursprung des Kunstwerkes* and "Wozu Dichter?" appear in English translation as part of *Poetry, Language, Thought,* trans. Albert Hofstadter (New York: Harper & Row, 1971). At the time of this book's compilation, Hofstadter's translations were unavailable. I have been able, however, to incorporate the appropriate cross-references to them under the abbreviation PLT. The above citation is translated at PLT, p. 29.

74. Cf., *Ibid.,* pp. 33-39. (PLT, pp. 44-50).

75. *Ibid.,* p. 32. (PLT, p. 42). My own translation. For an excellent commentary on *The Origin of the Art Work,* confer C. D. Keyes, "Truth as Art: An Interpretation of Heidegger's *Sein und Zeit* and *Der Ursprung des Kunstwerkes,*" *Heidegger and the Path of Thinking,* pp. 65-84.

and all other specific characters of the demarcated earth. The temple creates a world; it opens up space within the place of the earth. The two—earth and world—are internally related, yet intelligibly distinct. "World and earth are essentially different from each other, and yet are never separable. The world founds itself in the earth, and the earth towers through the world."[76] Earth is that primordial ground which opens and reveals through man a world; world is structured by man. He is central to any concept of worldhood. "The stone lacks a world," Heidegger relates, "Plant and animal also have no world. . . ."[77] Yet, they have the earth.

When Heidegger maintains that man through language creates Being, Being has to be understood, as Heidegger always remarks, as the Being of beings. To create Being is tautological with creating entities in the sense of demarcating and intelligibly shaping the earth. Being is equally primordial with the world, but ontologically prior to both is the earth, which is *not* created by man. World for Heidegger is an articulated structure, receiving its intelligibility through man, but not its substantivity.

This same view of "world" can be predicated of Wittgenstein's system. Although he never explicitly makes such a statement, the term "world" [*die Welt*] is used equivocally in his philosophy, especially in the *Tractatus* wherein it assumes the status of a technical term. David Weissman calls attention to a distinction within the *Tractatus* between the world of facts, the world which is the case, and the world of logic.[78] In addition, there can be assumed in Wittgenstein's system the distinction between world, as the totality of existing states of affairs, and world as the brute facticity of things, a distinction paralleling Heidegger's differentiation between world and earth.

Although the phrase "brute facticity of things" is foreign to Wittgenstein's vocabulary, I believe it has a definite place therein. In *Tractatus* 6.341 and 6.342, he speaks of language

---

76. *Ibid.*, p. 37. My own translation. (PLT, pp. 48-49).
77. *Ibid.*, pp. 33-34. My own translation. (PLT, p. 45).
78. Cf., David Weissman, "Ontology in the *Tractatus*," *Philosophy and Phenomenological Research*, XXVII (June, 1967), pp. 475-501.

as a grid through which the world is described. The description of the world is then an articulation of how its brute facticity appears through the grid. The articulated world is the combined structure of the grid and what appears through it. We will call this world$_1$. By itself, that which appears through the grid we will designate as world$_2$. Clearly, they are not the same. World$_2$ is the brute facticity of things, similar to Heidegger's earth, and world$_1$ is the articulated structure of the brute facticity of things, similar to Heidegger's world.

A Human Character

One final characteristic of technique which is common to Heidegger's and Wittgenstein's philosophical approaches is their emphasis upon man as the center of philosophical investigation. This does not mean necessarily that either man's philosophy can be classified as a kind of philosophical anthropology. Rather, man and his activities are revealed as essential underpinnings for the two thinkers' investigations.

Heidegger's philosophy, insofar as we have discussed it, is Dasein-centered, that is, man-centered from the existential viewpoint. Man is essentially that central point of reference around which the totality-matrix of worldly relations revolves. This fundamental structure takes its form as a system of relations only through *human* concern. All items of equipment occur in a context of double reference: they refer to other items of equipment and also to man. Heidegger's illustration of shoe-mending refers to the nails, the leather, and glue used to mend the shoe and also to the man for whom the shoe is being made.[79] Existential man (Dasein) can exist only in this particular mode of being (i.e., within these referential relations), and reciprocally man is the source from which this system as a whole is generated. The possible ways in which man can utilize things constitute their relational totality. Molina makes these important comments:

> The being of worldly entities can be considered as one with the being of the Person in the sense that entities can have a meaning in virtue of their being set in a

79. BT, pp. 98ff. (SZ, p. 69). Cf., Richardson, pp. 54-55.

matrix of significance determined by the concern over the world on the part of a Person (viewed as being-in-the-world). This matrix of meaning, essentially characterized by *relations of reference,* constitutes the worldliness of the world.[80]

. . . Heidegger's statement that the constitution, the make-up, of the utensil which is grounded in one of its aspects in its reference to other utensils, must ultimately be understood as a *for the sake of* the being of the Person. Utensil, Person, and utensility are all but links of a concatenation, but it is the Person who provides the telos, the end, with respect to which the relations of reference among utensils achieve a *total* significance.[81]

In his later works, Heidegger no longer utilizes the term "Dasein" as he searches out Being and lays bare its ontological significance. Some writers and commentators see this as a reversal of Heidegger's Dasein-centered philosophy of *Being and Time.* Such an interpretation, however, is unsound. Certainly, differences can be shown between Heidegger's earlier and later works, so much so that Richardson refers to Heidegger's *Being and Time, Kant and the Problem of Metaphysics,* and various minor works written in 1929 as "Heidegger I" and the works following these as "Heidegger II."[82] The early Heidegger sought to uncover, search out, and disclose Being, using Dasein as its starting point; the later Heidegger viewed Being as opening itself and revealing itself to Dasein. Such a difference between Heidegger I and Heidegger II cannot be denied; nevertheless, man's existential role is crucial to both periods of Heidegger's thought. In Heidegger II, it is to Dasein, that is, to man in his existential character, that Being reveals itself. Man is that nodal point through which Being is primordially made manifest. Moreover, once Being has made itself manifest to man, it is man himself who preserves and promulgates this manifestation.

In the next chapter of this work, Chapter 7, the writings

---

80. Molina, p. 60.
81. *Ibid.,* p. 61.
82. Cf., Richardson, p. 230.

of Heidegger II will be discussed at length, and our present position will therein be confirmed. We shall find that that through which Being makes itself principally manifest is language. The language of the poets first reveals Being and the language of the philosophers preserves it. It is through the word that Being becomes manifest in Heidegger II. Once again, then, Being is revealed through a genuinely *human* characteristic: language. As Richardson observes: ". . . in Heidegger I, it is the process of there-being [Dasein], in Heidegger II, it is Being, that is fundamental history. The structure of the process, however, is the same in both: . . . in both cases, the process comes to its fulfillment only when man endorses it with his liberty. . . ."[83] It is in and through Dasein that Being reveals itself. Only Dasein has the capacity to receive Being's revelation. In the writings of both the early and the late Heidegger, the human factor is central and pivotal.

In Wittgenstein's writings, the human element is likewise present and presupposed, though its relevance is not as immediate to Wittgenstein's position as it is to Heidegger's; moreover, its relevance is more specifically directed to the *Investigations,* although certain *Tractatus* texts suggest the human character of language. At 4.002 he states: "Everyday language is a part of the human organism and is no less complicated than it." So also, he remarks that "with propositions, however, *we* make *ourselves* understood."[84] As Max Black relates, texts as these mean that "Wittgenstein constantly suggests that he is using 'language' in such a way that to say there is a language implies that there are users of the language."[85]

In the *PI* this human element is made evident through first the "meaning is use" dictum and second the "life form" terminology. According to the dictum, linguistic meaning is determined by actual language activity; this presupposes the possibility of that activity which further presupposes users of the language. These users constitute the human element of the *PI*. As De Mauro remarks:

---

83. *Ibid.,* p. 624. Cf., Vycinas, pp. 90-91.
84. *Tractatus* 4.026. Italics are mine. Cf., Pears, pp. 179ff.
85. Black, *Language and Philosophy,* p. 148.

In the *Philosophical Investigations* Wittgenstein showed that it is not words which mean things but men who, by words, mean things, that a statement does not represent a fact, but that men, by a statement, mean facts: he also showed that by propositions men not only represent facts, but also live.[86]

"Words, symbols, sentences do not do things or have meanings by themselves, but words, symbols, sentences (the language) have things done with them."[87] Words are linguistic tools; they are utilized by man. It is man who gives them their meaning. "Every sign *by itself* seems dead. *What* gives it life?—In use it is *alive*."[88] This use is man's use. High sums up this human element best by stating:

> In all our talk about language as an instrument or words and sentences as tools, we can be misled (much ordinary-language philosophy has fallen victim to this) in over-looking the user—a *conditio sine qua non* for anything (including language) having a use. Wittgenstein, I maintain, has not overlooked this feature. Indeed, it is the basis for his talking about language as an activity or arguing specifically, for example, that an "arrow points only in the application that a living being makes of it."[89]

It must be kept in mind, however, that Wittgenstein is concerned chiefly with language activities as activities. Thus, the users and generators of the specific language-game in question are not *immediately* important to Wittgenstein's purpose.

This brings us to our second point: language as a "life form." "And to imagine a language means to imagine a form of life."[90] Wittgenstein uses the term only five times in the

---

86. De Mauro, p. 2.
87. Dallas M. High, *Language, Persons, and Belief* (New York: Oxford University Press, 1967), p. 97.
88. *PI* 432.
89. High, p. 64.
90. *PI* 19.

PI and nowhere does he explicitly define it.[91] As a consequence, commentators have given a wide variety of meanings to it. Some have considered it to be "one of the three cardinal elements in Wittgenstein's latter thought."[92] Whereas, others consider it so insignificant that they fail to make any mention of it.[93] We maintain that this notion of life form is indeed an important one in the *PI*.

Words and sentences alone are mere marks on paper or noises in the air; they do not *mean* anything of themselves. It is man who means something by them via the ways in which he uses them. Only those combinations of marks and noises which are chosen by man mean something. Sometimes this choice is a conscious deliberate one, other times not. But it is man who has made the choice. He has given linguistic expressions life, a human life, through his utilization of them. Language-games are human activities; they belong to man's natural history.

---

91. High attempts to correlate its meaning with the terms "conventions" and "forms of culture" as used in *The Blue and Brown Books* and *Remarks on the Foundations of Mathematics*. Cf., High, pp. 100ff. Stanley Cavell similarly hypothesizes the synonymy between the terms "form of life" and "conventions" as they respectively appear in *The Blue Book* and the *PI*. Cf., "Availability of Wittgenstein's Later Philosophy," *Wittgenstein, the Philosophical Investigations: A Collection of Critical Essays*, ed. George Pitcher (Garden City, New York: Anchor, Doubleday, 1966), pp. 158ff. Although such correlations are indeed plausible, there is no substantial text explicating such a view. Thus, our concern will be solely with the term "form of life" as appears in *PI*. Cf., J. F. M. Hunter, "Forms of Life in Wittgenstein's *Philosophical Investigations*," *American Philosophical Quarterly*, V (October, 1968), pp. 233-43.

92. P. F. Strawson, "Review of Wittgenstein's *Philosophical Investigations*," *Wittgenstein, The Philosophical Investigations: A Collection of Critical Essays*, ed. George Pitcher (Garden City, New York: Anchor, Doubleday, 1966), p. 62.
      Commentators have almost unanimously shied away from making a major statement on the meaning of Wittgenstein's "life form" terminology. Such silence on their part is understandable given the sparsity of its use and the ambiguity which does surround its occurrences. Dallas M. High's work, *Language, Persons, and Belief*, presents the best attempt, as far as I can determine, of surpassing these difficulties and of presenting a coherent explanation of this terminology. Cf., High, pp. 99-130. The hypothetical character of this attempt, however, must always be kept in mind.

93. Cf., Justus Hartnack, *Wittgenstein and Modern Philosophy*, trans. Maurice Cranston (New York: Anchor, Doubleday, 1965), pp. 59-104.

> What we are supplying [in the *PI*] are really remarks on
> the natural history of human beings; we are not con-
> tributing curiosities, however, but observations which no
> one has doubted. . . .[94]

Wittgenstein is proposing in the *PI* that the life form of language is a human one. Linguistic meaning rests upon man's
interpersonal communication. The human being is the actual
condition for any linguistic activity; he is the requirement
for linguistic comprehension and meaning. It is the *human*
form of life which constitutes the bedrock of actual linguistic
usage; here, one's spade is turned. Here is the ultimate justification of usage. It is the given, that which must be accepted.

*   *   *

Given this man-centered relational view of significance,
it could be argued that logical and ontological meaning have
respectively for Heidegger and Wittgenstein a subjective,
whimsical meaning. Such an interpretation, however, is ungrounded.

Looking at Wittgenstein's view, we observe that language
is relative to man as speaker, but an objectivity remains. Even
though the limits of *my* language are the limits of *my* world,
there is a presupposition that my world is your world, my
language your language, from the viewpoint of everyday language.

Language—my language—is a *social* phenomenon. Linguistically, solipsism coincides with pure realism.[95] Language
is part of man's *social* history. Wittgenstein makes this most
clear in his remarks on private languages in the *PI*. Private
languages, being so named, are apart not only *de facto* but
also *de jure* from public discourse. Consequently, Wittgenstein argues that such a state of affairs is a logical impossibility.
This does not, however, rule out *a priori* that one cannot
invent a personal language, that is, a system of signs such that
de facto some and only some persons know its projected sense.
There is nothing impossible about that. Rather, the logic of

---

94. *PI* 415.
95. *Tractatus* 5.64.

language is such that what Wittgenstein is objecting to is a use of signs which is prescribed as so esoteric that its sense is necessarily unintelligible except for the "chosen few." To reword this, there can exist—and in fact do exist—various languages or jargons which are spoken by only a few people; to the rest of mankind, unknowing of the languages, they are private and unintelligible. Nevertheless, there is nothing *a priori* within the logical structure of any language barring the "outsider" from learning it—if he so desires and has the aptitude. "The possibility of a private language, a language that does not build into it or depend upon the social matrix of use, must be rejected, as indeed Wittgenstein does."[96] A language which is theoretically incommunicable is impossible, though it is possible that there exist languages which in fact have not been communicated to all.

Directing our attention to Heidegger and the charge of subjectivism, we find such a charge more serious. Whereas for Wittgenstein's investigations, the human element is man in the collective; in the writings of Heidegger, however, the human element is man as individual.

Dasein, human existence, is always that of a particular individual. "Dasein" is not a categorical word indicating a class of entities; it is an *existentiale*. "Thus Dasein," Heidegger emphasizes, "is never to be taken ontologically as an instance or special case of some genus of entities as things. . . . Dasein has *in each case mineness,* one must always use a *personal* pronoun when one addresses it: 'I am,' 'you are.' "[97] The "who" of Dasein, as Heidegger words it, is an individual "who" in all its existential particularity.

To lose such particularity means that Dasein has become inauthentic and that it has become part of the "they"—*das Man.* The "they" live in accordance with the customs and practices of the masses; their rules of conduct are determined by the general dictates of society. The "they" have lost their authentic existential distinctiveness, grounding their being in conventions. The authentic Dasein is the Dasein as individual. This does not mean, however, that the authentic Dasein is

96. High, p. 62.
97. BT, pp. 67-68. (SZ, p. 42). Cf., pp. 150ff. (SZ, pp. 115ff).

an isolated entity. To the contrary, Dasein in its individuality is being-in-the-world; as a result, its being includes co-existence with other Daseins. To be-with other Daseins (*Mitsein*) is a genuine *existentiale* of Dasein. "In clarifying Being-in-the-world," Heidegger states, "we have shown that a bare subject without a world never 'is' proximally, nor is it ever given. And so in the end an isolated 'I' without Others is just as far from being proximally given."[98] Nevertheless, we must ask: What is the ontological status of the world and of the *Mitsein* for Heidegger? Concerning the *Mitsein*, he states: "Thus in characterizing the encountering of *Others,* one is again still oriented by that Dasein which is in each case one's own. . . ."[99] Concerning the world, Heidegger, states: "As totality, world 'is' no particular being but rather that by means of and in terms of which Dasein *gives itself to understand* what beings it *can* behave toward and how it *can* behave toward them."[100] Heidegger maintains that the "disclosure of that for which what we encounter within-the-world is subsequently freed, amounts to nothing else than *understanding* the world. . . ."[101] ". . . the understanding," he continues, "projects Dasein's Being both upon its 'for-the-sake-of-which' and upon significance, as the worldhood of its current world."[102]

If the authentic Dasein is the Dasein in all its particularity and each Dasein's world and relationship to other Daseins are projections of this particularity (as the above texts indicate), then it is true that the world and its inhabitants are different for each Dasein; the world is a creation, of sorts, of each Dasein. As a result, charges of subjectivism and psychologism are somewhat justified within Heidegger's earlier writings. This does not mean, however, that Heidegger fits into the

---

98. *Ibid.,* p. 152. (SZ, p. 116).

99. *Ibid.,* p. 154. (SZ, p. 118).

100. Martin Heidegger, *Essence of Reasons,* trans. Terrence Malick (Evanston: Northwestern University Press, 1969), p. 85. Cf., pp. 87-91 of the work for a more detailed account of Heidegger's views on "subject" and "subjectivity." This work is a bilingual edition; the original German texts appear on the pages opposite the respective English translations.

101. BT, p. 118. Italics are mine. (SZ, p. 86).

102. *Ibid.,* p. 185. (SZ, p. 145).

camp of Berkeley's idealism. Certainly, the contents of Dasein's intentional assignments and references as a totality are
existentially constitutive of the world, but, as Heidegger emphasizes, they are not "merely something thought, first posited
in an 'act of thinking.' They are rather relationships in which
concernful circumspection as such already dwells."[103] Dasein's
organizational projection into the world structures the world
relative to itself, but it still needs a given substratum to structure. Heidegger's philosophical starting point is Dasein's being-in-the-world. Dasein is the *There*-being, and the ontological substratum of this "There" is *not* a creation of the subject or consciousness. It is a foundation supporting consciousness. Once again, the notion of earth, of which Heidegger
speaks in his later writings, must be brought into the picture.
Earth is the given substratum fundamental to both Dasein
and the world. It is not a creation of Dasein. As a result, Heidegger's subjectivism must not be blown out of proportion.
The subjective element of Heidegger's philosophy is nec-
essitated by the content of his investigation in *Being and
Time:* the radical individual character of human existence.
Heidegger's subjectivism is not due to some haphazard or chaotic element in Heidegger's methods. His method of revealing
Being is highly systematic. What lacks systematization—that
is, categorization—is human existence and the earth as the
ground of such existence.

The Relation of Descriptive Language and the World

Having pointed out common characteristics of technique
within Heidegger's analysis of the world and Wittgenstein's
analysis of language, let us proceed and examine how Heidegger relates his world to language in *Being and Time* and
how Wittgenstein relates descriptive language to the world.
Basically, I believe, we can call this relation one of representation. From our exposition on the "relational character" found
within this chapter we recall that both for Wittgenstein and
for Heidegger the world and descriptive language in their
ultimate analyzable states of significance have relatable struc-

---

103. *Ibid.*, p. 122. (SZ, p. 88).

tures. The correlation of these structures in the sense of an isomorphic re-presentation, or mirroring, constitutes their interrelatedness.

As we recall, for Heidegger, the world in *Being and Time* is the totality of ways by which Dasein can engage and involve itself with things, ontologically speaking. Dasein is a being-in-the-world which manipulates and utilizes the entities of this totality in practical situations. To be specified and articulated in activities, this totality of involvements must be intelligibly demarcated. Such delineation is the function of language; it is "the articulation of intelligibility."[104]

Representational language, then, systematizes upon the level of intelligibility the referential structure of the world by articulating the latter's structural relation to Dasein; it represents that structure and consequently possesses it. "What the discourse is about is a structural item that it necessarily possesses; for discourse helps to constitute the disclosedness of Being-in-the-world, and in its own structure it is modelled upon this basic state of Dasein."[105] Any linguistic statement which is descriptive of Dasein's relation to the world is an articulation of an aspect of that relation and thus is a representational mirroring of it.

In Wittgenstein, one finds this same mirroring structure linking together the world and representational language. The picture theory of language is a depiction of existing states of affairs by propositions. States of affairs are isomorphic, mirrored images of propositions, and both are congruently structured since they possess a common logical form between them. True propositions picture existing states of affairs; to picture denotes an isomorphism of the proposition's elements and the state of affairs'. And the world is congruently structured to language. This is Wittgenstein's conclusion; furthermore, it is a necessary conclusion if the picture theory is to be valid. Whereas Russell's philosophy of language unites the world with language through names, Wittgenstein accomplishes the task through formal structure. For Russell, the naming function was the ultimate link of language to the world; for Witt-

---

104. *Ibid.*, p. 204. (SZ, p. 161).
105. *Ibid.*, p. 205. (SZ, p. 162).

genstein names also stand for objects and objects are their meaning. Nevertheless, this naming function is not ultimate; to be significant, it presupposes that the names in question occur in a concatenation with other names in propositional contexts.[106]

An Unmethodological Remark

Thus far we have shown that the way in which Heidegger structures the world and relates it to language is methodologically congruent to the way Wittgenstein structures language and relates it to the world. Such is all that our methodological approach can accomplish. Methodology, as we have utilized the term, proposes no new philosophical position nor does it justify or criticize an existing one; it merely explicates and compares specific philosophical techniques. Having accomplished this, we have, methodologically speaking, reached the end of the exposition for this part of our study. Yet, I believe there is even a greater unification between the two men's perspectives concerning the relation of language and the world than our methodological approach allows us to assert.

We have as methodologists concerned ourselves totally with the structures of Heidegger's way of approaching the world and of Wittgenstein's way of approaching language. We have shown a structural congruity between Wittgensteinian language and the Heideggerian world and between their relations to each other.

However, this is not to be seen as a mere coincidence. Stepping out of our role as methodologists, we must show that the two—language and the world—so permeate each other that to talk about one is to talk of the other. Yet, what is their precise relation? John Wild states the problematic very well in the following excerpt from a 1961 address. Referring to an approach to philosophy (similar to Heidegger's ontology) as an exploration of the "life-world," he states:

> The life-world is a distinct horizon with an order of its own. This can no more be reduced to the abstract perspectives of science than can the open structures and meaning of ordinary language be reduced to the abstract

---

106. *Tractatus* 2.0122, 3.3, 4.22, 4.23 and 5.55.

grammar of an ideal language or logic. The two worlds are quite different. But which world is prior and more inclusive? Which is less inclusive and derived? These questions concern a conflict of attitudes, a war of worlds, as we may call it, which is now proceeding, and which I believe, confronts us with a most basic philosophical issue of our time.[107]

This is indeed a most basic philosophical issue. Putting this conflict of attitudes into Heidegger's and Wittgenstein's philosophical terminology, we can observe that Heidegger sees language (Dasein's projective relation with the world) as presupposing Dasein's pre-predicative being-in-the-world; language's logical structure presupposes a world. ". . . there emerges the necessity," Heidegger affirms, "of re-establishing the science of language on foundations which are ontologically . . . primordial. The task of *liberating* grammar from logic requires *beforehand* a *positive* understanding of the basic *a priori* structure of discourse in general as an *existentiale*.[108] For Heidegger the *logos* of present-day discourse implies an ontology.

Wittgenstein, on the other hand, sees man's relation to the world as dependent upon, and therefore as presupposing, the logic of everyday language. For him, the logic of language is fundamental to the world's facts. ". . . the harmony between thought and reality is to be found in the grammar of the language."[109] Again, he states: "My work has stretched out from the foundations of logic to the nature of the world."[110]

The question is, then, one of priority, To echo John Wild's words: Which point of view is more fundamental, which derived? Is the logic of language, as Heidegger maintains, dependent upon being-in-the-world, or is the world, as Wittgenstein maintains, grounded upon the logic of lan-

107. John Wild, "The Exploration of the Life-World," *Proceedings of the American Philosophical Association*, XXXIV (October, 1961), p. 22.
108. BT, p. 209. (SZ, p. 165). Cf., Borgmann, p. 141.
109. Ludwig Wittgenstein, *Zettel*, ed. G. E. M. Anscombe and G. H. von Wright, trans. G. E. M. Anscombe (Berkeley and Los Angeles: University of California Press, 1967), p. 55e. Hereafter this work will be cited as *Zettel*.
110. *Notebooks* 2.8.16.

guage? Wild contends that these two approaches "are so similar that these two tendencies of 20th century philosophy are
basically one."[111] I personally hesitate to say this since such
a statement applied to Heidegger's and Wittgenstein's writings would blot out or obscure many genuine differences between the two men's thoughts. The two perspectives are not
one. Heidegger sees language as an offspring of man's relationship to the world; Wittgenstein sees the world as the
result of language. These positions are different. However—
and this is the point I wish to emphasize—these positions,
though not one and the same, are not antithetical or contrary to each other. They are not mutually exclusive; quite to
the contrary, they are complementary. The logic of language
and the existence of the world are not totally independent;
the one is not "absolutely" prior to the other. To ask which
one is prior to the other is not answerable upon a simple
either-or basis. Let me explicate the position. I will use as
a starting point texts of Wittgenstein's *Tractatus.*

In the early glosses of the *Tractatus,* Wittgenstein speaks
of the "world" and of "logic." What is the meaning of these
glosses? Is Wittgenstein here alluding to a certain "ontological element" in logic? The 1's and 2's of the *Tractatus* do
indeed deal with the world. De Mauro refers to them as "a
solemn sequence of ontological assertions."[112] Black similarly
refers to them as "Wittgenstein's ontology," insisting that
"the ontology of the *Tractatus* . . . is too prominent in the
text to have escaped the attention of even the most casual
commentators."[113] Black emphasizes that Wittgenstein

> . . . did not regard the ontology to which he was led by
> his logical investigations as irrelevant or unimportant. . . .
> It is characteristic of Wittgenstein's thought that nearly
> every one of his main remarks about language or logic
> has an ontological counterpart, while, conversely, each
> ontological remark is reflected in some truth about the
> essence of language.[114]

111. Wild, p. 22.
112. De Mauro, p. 25.
113. Black, *A Companion to Wittgenstein's 'Tractatus,'* pp. 8-9.
114. *Ibid.,* p. 27.

I disagree with Black's views that "nearly everyone of his main remarks about language or logic has an ontological counterpart." Certainly, in the early texts of the *Tractatus* Wittgenstein speaks of propositions and their constituent names mirroring existing states of affairs and their constituents. World-language counterpart statements are found in these texts, but after the 3's they disappear. What are the ontological counterparts for Wittgenstein's presentation of truth-functions, tautological and contradictory propositions, the method of philosophy, the constituents of scientific laws, etc.? There are none. Black's statement is much too encompassing. He is, however, correct in calling attention to the 1's wherein the constitution of the world is discussed.[115]

Anscombe, on the other hand, interpreting the *Tractatus* as a purely logical work, plays down the importance of these commencing texts and asserts that the *Tractatus* really begins in the middle where its obviously logical subject matter is found. "The *Tractatus* is not presented in an order of demonstration from premises," Anscombe states; "if we want to find the grounds for its contentions, we must look in the middle and not at the beginning."[116] But, in answer to Anscombe: Wittgenstein in writing the *Tractatus* surely must have known what he was doing; surely he would not have made so gross a mistake as to put the opening remarks of the work in the middle of the text! Nevertheless, I tend to agree with Anscombe that the work is primarily logical.

M. T. Charlesworth maintains that the very beginning texts of the *Tractatus* "are statements about the *logical* conditions necessary for propositions to have sense, and though they do indeed 'show something about the world,' namely that the world is such that these logical conditions are necessary, they have, as such, no direct ontological implications."[117]

---

115. Black surmises that these texts with which the book opens were probably the last to be composed (*Ibid.*). Yet, Wittgenstein begins the *Tractatus* with them.
116. Anscombe, *An Introduction to Wittgenstein's 'Tractatus,'* p. 18.
117. M. T. Charlesworth, *Philosophy and Linguistic Analysis* (Pittsburgh: Duquesne University Press, 1959), p. 84. Charlesworth modifies this position; he in later texts admits that "the very insufficiency of his

By this is meant, as I interpret the matter, that the beginning glosses of the *Tractatus* say nothing significant about the *de facto* world in which we live. The world of the opening texts is any possible world. Griffin states:

> First, for "world" we should understand "any world." When Wittgenstein says in the 1's that "the world is all that is the case" or that "the world divides into facts," this is not intended as a truth about the world as in fact it is. He does sometimes speak of "the world" meaning "the world as in fact it is" but only to say, in effect, that describing "the world" in this sense is not his business.[118]

Whether or not Griffin is correct in his interpretation, we are now not in a position to say; nevertheless, his remark does lead to some interesting questions: What would it mean to speak of "a possible world" in a Wittgensteinian context? What would an "impossible world" be like? What are the implications of such terminology? These are indeed crucial questions, and their answers will hopefully reveal the complex, interrelated status of the world, language, and logic.

At *Tractatus* 3.02 Wittgenstein remarks: "What is thinkable is possible, too." And, at *Zettel* 263 he makes the related comment: "Hence there is something right about saying that unimaginability is a criterion for nonsensicality."[119] If something is nonsensical, then it is unimaginable; therefore, if something is imaginable, it is sensical. Likewise, if something

---

[Wittgenstein's] purely 'logical' enquiry *forces* him to make certain extra-logical commitments. For, if we interpret that *Tractatus* as a purely logical theory, where terms like 'fact,' 'the world,' etc., have no direct ontological significance, then, as I have already suggested, the doctrine of the *Tractatus* becomes no more than a collection of truisms, illuminating truisms in many cases, but still truisms" (*Ibid.*, p. 98). Perhaps Charlesworth has underestimated the values of truisms —which in this context I take to mean tautologies.

118. Griffin, p. 29.

119. Cf., *Zettel* 250. Obviously, there is a difficulty with this text; it contradicts the gist of the *Tractatus*. Note *Tractatus* 4. The *difficulty* seems to revolve about Wittgenstein's equating in meaning the propositions, "One can think of the rose in the dark as red" and "One can think of a red rose in the dark." The two propositions can mean in two different ways. For an interestingly related discussion, cf. Charles S. Peirce, *The Principles of Phenomenology*, 1.422.

is thinkable, it is possible, indicating that one cannot think the impossible. ". . . thought can never be of anything illogical, since, if it were, we should have to think illogically."[120] Moreover, since language is the same as thought,[121] Wittgenstein likewise concludes that "it is impossible to represent in language anything that 'contradicts logic.' "[122] As a result, one cannot conceive of or sensically articulate what an illogical (impossible) world would be like.[123] The second question, which we posed in response to Griffin's commentary, is then a pseudo-question; no answer can be given.

This, however, still leaves unanswered the more primary question: What is the structure of a possible world? By what criterion can be determined an imaginable world? At 2.022 of the *Tractatus,* Wittgenstein makes a very revealing statement in reference to this point: It is obvious that an imagined world, however different it may be from the real one, must have *something*—a form—in common with it. And, "objects are just what constitute this unalterable form."[124] Possible worlds share with the real world a form, the form of objects, which are the unanalyzable constituents of states of affairs. This is obvious since the form of an object is the "possibility of its occurring in states of affairs."[125] Objects contain the possibility of all situations.[126] In *The Blue Book,* Wittgenstein remarks:

> Supposing we asked: "How can one *imagine* what does not exist?" The answer seems to be: "If we do, we imagine non-existent combinations of existing elements." A centaur doesn't exist, but a man's head and torso and arms and a horse's legs do exist. "But can't we imagine an object utterly different from any one which exists?"—We should be inclined to answer: "No; the elements, individuals, must exist. . . ."[127]

120. *Tractatus* 3.03.
121. *Ibid.,* 4.
122. *Ibid.,* 3.032.
123. *Ibid.,* 3.031.
124. *Ibid.,* 2.023.
125. *Ibid.,* 2.0141.
126. *Ibid.,* 2.014.
127. *The Blue Book,* p. 31.

Of this text, two observations must be made. First, the word "object" is not being used in the technical sense of the *Tractatus*. Therein, at 2.02 and following, it is asserted that objects are the ultimate, substantive elements which concatenated constitute states of affairs. Being irreducible to more basic units, they are simple, non-composite; whereas, the word "object" in the above quotation refers to a composite, partified whole. As a result, according to the strict use of *Tractatus* terminology, the above use of the word "object" is a misnomer and it should be replaced by the phrase "state of affairs." The latter is a composite, partified whole, a concatenation of elements.

Strictly speaking, one cannot speak of a possible object in the context of the *Tractatus;* one can only speak of possible states of affairs, although one can speak therein of the possible *use* of objects, and mean objects' constituent occurrences in states of affairs.

In a similar manner, in the context of the *Tractatus,* the word "impossible" has no meaning in reference to objects. It makes no sense to speak of actual examples of objects as if, in contradistinction to them, somewhere "behind the scenes," there are other examples of objects some of which are possible, others impossible. We can speak only of those examples of objects which are part of our language system. This does not mean that new words and thereby new examples of objects cannot be generated to function as simples. Language as a growing phenomenon—life form—is obviously undergoing development. However, these new words and their respective meanings were not previously "possible names" and "possible objects" before their incorporation into the totality of the linguistic system. As Wittgenstein remarks: "If all particular objects are given, 'all objects' are given. In short with the particular objects all objects are given."[128]

Possibility is referent, then, of only sensical combinations of *existing* elements. The type of possibility of which Wittgenstein speaks is *not* a possibility of entities existing, but a possibility of existing entities being combined into states of

---

128. *Notebooks* 11.7.16. Cf., *Tractatus* 5.524.

affairs. This insight into Wittgenstein's position reveals something quite significant about the status of logic. If logic is the study of possibility and if possibility consists in the total concatenations of *existing* objects, then possibility together with logic (as the study of possibility) have an ontological foundation. The contents of possible worlds are generated from the objects existing in the *de facto* world.

In view of this finding, we must reformulate our interpretations of *Tractatus* 3.02 and of *Zettel* 263. The first must be interpreted to mean that a proposition is thinkable if and only if it is possible. And *Zettel* 263, to mean that a proposition is unimaginable if and only if it is nonsensical. Examine the following text from the *Tractatus:*

> 5.552 The "experience that we need in order to understand logic is not that something or other is the state of things, but that something *is*: that, however, is *not* an experience.
> Logic is *prior* to every experience—that something *is so.*
> It is prior to the question "How?," not prior to the question "What?"

A logic depictive of all possible worlds obviously presupposes the existence of a world in that it presupposes that existing indefinables are in fact given. This means that objects are given as instantiated with a specific content; this content consists in the substance of the world, its *what*. The postulation of this *what* is necessary in order to speak of a logic of all possible worlds, so as to determine what constitutes possible worlds. In this sense, then, the *what* of the *de facto* world is required for the generation of logical propositions and logic thereby reveals something about the world.

"Logic . . . is a mirror-image of the world."[129] Note, Wittgenstein is *not* saying that the world is an image (re-presentation) of logic; to the contrary, it is logic which mirrors (re-presents) the world. A mirror-image is always dependent upon that which it mirrors. It is a copy and thus presupposes

---

129. *Tractatus* 6.13.

the original; without the original first given, it makes no sense to speak of a copy. The copy is something secondhand and dependent upon the original; it is a representation in the literal sense of the word—a re-presentation, a presenting again. This relation of representor to represented likewise occurs in the relation of the propositions of logic to the world. "The propositions of logic describe the scaffolding of the world, or rather they represent it . . . and that is their connexion with the world."[130] This means that the propositions of logic, though presupposing a world, do not reveal or describe any of the latter's material properties as such. Logic then does not concern itself with *how* in fact objects are concatenated into states of affairs. Logic cannot tell what is the case, but it does tell what can be the case.

As a result, though dependent upon the elements of the existing world for its form, logic is not refutable by any experience. The latter shows that something *is so,* that it is in such and such a concatenation. Experience shows *how* things stand. Given this function of experience, logic is prior to every experience. That to which it is not prior, however, is the substantial *what,* that something is. Logic does not dictate the actual states of affairs of the world, yet the formal structure of the world must conform to logic since the latter is generated for the former. The logic of language deals with all possibilities as its facts; the structure of the *de facto* world (as a possible world) is likewise elucidated by logic.

> A particular mode of signifying may be unimportant but it is always important that it is a *possible* mode of signifying. . . . again and again the individual case turns out to be unimportant, but the possibility of each individual case discloses something about the essence of the world.[131]

Thus far, we have been saying that logic presupposes something about the world as in fact it is. Another way of saying this is that logic reveals something about the *actual* way that language is used. After all, my language determines my world.

130. *Ibid.,* 6.124.
131. *Ibid.,* 3.3421.

As stated in the famous, often quoted, text of *Tractatus* 5.6, *"the limits of my language* mean the limits of my world." Yet seldom quoted in conjunction with it is the text immediately following which maintains that "logic pervades the world: the limits of the world are also its limits."[132] Taken together, these texts indicate that not only does logic reveal something about the world, but also it reveals something about my language. In fact, the limits of my language are likewise the limits of logic.

> 5.473   Logic must look after itself.
>
> If a sign is *possible,* then it is also capable of signifying. Whatever is possible in logic is also permitted. (The reason why 'Socrates is identical' means nothing is that there is no property called 'identical.' The proposition is nonsensical because we have failed to make an arbitrary determination, and not because the symbol, in itself, would be illegitimate.)
>
> In a certain sense, we cannot make mistakes in logic.

Within this linguistic context, what is presupposed of the world in logic is that names have meanings, i.e., uses.[133]

Thus logic is not a study of possible worlds, as though they had a substantive status to be sought out and described. The language of possible worlds (logic) does not tell us or reveal to us information about other planets, other galaxies, or other universes existing in some unknown dimension—whatever this might mean: Rather, it tells us about the ways actual language allows us to speak about planets, galaxies, universes, etc. Possible worlds are nothing more than the totality of ways of speaking about objects in concatenation. Consequently, as the investigation into the necessary structure of possible worlds, logic is an investigation into the uses of language. The generating factor (and likewise the limiting factor) of possible worlds and logic itself is linguistic structure. *De facto* language becomes the basis of talking about

---

132. *Ibid.,* 5.61.
133. *Ibid.,* 6.124.

possible worlds. "The 'pervasive traits' and 'limiting structures' of all 'possible worlds' which logic is alleged to formulate," Ernest Nagel remarks, "thus appear to be traits of discourse. . . ."[134]
Though born within actual linguistic usages, logic is not
refutable by any particular factual statement. Logic says nothing about this fact as opposed to that one; facts are to be
discerned only by observation. Logic's propositions are purely
formal. To say that $\sim$ (p $\cdot$ $\sim$ p) is tautological, says nothing
significant about the world; it does, however, say that *de facto*
language is precisely used in such a way that when "p" is
given a definite sense, "$\sim$" means the negation of "p." Thus,
to assert the truth of "p" means that "$\sim$ p" is *not* true or to
assert the truth of "$\sim$ p" means that "p" is *not* true; consequently, both "p" and "$\sim$ p" cannot be said simultaneously
and under the same circumstances and still have a determined
sense. *De facto* language just does not function in this way.
Consistency and coherence are characteristics of speaking
about the world and not of the world itself; the same can be
said of inconsistency and incoherence. If pv $\sim$ p is to be a necessary truth, that is, true for all possible worlds, it must be part
of a given system of symbols. By itself, pv $\sim$ p expresses nothing necessary; it is its integration into a given symbolic system
which makes it tautological.

---

134. Ernest Nagel, "Logic Without Ontology," *Readings in Philosophical
Analysis*, ed. Herbert Feigl and Wilfrid Sellars (New York: Appleton-
Century-Crofts, Inc., 1949), p. 197. Max Black remarks: "In the case
of a simple tautology such as pv $\sim$ p, it might be thought that what is
'presupposed" is that propositions have sense (to speak in the style of
the present section); but propositions have sense only because the
names of which they are composed have meaning—and *vice versa.*
Thus, to understand a tautology, we must know the range of values
of the variable that occurs in the tautology" (Black, *A Companion to
the 'Tractatus,'* p. 330).
    Black has the correct idea, except for the last sentence of the quota-
tion. To understand that pv $\sim$ p is a tautology does not in the least
require that there be known the value domain of "p." It *does* require,
however, that it be known that the above "p" when incorporated
into a symbolism indicates propositions with a determinate sense and
that whatever "p" is, "$\sim$ p" indicates the opposite of "p" in the domain
(without stipulating its range), and that in this disjunctive form, the
statement asserts either "p" or "$\sim$ p"—again without stipulating the
range of the variable's domain.

Returning to Griffin's viewpoint that the world of which Wittgenstein speaks in the initial texts of the *Tractatus* is any world—the remark which initiated this discussion—we are now in a position to comment upon it intelligibly. Griffin has misinterpreted Wittgenstein. The latter's starting point of a world which is all that is the case and which divides into facts cannot be any and all possible worlds since the very notion of "possible worlds" presupposes the world as in fact it is.

To rephrase this upon the linguistic level, talking about possible worlds presupposes that names *in fact* have meanings. There is indeed an ontological presupposition in Wittgenstein's *Tractatus*. It is not, however, an ontology of possible worlds; rather, it is an ontology of that something is, that names in fact mean objects. This is the presupposition of any discourse, including that of logic. This is not to say, however, that the *Tractatus* is *not* a work logical in character. It is a logical treatise; however, the interpreting of the phrase "the world" appearing therein as divested of all ontological significance leads to certain insurmountable difficulties.

To take an example, let us assume with Griffin that *Tractatus* 1 means: Any world is all that is the case. Given proposition 2, it must be further maintained that "Any world is the existence of states of affairs." The consequence of this assertion is the reduction of all contingent propositions to tautologies. On Griffin's interpretation, it makes no sense to speak of a contingent proposition picturing what is not the case; the latter would have to be an impossible situation. This is easily seen in that a proposition represents a state of affairs in logical space. Since this state of affairs is a constituent of a world, and, according to Griffin, *any* world is all that is the case, then this possible state of affairs necessarily is the case and the proposition picturing it is thus a tautology, an untenable conclusion within the context of the *Tractatus*.[135] Moreover, any picture, on Griffin's terms, is true *a priori*, a further untenable conclusion within the context of the *Tractatus*.[136]

---

135. *Tractatus* 4.022.
136. *Ibid.,* 2.225.

Griffin is incorrect in maintaining that "Any world is all that is the case." One can say on Wittgenstein's terms that *any* complex of states of affairs constitutes *a* world; Wittgenstein at times does speak of "a world."[137] However, such references are exiguous, and they are radically different in meaning from that of his continually reoccurring phrase "the world." The latter specifies a unique complex of states of affairs; it refers to the *de facto* viewpoint from which Wittgenstein entered the realm of logic, the presupposed viewpoint of the world as in fact it is.

Summing up our above remarks, we can say that there is a reciprocally grounded relation between the logic of representational language and the world, the ontological given. Logic and all possible worlds cannot be thought of as totally independent of the world. The logic of representative language and the world are inextricably bound to each other, grounding each other reciprocally.

It is, as Heidegger points out, the ontological given of the world which makes the logic of language a *fact*. Similarly, it is, as Wittgenstein points out, the logic of language which makes a world possible. The world is such because of language. An investigation of the logical structure of language is simultaneously a searching out of the formal structure of the world. The logic of language permeates and constitutes the structure of the world. "To give the [logical] essence of a proposition means to give the essence of all description, and thus the essence of the world."[138] "The propositions of logic describe the scaffolding of the world. . . ."[139]

This "scaffolding of the world" is included in the relational structural possibilities exhibited when the domain of existing objects (in totality) is stipulated. Being formal, this scaffolding exhibits no subject matter. ". . . Is there an order in the world *a priori,* and if so, in what does it consist?" Wittgenstein asks in the *Notebooks*.[140] There indeed is this *a priori:* "Logic is *prior* to every experience—that something

---

137. Cf., *Ibid.,* 4.023, 5.123, 5.5521, and 6.1233.
138. *Ibid.,* 5.4711.
139. *Ibid.,* 6.124.
140. *Notebooks* 1.6.15.

is so," Wittgenstein remarks; "it is prior to the question 'How?' "[141] Logic is prior to this experience; it tells nothing significant about the contingent facts of the world. Logic does not presuppose that states of affairs are "such" and "so" for its logical propositions.

Yet, on the other side of the problematic there is Heidegger's view, a view showing the necessity that an ontological given be presupposed for the logic of language to be determined. Language's logical structure which is true for all possible worlds presupposes a world. As Anscombe remarks: "It is essential to see that logic does not describe any facts. . . . But logic cannot be thought of as something quite independent of the world either."[142]

According to Heidegger, logic must be predicated upon an ontology if it is to be properly understood. There exists a necessity of founding logic upon the existential structure of language.[143] Wittgenstein's view is complementary; for him, logic can be used only within the confines determined by language itself. The "What," the substance of the world, in the form of instantiated objects is a necessary requirement for the logic of Wittgenstein's *Tractatus.* "The propositions of logic . . . presuppose that names have meaning . . . and that is their connexion with the world."[144] For, it is the objects of our language which "contain the possibility of all situations."[145]

We must remember, therefore, that logic is not the science of *things,* but of the totality of ways of speaking about things. If logic were the science of things and existing, contingent states of affairs, then its necessary character would be unexplainable and unjustifiable. The certainty and necessity of logic is found in the *way* things are spoken of and not in things themselves. Consequently, there is an ontological given

---

141. *Tractatus* 5.552.
142. Anscombe, *An Introduction to Wittgenstein's 'Tractatus,'* p. 165.
143. Cf., BT, p. 209. (SZ, p. 165).
144. *Tractatus* 6.124. Ernest Nagel maintains that "the interpretation of logical principles as ontological invariants seems, therefore, on closer view, to be an extraneous ornamentation upon the function they actually exercise" (Nagel, p. 179).
145. *Ibid.,* 2.014. Cf., Maslow, p. 26.

in Wittgenstein's logic of representational language—it is not
an ontology of things but of language. The logic of representation presupposes and is predicated upon the *fact* of representational language. Such language as a fact must be presupposed so the terms "logic of language" and "all possible
worlds" convey sense.[146] The necessity of the logic of descriptive language is born in actual linguistic conventions. Logical
necessity is not an absolute; it is relative to actual linguistic
conventions. The logic of descriptive language presupposes
that language is a fact, and its facticity consists in its being
part of man's social history.[147]

Logic presupposes the contingent fact of human past
events, just as does mathematics, its applied counterpart. "For
mathematics is after all an anthropological phenomenon,"[148]
Wittgenstein observes. The mathematical proposition like
that of the logic of language, "is *grounded in* a technique.
And, if you like, also in the physical and psychological facts
that make the technique *possible*."[149] Logic and mathematics
are possible because certain *facts* make them possible; they
are part of language-games which are forms of human social
life.

How else could the propositions of logic be justified? Certainly not by logic—what sense does it make to justify logically
the propositions of logic? If logic is identified as discourse
about possible worlds, and possible worlds are so identified
as what logic talks about, then a vicious circle is generated.[150]
To the contrary, logical propositions are justified ontologically, or more properly, their structural validity is given as
the coherence of actual language activities. In *Remarks on
the Foundations of Mathematics*, Wittgenstein states: "The
danger here, I believe, is one of giving a justification of our

146. Cf., Hans Hahn, "Conventionalism," in *Logic and Philosophy*, ed. Gary
     Iseminger (New York: Appleton-Century-Crofts, Inc., 1969), p. 46
     and Arthur Pap, "Laws of Logic," in *Logic and Philosophy*, ed Gary
     Iseminger (New York: Appleton-Century-Crofts, Inc., 1969), pp.
     52-53.
147. Cf., *Remarks*, I, 141.
148. *Ibid.*, V, 26.
149. *Ibid.*, V, 1.
150. Cf., Nagel, pp. 196-97.

procedure when there is no such thing as a justification and we ought simply to have said: *That's how we do it.*"[151] The ultimate justification of the logic of language is simply that *this* is the way language functions; its structure is a given, that which must be accepted. "What has to be accepted, the given, is—so one could say— *forms of life.*"[152] Logic is possible because actual discourse makes it possible. If such were not the case, then the necessary character of logic would become unduly enigmatic; for, the entire subject would degenerate into a study of the occult, and its necessary character would be relegated to the mysterious. Whereas for Wittgenstein, what makes logic *a priori* is the *impossibility* of illogical thought.[153] Language, the world, and the logic of descriptive assertions are intricately bound together, defining and determining one another reciprocally.

151. *Remarks*, II, 74.
152. *PI*, p. 226e.
153. *Tractatus* 5.4731.

PART III

LANGUAGE AND BEING

Chapter VII

HEIDEGGER'S BEING OF LANGUAGE

> Real poetry is never only a higher
> way of everyday language. Rather
> vice versa, everyday speech is a for-
> gotten and therefore well used
> poem, from which scarcely still
> sounds a call.
>
> —Heidegger, "Language," *Unter-
> wegs zur Sprache*

Like most creative and original thinkers, Martin Heidegger as a philosopher of language has been received by today's
established philosophical circles with mixed judgments. Heidegger has been proclaimed a "prophet"[1] by some and a "pre-
tentious verbal philosopher"[2] by others. "A close examination
[of Heidegger's philosophy]," Marjorie Glicksman maintains,
"seems rather to expose, within the ponderous sentences of
essay and lecture, a very unsubstantial basis for a superstruc-
ture. Heidegger's philosophy is unique only in its rampant
misuses of language and its own emphatic claim to uniqueness."[3]

It is the goal of this chapter to point out that a cogent
and coherent philosophy of language is discoverable within
Heidegger's writings and that various of the commentators'
derogatory remarks on this matter (such as the above) are
unfounded.

---

1. Marjorie Grene, "Heidegger: Philosopher and Prophet," *Twentieth
   Century*, CLXIV (December, 1958), p. 545.
2. Marvin Farber, *Naturalism & Subjectivism* (Springfield, Illinois:
   Charles C. Thomas, 1959), p. 334.
3. Marjorie Glicksman, "A Note on the Philosophy of Heidegger," *Journal of Philosophy*, XXXV (February 17, 1938), p. 93.

In Chapter IV, the last expository chapter of Heidegger's thought, our concern focused mainly upon Heidegger's structure of the world since this is chronologically—and also ontologically—how Heidegger himself comes to grips with philosophical problems concerning language. Heidegger's main philosophical purpose is to grasp that pre-predicative ground of worldly beings, namely Being. As a result, his approach to language centers around this concern; his encounters with language are always through ontological (and etymological) investigations; his expositions on language are always done for the sake of and subjugated to the primary task of revealing Being—or more properly, of allowing Being to reveal itself.

Despite this subordination of questions concerning language to the Being-question within Heidegger's overall thought, Heidegger in no way minimizes the impact of language to philosophical inquiry. He remarks that "without a sufficient consideration of language, we never truly know what philosophy is . . . nor what philosophy is as a distinctive manner of language."⁴ Definitely language plays a crucial role in his philosophy. As J. Glenn Gray points out in his "Introduction" to the English translation of *Was heisst Denken?*, even though the nature of language "has come to hold the center of his attention till the present and has received its fullest treatment in the book *Unterwegs zur Sprache*, 1959. . . . To be sure, Heidegger has long before this reflected on the mysterious nature of language in its relation to thinking and Being."⁵ Heidegger himself asserts this fact; he relates that within all his works from *Being and Time* onward he had

---

4. Martin Heidegger, *What is Philosophy?*, trans. with an introduction by William Kluback and Jean T. Wilde (New Haven, Connecticut: College & University Press, 1956), p. 95. German text: p. 94 of the same edition.
5. J. Glenn Gray, "Introduction" to Martin Heidegger's *What is Called Thinking?*, trans. Fred D. Wieck and J. Glenn Gray (New York: Harper & Row, 1968), p. xix. Hereafter this work will be cited as WT; this translation will be used throughout. Abbreviated as WD, corresponding references to the German edition *Was heisst Denken?* (Tübingen: Max Niemeyer, 1954) appear in parentheses following the WT citation.

been concerned with the problem of language, though this concern had not always been made evident. ". . . because the recollection over language and Being determined my way of thought from the beginning, therefore the discussion [of them] remains as much as possible in the background."[6] It was, Heidegger relates, due precisely to the failure of an adequate linguistic framework that he suppressed publication of the third section of the first part of *Being and Time*.[7]

Language, then, has a profound and integral role within Heidegger's existential philosophy. Language is not just a tool lying at man's side for his convenience, nor is it a mere conveyance of information. Language, to the contrary, is *man's* way of Being.

> Language serves to give information. . . . But the essence of language does not consist entirely in being a means of giving information. This definition does not touch its essential essence, but merely indicates an effect of its essence. Language is not a mere tool, one of the many which man possesses; on the contrary, it is only language that affords the very possibility of standing in the openness of the existent. Only where there is language, is there world. . . . Language is not a tool at his [man's] disposal,

---

6. Martin Heidegger, *On the Way to Language*, trans. Peter D. Hertz (New York: Harper & Row, 1971), pp. 7ff. Hereafter this work will be cited as WL. This work is a translation of essays in Heidegger's *Unterwegs zur Sprache* (Pfullingen: Neske, 1959). Abbreviated as US, corresponding references to this German edition appear in parentheses following the WL citation. (US, pp. 93ff). At the time of this book's compilation, the English translation of the essays in US was unavailable to me. As a result, all citations of US are my own translations. I have, however, been able to incorporate the pagination of texts in WL for the reader's reference.

7. "The section in question was suppressed because the thinking failed to find language adequate to this reversal and did not succeed through the aid of the language of metaphysics." Martin Heidegger, "Letter on Humanism," *Philosophy in the Twentieth Century*, III, edited by William Barrett and Henry D. Aiken (New York: Random House, 1962), p. 280. Hereafter this work will be cited as LH; this translation will be employed throughout. Abbreviated as PLW, corresponding references to the German edition *Platons Lehre von der Wahrheit* (Bern: Francke, 1954) appear in parentheses following the LH citation. (PLW, p. 72).

rather it is that event which disposes of the supreme possibility of human existence.[8]

For Heidegger "language is not merely and not seriously a verbal and written expression which ought to become propagated."[9] "Language is neither merely the field of expression, nor merely the means of expression, nor merely the two jointly."[10] Language is not a simple aggregation of words either spoken or written. It is man's primary way of Being. "The being of men is founded in language," Heidegger relates; "language is the supreme event of human existence. . . ."[11] Even though the Being-question is Heidegger's pivotal philosophical theme, another theme has been working its way side-by-side with that of Being—the query into language, its meaning, scope, and function.

Because of the importance of this aspect of Heidegger's works, especially in relation to our own topic, it was my original intent to discuss individually, in the order of their original publication, those works of Heidegger which deal primarily with his philosophy of language. However, such a procedure would be repetitious and obscurant of Heidegger's basic thought. At times one work is, except for terminological differences, repeating the point of exposition of another work. At other times, works which should be studied together for the sake of contentful continuity are published at different periods of Heidegger's career. As a result, it is best to discuss Heidegger's thought on language according to subject matter. Though a certain *general* chronological progression still remains within the exposition, our aim is to illustrate the basic progression and continuity of Heidegger's philosophy of language.

---

8. Martin Heidegger, *Hölderlin and the Essence of Poetry*, trans. Douglas Scott, *Existence and Being*, ed. with an introduction by Werner Brock (Chicago: Regnery, 1949), pp. 276-77. Hereafter this work will be cited as HEP; this translation will be employed throughout. Abbreviated as HD, corresponding references to the essay as it appears in the German edition *Erläuterungen zu Hölderlins Dichtung* (Frankfurt am Main: V. Klostermann, 1951) are placed in parentheses following the HEP citations. (HD, p. 35).
9. H, p. 60. My own translation. (LPT, p. 73).
10. WT, p. 128. (WD, p. 87).
11. HEP, pp. 277 and 280. (HD, pp. 36 and 38).

The Structure of Representational Language

In our last chapter we observed how Heidegger structured the world and the role of language in such a structuring. Now let us investigate in detail Heidegger's proposal: ". . . philosophical research must resolve to ask what kind of Being goes with language in general."[12] His answer to this question is found primarily in his later works and we will examine these very closely; however, let us briefly see how the early Heidegger answers this question in *Being and Time* since his answers in this work are indicative of the direction of his later thought.

As we recall, language together with states-of-mind and understanding are discussed in *Being and Time* as the three modes by which Dasein is being-in-the-world; language is that existentiale by which Dasein projects itself into the world and integrates itself with it by intelligibly articulating its possibilities. The key word in this context is "articulate." What precisely does articulation of the world mean? It means the exhuming of objects from the totality-matrix of the world's possible relations to Dasein and focusing upon them so as to clearly delineate their specific thingly outlines. In other words, language in its depictive function makes explicit the thinghood of objects; it demarcates the structures of some-*thing* precisely as a thing. Language is an assertion and the "primary significance of 'assertion' is *'pointing out.'* [It is a] letting an entity be seen from itself."[13]

This pointing out, or letting be, is principally accomplished through predication. " 'Assertion' means no less than *'predication.'* We 'assert' a 'predicate' of a 'subject,' and the 'subject' is *given a definite character* by the 'predicate.' "[14] What is exhumed from the totality of world relations is the subject of the proposition and that which clearly delineates it or gives it a status of differentiation is the predicate. As a result, a proposition can strictly speaking articulate only entities which are present-at-hand. Articulation takes a sub-

---

12. BT, p. 209. (SZ, p. 166).
13. *Ibid.*, p. 196. (SZ, p. 154). Cf., Richardson, p. 384.
14. *Ibid.* (SZ, p. 154).

ject and delineates it *as* something. This "as" structure demarcates it within explicit contextual boundaries of the present-at-hand and consequently obscures the network of worldhood reference-relations in their pristine undifferentiated-
ness. ". . . that which is *explicitly* understood—has the structure of *something as something.*"[15] The "as" indicates the explicit disclosure in question and makes it articulate. Heidegger states:

> When an assertion has given a definite character to some-
> thing present-at-hand, it says something about it *as* a
> "what"; and this "what" is drawn *from that* which is
> present-at-hand as such. . . . In its function of appro-
> priating what is understood, the "as" no longer reaches
> out into a totality of involvements. As regards its possi-
> bilities for Articulating reference-relations, it has been
> cut off from that significance which, as such, constitutes
> environmentality. The "as" gets pushed back into the
> uniform plane of that which is merely present-at-hand. It
> dwindles to the structure of just letting one see what is
> present-at-hand, and letting one see it in a definite way.[16]

The limitation of the word is that it "gets experienced as
something present-at-hand and Interpreted as such, while at
the same time the entities which it points out have the meaning of presence-at-hand."[17]

Being as the pre-predicative ground of the world is constituted by this totality of reference-relations; as a result, it
is inarticulable. Neither is it an entity nor is it present-at-
hand. Being cannot be authentically predicated of, and thus
remains unsayable from the viewpoint of representational
propositions.

> The Being of entities "is" not itself an entity. If we are
> to understand the problem of Being, our first philo-
> sophical step consists . . . in not "telling a story"—that
> is to say, in not defining entities as entities by tracing

---

15. *Ibid.*, p. 189. (SZ, p. 149).
16. *Ibid.*, pp. 200-01. (SZ, p. 158).
17. *Ibid.*, p. 203. (SZ, p. 160).

them back in their origin to some other entities, as if Being had the character of some possible entity. Hence Being, as that which is asked about, must be exhibited in a way of its own, essentially different from the way in which entities are discovered. Accordingly, *what is to be found out by the asking*—the meaning of Being—also demands that it be conceived in a way of its own, essentially contrasting with the concepts in which entities acquire their determinate signification.[18]

Heidegger continues this line of thought in his later works. He continually emphasizes that the thinking of Being is non-representational in character; whereas, the thinking of entities is representational in character. The two demand language techniques and conceptual processes characteristically different.

The Language of Ontology as Non-Representational

Distinct from the assertional character of representational language, is the structure of non-representational language, as expressed in *Discourse on Thinking*. The work consists of a memorial address commemorative of the 175th birthday celebration of composer Conradin Kreutzer on October 30, 1955 in Messkirch and a "conversation" between a teacher, a scientist, and a scholar elaborating on the theme of the address. As in all of Heidegger's writings, we find here a continuing search for the meaning of Being. Within the work, Heidegger's approach to Being is not so much through language, as through thought. If, however, we assume no structural differentiation between modes of thought and varieties of language, then Heidegger's approach to Being in this work is an excellent introduction to his views on language. We will make such an assumption; the terms "thought" and "language" will be used interchangeably in this section.

A central theme within *Discourse on Thinking* is Heidegger's distinction between meditative thinking and calculative thinking, a distinction reminiscent of texts in *What is Metaphysics?* wherein Heidegger distinguishes the scientist's

---

18 *Ibid.*, p. 26. (SZ, p. 6).

calculative and manipulative methods from the more "original" or "essential" methods of metaphysics, and thus of philosophy. In *What is Metaphysics?*, we recall, Heidegger tells us that science concerns itself with "what-is," that is with objective units of measurable and calculable entities. Philosophy, on the other hand, utilizes methods of approach to search out that undifferentiated ontological ground of the calculable world; philosophy deals with Being. Heidegger has, thus, distinguished two types of inquiry each utilizing a different method: philosophy, or metaphysics, employs the methods of essential, or original, thinking and science, the method of calculation. In *Discourse on Thinking,* Heidegger, having recourse to this same distinction (with the terminological substitution of "meditative thinking" for "essential thinking") , proceeds to show that not only do these two disciplines have different methods, but also they have different linguistic structures: non-representational and representational language respectively. Non-representational language does not deal with entities, things. Representational language, on the other hand, pictures; it deals with entities, things.

The language of the representable is the language of calculation; it is the language of the object. ". . . in re-presenting, everything has become an object that stands opposite us. . . ."[19] Within representative language, "the world now appears as an *object*. . . ."[20] Recall that in the essay *On the Essence of Truth* Heidegger resorts to the proposition "This coin is round" (referring to a half-crown lying on the table) as an example of a depictive proposition. The make-up of this proposition is "the letting something take up a position opposite to us, as an object."[21] A representative proposition deals with objects; it asserts what-is. It frees and thereby objectifies a specific concatenation of objects from its surrounding ones and (relative to Dasein) "reveals itself as the 'letting-be of what-is.' "[22] Reference to the proposition is "only relative to objects and our *representing* them."[23]

---

19. DT, p. 67. (G, 43).
20. *Ibid.*, p. 50. Italics are mine. (G, pp. 19-20).
21. ET, p. 300. (WW, p. 11).
22. *Ibid.*, p. 305. (WW, p. 15).
23. DT, p. 64. Italics are mine. (G, p. 39).

Likewise, recall that in *On the Essence of Truth* Heidegger maintains that the truth of the proposition "This coin is round" presupposes a horizon of relational structures surrounding the coin in question. It is this horizon which constitutes the pre-predicative ontological ground of representative *language;* it is this horizon which constitutes the worldhood of the world as discussed in *Being and Time;* it is this horizon which is the Heideggerian notion of Being. Can this horizon—Being—representationally be portrayed? Obviously not. The specific character of depiction is that what is pictured is objectified within an articulated structure; whereas, the character of the horizon as Being is a surd-like matrix of relations. It does not have the character of objects.[24] Consequently, the language of philosophy, which is meditative language, is non-representational. Any language attempting to *represent* Being as a horizon, or region, "is no longer suitable; it could make clear to us that meanwhile we have come to confront something [factually] ineffable."[25] Heidegger makes this quite explicit in the "conversation" of the *Discourse:*

> Scientist: I must confess that I can't quite re-present in my mind all that you say about region [Being]. . . .
>
> Scholar: Probably it can't be re-presented at all, insofar as in re-presenting everything has become an object that stands opposite us within a horizon.
>
> Scientist: Then we can't really describe what we have named?
>
> Teacher: No. Any description would reify it.
>
> Scholar: Nevertheless it lets itself be named, and being named it can be thought about. . . .
>
> Teacher: . . . only if thinking is no longer re-presenting.[26]

Being cannot be represented since it is no-*thing* to be depicted. ". . . in the word 'Being,' in its meaning, we pass through word and meaning and aim at Being itself, except

24. *Ibid.* (G, p. 39).
25. *Ibid.,* p. 88. (G, p. 70).
26. *Ibid.,* p. 67. (G, p. 43).

that it is not a thing, if by thing we mean something that is in any way essent."[27] As a result, one cannot predicate of Being as one predicates of a piece of chalk.[28] Being has no color, or shape; it is not tangible or accessible to any of the senses as such. ". . . when we wish to apprehend Being, it is always as though we were reaching into the void."[29] From the perspective of representation, "Being" is an empty word; it points out or ostensibly manifests nothing. Yet, our language deceives us into thinking that the word "Being" does in fact represent some-*thing*.

> We say "das Sein." This form arises when by prefacing it with an article we transform the abstract infinitive into a substantive: *to einai*. The article was originally a demonstrative pronoun. It signifies that the object indicated stands as it were for itself, and is. This function of demonstration and indication always plays an eminent role in language. If we say only "sein," what is named is already indefinite enough. But the transformation of the infinitive into a verbal substantive further stabilizes as it were the emptiness that already resided in the infinitive; "sein" is set down like a stable object. The substantive "Sein" implies that what has thus been named itself "is." Now "being" itself becomes something that "is," though manifestly only essents are and not being in addition.[30]

It is Heidegger's contention that the history of western metaphysics from Plato onward is guilty of this reductive error.

The Linguistic Error of Western Metaphysics

The problem with traditional metaphysics, according to Heidegger, is that it has failed to utilize the proper manner

---

27. Martin Heidegger, *Introduction to Metaphysics*, trans. Ralph Manheim (Garden City, New York: Doubleday and Company, Inc., 1961), p. 74. Hereafter this edition will be cited as IM; this translation will be employed throughout. Abbreviated as EM, corresponding references to the German edition *Einführung in die Metaphysik* (Tübingen: Max Niemeyer, 1953) appear in parentheses following the IM citations. (EM, p. 67).
28. *Ibid.*, p. 28 (EM, p. 26).
29. *Ibid.*, p. 29. (EM, p. 27).
30. *Ibid.*, p. 57. (EM, pp. 52-53).

of expressing its subject matter, Being. Traditional philosophers linguistically have allowed Being to slip from their grasp by entifying it; metaphysicians have failed to think of and articulate Being correctly since their language and their thoughts have approached Being from a literal, representational viewpoint.

> . . . the traditional nature of thinking has received its shape from representations, that thoughts are a kind of representational idea. That is true. But at the same time it remains obscure how this shaping of the nature of traditional thinking takes place. The source of the event remains obscure. . . . Our own manner of thinking still feeds on the traditional nature of thinking, the forming of representational ideas. But we still do not think inasmuch as we have not yet entered into that nature which is proper to thinking, and which is still reserved, withheld from us.[31]

The *proper* content of metaphysics [Being] has fallen into oblivion. "Metaphysics thinks about beings as beings. Whenever the question is asked what beings are, beings as such are in sight. . . . [Traditional] metaphysics always represents beings only as beings."[32] The question about Being, or the prepredicative ground of things, has lapsed into an inquiry about things.

> . . . if we consider the question of Being in the sense of an inquiry into Being as such, it becomes clear to anyone who follows our thinking that Being *as such* is precisely hidden from metaphysics, and remains forgotten —and so radically that the forgetfulness of Being, which itself falls into forgetfulness, is the unknown but enduring impetus to metaphysical questioning.[33]

---

31. WT, pp. 44-45. (WD, p. 60).
32. Martin Heidegger, *The Way Back Into the Ground of Metaphysics*, in *Existentialism from Dostoevsky to Sartre*, trans. and introduced by Walter Kaufmann (Cleveland: The World Publishing Company, 1956), p. 207. Hereafter this work will be cited as GM.
33. IM, pp. 15-16. (EM, p. 15). "The history of Being begins and indeed necessarily with the oblivion of Being" [H, p. 243]. My own translation. Cf., Vycinas, pp. 90ff.

Heidegger's philosophical aim is to overcome the mistakes and misunderstandings of traditional metaphysics and re-discover the real meaning of Being.

> If the question of Being is to have its own history made transparent then this hardened tradition must be loosened up, and the concealment which it has brought about must be dissolved. . . . we are to *destroy* the traditional content of ancient ontology until we arrive at those primordial experiences in which we achieved our first ways of determining the nature of Being. . . .[34]

From Heidegger's viewpoint, a genuine inquiry into Being took place within pre-Socratic thought. The philosophical perspectives of especially Parmenides and Heraclitus manifest authentic thinking concerning Being. With Plato, however, western metaphysical thought deteriorated and was reduced to an inquiry into beings. Plato proposes to speak of *Being* as an Idea, or Form, yet all he speaks of are beings, that is entities. By making the Idea the ontological underpinning of things, Being has become an Essence—Being is solidified into an ideal unchanging entity. Following in like manner, Aristotle objectified the ground of beings; however, unlike Plato, he reduced it to substance. Aristotle and Plato sought the explanation of sensible things in *objective* structures. As Langan remarks:

> . . . failing to see the importance of the Dasein as the opening within which the unveiling [of Being] could take place, they sought for a *"thingly"* explanation for the presence of the things-that-are. They concluded that *something* of a different nature, beyond the "physical" world of the things-that-are, must sustain and hence account for their intelligibility.[35]

The philosophers of the Middle Ages, Heidegger maintains, held fast to this searching out of a *thingly* explanation

---

34. BT, p. 44. (SZ, p. 22).
35. Langan, p. 162. Cf., Richardson, p. 306. For a thorough and comprehensive study into Heidegger's relation with pre-Socratic thought, see *Martin Heidegger and the Pre-Socratics: An Introduction to his Thought* by George Joseph Seidel (Lincoln, Nebraska: University of Nebraska Press, 1964).

of beings. James Anderson refers to this criticism against the medievalist tradition as directed against a "straw man."[36] And, to a great extent, I agree. In medieval philosophy one finds within the writings of Thomas Aquinas, for example, a clear distinction between *ens* and *esse*. One wonders how Heidegger could overlook such a giant within the medieval tradition. It would seem that Heidegger's knowledge of medieval philosophy is not clearly in focus. Thomas Langan makes an interesting comment in confirmation of such an hypothesis. He calls attention to a series of lectures and seminars conducted by Heidegger in 1955 as guest of the Foyer Culturel International de Cerisy, maintaining that they laid bare an important *lacuna* in Heidegger's historical knowledge. Although it has been written that from his youngest days Heidegger was trained in Thomistic thought, relates Langan, Heidegger's interpretations of typical Scholastic texts during the lectures were *consistently* Scotistic in flavor.[37] It would seem that Heidegger's thesis of 1915 on *The Doctrine of Categories and Meanings of Duns Scotus* dominantly tinted the perspective from which he interprets the whole of medieval philosophy. Indeed, if Heidegger were more aware of Aquinas' philosophy, he would be less critical of the medieval tradition.

Turning now to modern philosophy, Heidegger finds in this tradition, beginning with Descartes and proceeding onward, a continuation of the forgetting of Being. Referring to Descartes' analogy of philosophy to a tree in which the roots are metaphysics, the trunk physics, and the branches the other sciences, Heidegger questions:

---

36. James F. Anderson, "Bergson, Aquinas, and Heidegger on the Notion of Nothingness," in *Proceedings of the American Catholic Philosophical Association*, XLI, ed. George F. McLean and Valerie Voorhies (Washington, D.C.: The Catholic University of America, 1967), pp. 147ff.

37. Cf., Thomas D. Langan, "Heidegger in France," *The Modern Schoolman*, XXXIII (January, 1956), pp. 114-17. Richardson warns against any attempt to correlate Heidegger's meaning of *Sein* with various scholastics' use of *esse*. [Cf., Richardson's footnote on p. 320.] Anderson, on the other hand, draws such an analogy (Anderson, p. 147). His correlation between Heidegger's *Seiende* and Aquinas' *essentia* (*Ibid.*) is clearly wrong. If anything, Heidegger's *Seiende* approximates Aquinas' *ens*.

In what soil do the roots of the tree of philosophy have
their hold? Out of what ground do the roots—and through
them the whole tree—receive their nourishing juices and
strength? What element, concealed in the ground, enters
and lives in the roots that support and nourish the tree?
What is the basis and element of metaphysics?[38]

The ontological ground of beings remains obscured within
Descartes' philosophy; the ground of the tree is never sought
out by him. Descartes' approach to philosophical inquiry did
instead lay emphasis upon the notion of "subject"; however,
this in no way uncovered its ontological grounding character.
The Being of the subject became objectified into a *res cogitans*. This laid the way for future philosophical reductions
of the ontological character of the subject into a thingly
status.

In the course of this history certain distinctive domains
of Being have come into view and have served as the primary guides for subsequent problematics: the *ego cogito*
of Descartes, the subject, the "I," reason, spirit, person.
But these all remain uninterrogated as to their Being
and its structure, in accordance with the thoroughgoing
way in which the question of Being has been neglected.
It is rather the case that the categorical content of the
traditional ontology has been carried over to these entities . . . for the purpose of Interpreting the substantiality of the subject ontologically.[39]

The philosophies of the modern period are, for Heidegger,
characterizable according to the divergent ways from which
they view the meaning of the subject. Each is a different form
of objectifying the ontological ground of the subject.[40] Moreover, this objectification of the ontological ground of the subject is carried over through Hegel and, according to Heidegger, culminates in Nietzsche. At first glance, one would
think that Nietzsche's philosophy is an attack upon the metaphysical tradition of western philosophy, and indeed it is.

38. GM, p. 207.
39. BT, p. 44. (SZ, p. 22).
40. Cf., Richardson, p. 326, notation 1.

Nevertheless, it is *not* a complete dissolution of this tradition; it preserves the error of traditional metaphysics by grounding beings in an essence-like characteristic of beings—The Will to Power.[41] Such an absolute, ontic structure has no place within Heidegger's ontology. Representational thought and representational language play no part within his philosophy. Philosophy *presents* its subject—Being—in a manner akin to poetry.

The Kinship of Philosophical and Poetical Linguistic Activities

Given Heidegger's illuminative interest in language, one would surmise his writings to be the epitome of lucidity and coherence. Yet, like Wittgenstein's works, they are not. "But, it is the very nature of philosophy," Heidegger observes, "never to make things easier but only more difficult. . . . its language strikes the everyday understanding as strange if not insane."[42] Philosophical language is strange, if not insane, from the point of view of ordinary language because the latter is primarily understood as representational, the former non-representational. Any non-representational linguistic activity will always appear as nonsense from a representational viewpoint. Due to this non-representational characteristic of philosophical language, we have seen already that Heidegger has separated philosophy and science on a linguistic basis. Now, Heidegger introduces a new element within his philosophical scheme: poetry. Because poetry likewise utilizes non-representational language, Heidegger maintains there is a certain kinship between it and philosophy itself. Moreover, upon closer analysis, Heidegger discovers that not only are the two akin in their specific non-representational linguistic structures, but also they are akin in their aims: both poetry and philosophy search out Being.

We have already discussed at some length the non-representational character of Heidegger's philosophical lan-

---

41. For a compact presentation of Heidegger's criticism and analysis of Nietzsche's theme "The Will-to-Power," confer the former's essay "Nietzsche's Word, 'God is Dead.'" H, pp. 193-247.

42. IM, p. 9. (EM, p. 9).

guage. In a manner similar to this analysis, Heidegger discusses poetic language. Before explicating this point, however, a certain clarification should be made concerning what Heidegger means by poetry. One should not mistake Heidegger's primary meaning of poetry with the poet's actual writing in verse form. The mechanics of versification coupled with the complexity of meter, rhythm, and rhyme is not the primary meaning of poetry, as Heidegger uses the term. With such grammatical structures Heidegger does not concern himself. Grammatical terms, Heidegger relates,

> ceased long ago to be anything more than technical instruments with the help of which we mechanically dissect language and set down rules. Precisely where a pristine feeling toward language still stirs, we sense the deadness of these grammatical forms, these mere mechanisms. Language and linguistics have been caught fast in these rigid forms, as in a steel net. In the barren and spiritless doctrine of the schools, these formal concepts and terms of grammar have become totally uncomprehended and incomprehensible shells.[43]

Poetry [*Dichtung*] in its essential, original sense is for Heidegger the linguistic creation or allowing-to-be of things. Verse making, or poetry in its narrow sense [*Poesie*], depends upon *Dichtung* and is derived from it. As Heidegger remarks, it is poetry [*Dichtung*] as a way of thought which is "the original poetizing which precedes all poesie. . . ."[44] Language is not therefore [originally] poetry [*Dichtung*] because it is initially a speaking in verse [*Poesie*], rather speaking in verse occurs in language because this preserves the original essence of poetry [*Dichtung*]."[45]

Given this original poetry as the letting-be of what is, it becomes manifest that language in its pristine form is for Heidegger poetry. "The origin of language is in essence mysterious. . . . In this departure language was Being, embodied in the word: poetry. Language is the primordial poetry in

---

43. *Ibid.*, pp. 43-44. (EM, pp. 40-41).
44. H, p. 303. My own translation.
45. *Ibid.*, p. 61. (PLT, p. 74). My own translation. Cf., Seidel, p. 145 and Richardson, p. 410.

which a people speak Being."[46] "Language," Heidegger asserts, "is itself poetry in an essential sense."[47] Whereas verse-making employs *Dichtung, Dichtung* creates this language itself. *Dichtung* is the actual creation of language in and through its letting things be; this original "language brings the thing as a thing first into being overt. . . . [Primordial poetic] language names the thing for the first time; each name first brings the thing to the word and to appearance. This name designates the thing first in its Being this [which is named.]."[48] As a result, this primordial act of naming is a linguistic use radically different from the naming-activity of representational language. In everyday depictive language, a name refers to something already designated; in poetic use [*Dichtung*], the "name" creates the entity as named; in the ordinary sense of the word, "names" do not occur in poetic language. In the same sense, Being, as the subject matter of poetry and philosophy, cannot be named. Thus, Heidegger is quite insistent in "Remembrance of the Poet" that Being (the Holy) cannot be named; "Holy" words are not names.

The purpose of poetic language is to make things manifest; it is to make things appear in their unconcealment. Original poetic *Logos* means "to produce the unconcealed as such, to produce the thing in its unconcealment."[49] It is the poetic word which capsulates and delineates things. "The word, the name, restores the emerging essent from the immediate, overpowering surge to its Being and maintains it in this openness, delineation, and permanence."[50] Poetic language is that "departure into Being, as a configuration disclosing the thing. . . ."[51] As a result, its language is non-representational. In poetry there is no-*thing* to represent. Poetry, to the contrary, *presents* things in language *for the first time* by calling them into appearance and yet at the same time preserving the novel presentational characters of these appearances. In *Remembrance of the Poet* Heidegger speaks of this, the poet's

---

46. IM, p. 144. (EM, p. 131).
47. H, p. 61. My own translation. (PLT, p. 74).
48. *Ibid.*, pp. 60-61. My own translation. (PLT, p. 73).
49. IM, p. 143. (EM, p. 130).
50. *Ibid.*, p. 144. (EM, p. 131).
51. *Ibid.*, p. 143. (EM, p. 130).

function, as that which "makes the Near be near and yet at
the same time makes it the sought-after, and therefore not
near. . . . [T]he essence of proximity seems to consist in bringing near the Near, while keeping it at a distance."[52] Such
language seems paradoxical, if not nonsensical, from a literal,
representational viewpoint.

To say that something is near and that at the same time
it remains at a distance—this is tantamount either to
violating the fundamental law of ordinary thought, the
principle of contradiction, or on the other hand to playing with empty words, or merely to making a presumptuous suggestion. That is why the poet, almost as soon
as he has spoken the line about the mystery of the re-
serving proximity, has to descend to the phrase:

"Foolish is my speech."[53]

Foolish is the poet's speech, foolish from a literal, representational standpoint. Poetic language must remain a non-literal
medium. ". . . we never get to know a mystery by unveiling
or analyzing it; we only get to know it by carefully guarding
the mystery as mystery."[54] The mystery is *shown* (in the sense
of *zeigen*) in poetic language, rather than pictured as some
kind of entity in a representational context. A theory of showing, although not explicitly worked out by Heidegger—except to some extent in *On the Way to Language*[55]—is quite
fundamental to his overall position. This becomes apparent if
we recall that his basic approach to philosophical questions
is phenomenological. Phenomenology is a study of what appears, of what makes itself manifest, of what *shows* itself. To
show in the sense of to disclose Being within some immediate
experience is the essence of Heidegger's philosophical posi-

---

52. Martin Heidegger, *Remembrance of the Poet*, trans. Douglas Scott,
    Existence and Being, ed. with an introduction by Werner Brock (Chi-
    cago: Regnery, 1949), p. 259. Hereafter this work will be cited as
    RP; this translation will be employed throughout. Abbreviated as
    HD, corresponding references to the essay as it appears in the Ger-
    man edition *Erläuterungen zu Hölderlins Dichtung* appear in paren-
    theses following the RP citations. (HD, p. 23).
53. *Ibid.*, p. 260. (HD, p. 24).
54. *Ibid.*, p. 259. (HD, p. 23).
55. WL, pp. 111-38. (US, pp. 239-68).

tion. Moreover, language is the chief mode within which Being *shows* itself; poetic discourse discloses reality by making it manifest. " 'To say' means to show, to let appear, to open to seeing and to hearing."[56] Language in its primordial sense is essentially a manifestation. "The being of language is to say as to show."[57] To say something is Dasein's way of bringing it to Being, of showing it as revelation. This disclosure by man is his way of owning something; appropriation is a key characteristic of language. By uttering the word, Dasein becomes the owner and guardian of what manifests itself in language. Showing is the source of things' presence to man in language and the resultant appearance of Being as the existence of these entities.

"Language is the House of Being," Heidegger asserts. "In its home man dwells. Whoever thinks or creates in words is a guardian of this dwelling."[58] Who creates in words? Heidegger replies: "Speech of thinkers and poets creates language."[59] The philosophical thinkers and the poets are the guardians of the House of Being; they dwell therein. Because of this common dwelling, Heidegger sees a close and significant interrelation between the two. In fact, in *Holzwege* Heidegger proposes that "original poetry [*Dichtung*] is the subject matter of thinking. . . ."[60] And, in one of his most recent essays he more daringly asserts: "All reflective thinking is poetry, all poetry, thinking."[61] For Heidegger the philosophical-poetical chasm is a pseudo-one. The theoretical ap-

---

56. *Ibid.*, p. 122. My own translation. (US, p. 252). Cf., WL, pp. 119-25 and 47ff. (US, pp. 250-56 and 144ff).

57. *Ibid.*, p. 123. My own translation. (US, p. 254).

58. LH, p. 271. (PLW, p. 53). Similarly in *Holzwege*, Heidegger refers to language as "the district (temple) that is the House of Being" (H, p. 286. My own translation). In addition, for remarks upon the difference of the Oriental and the Western ways of dwelling within the House of Being, confer US, pp. 85-155.

59. WT, p. 88. (WD, p. 33).

60. H, p. 256. Cf., J. Glenn Gray, "Poets and Thinkers: Their Kindred Roles in the Philosophy of Martin Heidegger," in *On Understanding Violence Philosophically* (New York: Harper & Row, 1970), pp. 69-90.

61. WL, p. 136. (US, p. 267). My own translation. Richardson appropriately comments that what Hölderlin calls "poetizing" is (despite profound differences) one with what Heidegger calls "thought." Cf., Richardson, p. 588 and H, p. 303.

proaches of philosophy and the imaginative, creative modes
of poetry are intimately related. Heidegger states:

> This theoretical-poetical distinction springs from a
> confused [way of] thinking. . . . All philosophical think-
> ing—and even the most rigorous and most prosaic [think-
> ing]—is in itself poetical, and nevertheless never verse.
> On the other hand, a poetical work—as Hölderlin's
> Hymns—can be poetical in the highest degree; neverthe-
> less, it is a philosophy. Nietzsche's "Thus Spoke Zara-
> thustra" is in the highest degree poetical and, yet, is not
> an art-work, but rather "philosophy." Because all real,
> that is great, philosophy in itself is thoughtful-poetical,
> the distinction of "theoretical" and "poetical" can not
> serve, in addition, to distinguish philosophical notes.[62]

One must be careful, however, not to mistake this kinship
between poetry and philosophy as a complete identification of
the two, though Heidegger's words at times might so suggest.[63] Both philosophical thinking and poetry dwell within
the House of Being, yet they dwell in different manners. In
Lectures and Essays [Vorträge und Aufsätze] Heidegger asserts: "That which is said poetically and that which is said
thoughtfully are never equal. But the one and the other can
say the same thing in various ways."[64] In What is Called
Thinking? he more emphatically reasserts that "what is stated
poetically and what is stated in thought, are never identical;
but there are times when they are the same—those times when
the gulf separating poesie and thinking is a clean and decisive
cleft."[65] Likewise in Explanations of Hölderlin's Poetry
[Erläuterungen zu Hölderlins Dichtung] Heidegger affirms:
"The unusual opens itself and opens the open only in poetiz-

---

62. Martin Heidegger, Nietzsche, I (Neske: Pfullingen, 1961), p. 329. My
    own translation.
63. I am referring specifically to the above-quoted text of US, namely
    "All reflective thinking is poetry, all poetry thinking" (p. 267). This
    very recent text would indicate an identification of thinking and
    poetry. All of Heidegger's other texts which I have examined, how-
    ever, have to the contrary indicated a close relation between the two,
    but never an identification.
64. Martin Heidegger, Vorträge und Aufsätze (Pfullingen: Neske, 1954),
    p. 138. My own translation. Hereafter this work will be cited as VA.
65. WT, p. 20. (WD, pp. 8-9).

ing [*Dichten*] (or else in its own time in thought abyssly different from the latter)."[66] And finally, quoting Hölderlin, Heidegger in *What is Metaphysics?* maintains that although the poet and philosophical thinker dwell together within the House of Being, they "dwell near to one another on mountains farthest apart."[67]

Richardson hypothesizes that perhaps the difference between philosophy and poetry which Heidegger maintains is respectively one of a purely positive comprehension of Being versus one which has a certain negativity bound up with it. The language of the poet totally reveals Being; whereas, that of the philosopher reveals it, yet simultaneously conceals it.[68] Richardson never specifically attempts to justify this interpretation, though various texts of Heidegger (which Richardson considers) do imply that this is an incorrect solution to the problematic. If Richardson were correct in saying that the poet's language designates Being in its pure positivity, then poetic language would be an immediate revelation of Being. Yet, Heidegger relates that "the poet, however, can never of himself name the Holy [i.e., Being] immediately. . . . Poets must leave to the immediate its immediacy . . . and still take their mediation as the unique."[69] The immediacy of Being always remains unsaid in poetic or philosophical language. "Every original and authentic naming [poetic utterance] expresses something unsaid, and, indeed, in such a fashion that it remains unsaid. . . ."[70] The distinction between poetry and philosophy, then, is *not* one of an immediate versus a mediated, or positive versus a negative, revelation of Being.

Richardson does propose another way of differentiating the two, and this second interpretation is well grounded within the texts of Heidegger. Richardson states: "What differentiates them [poet and philosophical thinker], apparently, is that the poet's principal concern is to utter Being in words, the thinker's to attend to Being thus revealed in poetic ut-

66. HD, p. 66. My own translation.
67. WM, p. 360. (WIM, p. 31).
68. Cf., Richardson, pp. 544-45 and p. 637.
69. HD, p. 66. My own translation.
70. WT, p. 119. (WD, p. 84).

terance."[71] When the poet incarnates Being within the word,
Being therein appears in its fresh and vital creation. The constant utilization of the linguistic structure in which this creation appears can, however, make the latter static and solidify
its novelty into a literal depictive linguistic structure; it is the
thinker's, that is the philosopher's, task to preserve the metaphorical, presentational character of the language.

> But because the word, once it has been spoken, slips out
> of the protection of the care-worn poet, he cannot easily
> hold fast in all its truth to the spoken knowledge of the
> reserved discovery and of the reserving proximity. There-
> fore, the poet turns to the others, so that their remem-
> brance may help toward an understanding of the poetic
> word. . . .[72]

The philosophers are those kindred to poets. They are "the
others" who preserve in language the original appearance of
the Holy. "They are the people of writing *and* of thinking. . . . In hearkening to the spoken word and thinking about
it so that it may be properly interpreted and retained, they
are helping the poet."[73] In addition to preserving the poet's
non-representational presentation of Being within language,
the philosopher's job is to distinguish the authentic language
of Being from inauthentic uses. Both linguistic mediums
utilize the same words and a mere grammatical analysis will
not reveal their differences.

> The pure and the ordinary are both equally something
> said. Hence the word as word never gives any direct
> guarantee as to whether it is an essential word or a coun-
> terfeit. On the contrary—an essential word often looks
> in its simplicity like an unessential one. And on the other
> hand that which is dressed up to look like the essential is
> only something recited by heart or repeated.[74]

The literal, repeated language of everyday speech has as
its aim the conveyance of information; in it, the manifesting

---

71. Richardson, p. 471.
72. RP, p. 269. (HD, pp. 29-30).
73. *Ibid.*, p. 268. (HD, p. 29).
74. HEP, pp. 275-76. (HD, p. 35).

of Being, which is language's original creative role, is forgotten. As Richardson relates: ". . . when an authentic word is uttered as we know already, there is a risk that in thoughtless repetition it may lose its power to disclose the Holy and become a 'mere verbal expression.' "[75] The repetition of words in everyday speech solidifies them within a definitive confine which ultimately gives them a literal significance and obliterates the terms' original significance. Ordinary everyday language "plays in such a way with our process of language that it gladly lets our language wander astray in the more obvious meanings of words. It is as if man had difficulty in dwelling authentically in language."[76] Once the poet has linguistically revealed Being through non-representational, metaphorical language, that revelation can be concealed in the repeated usage of that language and the literal founding of it. It is at this point that the philosopher—the thinker—assumes his professional role of preserving the metaphorical, non-literal meaning of the poet's language.

Being as a Linguistic Revelation

In our past analysis of Heidegger's philosophy of language one point had been made and has been carried along throughout our discussion in a somewhat hidden manner. It has been lying underneath the surface of our discussion and now we must overtly bring it to this surface: man's contact with Being occurs *only* through beings and their activities. Being's revelation to man is always mediated. "The poet, however, can never of himself name the Holy immediately. . . . Poets must leave to the immediate its immediacy . . . and still take their mediation as the unique."[77] The point emphasized is: *Man's encounter with Being is always through beings; apart from beings Being is not manifest to man.* Being is *never* found alone in its purity, it is there reflected through beings. The existential appears through the existentiell.[78] The

---

75. Richardson, p. 470.
76. WT, p. 83. (WD, p. 31).
77. HD, p. 66. My own translation.
78. Or, as Richardson words it, "the ontological can come to us *only* through the prism of the ontic. . . ." Richardson, p. 430. My own emphasis. Cf., Richardson, pp. 429ff.

two are ontologically inseparable. In fact, for Heidegger it really makes no sense to *speak* of Being isolated from beings. To bring forth and disclose beings is simultaneously to bring forth Being, although the latter's positive disclosure to Dasein is not immediately evident in and through the noetic context of entities. This fashioning of Being does not put Heidegger into the camp of some radical idealism, as we have already discussed. Primordial to beings in their Being is the earth. Vycinas summarizes Heidegger's position quite well on this point:

> . . . Being reveals itself by letting beings appear; these can only appear in the light of Being. Being is always the "beingness" of beings. In other words, Being cannot appear without beings which appear; the appearing beings reveal Being. However, Being in its revelation does not appear itself as beings do. It remains hidden or it appears in its concealment.[79]

And, what is this primary mode of revelation of Being through beings? Language. Man's access to Being is primarily linguistic. As a result, when Heidegger speaks of man's pre-predicative encounter with Being, this encounter is *not* pre-linguistic. The pre-predicatedness of man's encounter with Being is a pre-representational or pre-literal encounter, as occurs within the language of poetry and meditative philosophy. *Yet this encounter is linguistic.* It is language in and through poetry and philosophy which makes not only beings appear but also Being. Heidegger makes this point quite clear in his later writings. "Poetry," he remarks, "is the establishment of Being by means of the word."[80] In its primordial sense, poetry founds Being through the word; "primitive language is poetry, in which Being is established. . . ."[81] Being, as a result, is in a certain sense contingent upon language. "Being itself is dependent on the word in a totally different and more fundamental way than any essent."[82] Language be-

---

79. Vycinas, pp. 90-91.
80. HEP, p. 281. (HD, p. 38). Cf., H, p. 61. (PLT p. 74).
81. *Ibid.*, p. 284. (HD, p. 40).
82. IM, p. 74. (EM, p. 67).

comes "the clearing-and-concealing advent of Being itself."[83] It makes Being appear, while in other contexts it conceals Being. In both situations, however, language is that indwelling by which man relates himself to Being. "According to this, language is the House of Being, owned and pervaded by Being. Therefore, the point is to think of the essence of language in its correspondence to Being and, what is more, as this very correspondence, i.e., the dwelling of man's essence."[84] "Being can be discovered through the investigation of, the listening to, and meditating upon the language of thinkers and poets."[85]

83. LH, p. 279. (PLW, p. 70).
84. *Ibid.*, p. 283. (PLW, p. 79). Cf., IM, p. 143. (EM, p. 130).
85. J. Glenn Gray, "Heidegger's Being," Journal of Philosophy, XLIX (June 5, 1952), p. 415.

CHAPTER VIII

WITTGENSTEIN'S LANGUAGE OF BEING

Do not forget that a poem, even though
it is composed within language of information, is not used in the language-
game of giving information.

—Wittgenstein, *Zettel*

Wittgenstein's position on the structure of ontological
language is not really presented *verbatum et literatum* in his
works—either the earlier or the later ones. His overall position on statements of ontology is, rather, intimated in his
works, and the direction of this implication is discovered by
determining the precise relation between the *Tractatus* and
the *Investigations*. If we examined one work and one alone,
we would get a one-sided interpretation of the matter; somewhat correctly, it could be said that Wittgenstein's views on
language point in opposing directions in the two works. We
must then determine to what extent the two works comple-
ment each other. How much of the *Tractatus* can still be
maintained within the context of the *PI*, and to what extent
has the *PI* traversed the bounds of the *Tractatus?*

Because the "picture-terminology" and other technical
terms of the *Tractatus* do not reappear in the *PI*, some commentators have interpreted the latter as a denial of what is
propounded in the *Tractatus*. Justus Hartnack, for example,
maintains: "No unbroken line leads from the *Tractatus* to
the *Philosophical Investigations;* there is no logical sequence
between the two books, but rather a logical gap. The thought
of the later work is a negation of the thought of the earlier."[1]

---

1. Justus Hartnack, *Wittgenstein and Modern Philosophy*, trans. Maurice
Cranston (New York: Anchor Books, Doubleday, 1965), p. 62.

Tullio De Mauro likewise holds that the *PI* "is the *Tractatus* turned upside down. It should be understood as such. This means that in it there are *also* a methodology and an ontology entirely different from that of the *Tractatus*."[2]

Albert W. Levi, on the other hand, assumes an opposite point of view; he maintains that there is "a synthetic or synoptic gospel demonstration that our philosopher is one and not two; that the "early" and the "later" Wittgenstein are a single and coherent mind at work which should command the same philosophical audience for a sympathetic reading alike for the *Tractatus* and the *Philosophical Investigations*."[3]

Which position is correct? Must the *PI* be looked upon as a destruction of the position assumed in the *Tractatus?* Indeed this has been the prevalent view. In recent years, studies into the *Tractatus* have diminished within philosophical circles because of the latter's interpretations of the *Investigations*. The feeling is that one work supplanted the other. If we accept this view at face value and literally deny any continuity between the *Tractatus* and the *PI,* then our remarks on the *Tractatus* become insignificant as illustrative

---

2. De Mauro, p. 43. Cf., A. M. Quinton, "Excerpt from 'Contemporary British Philosophy,'" *Wittgenstein: The Philosophical Investigations,* ed. George Pitcher (New York: Doubleday, 1966), pp. 9ff.

3. Albert W. Levi, "Wittgenstein as Dialectician," *Journal of Philosophy,* LXI (February 13, 1964), p. 127. Levi proceeds to unite the various works of Wittgenstein in a rather interesting and unique way. Looking at Wittgenstein's works, one sees that the three major ones in chronological order are the *Tractatus Logico-Philosophicus, Remarks on the Foundations of Mathematics,* and the *Philosophical Investigations.* Levi focuses upon the type of work which each is. The first consists in a treatise [*Tractatus*], that is a systematized exposition or argument reaching definite and certain conclusions. The second, a series of remarks, that is, definite comments and observations presented in a rather casual, unsystematized manner. The third, a series of investigations, that is, inquiries and examinations of facts which do not necessarily reach any definite or systematic conclusions. Thus, in the preface to the *PI,* Wittgenstein refers to the work as a travelling "over a wide field of thought criss-cross in every direction . . . a number of sketches of landscapes which were made in the course of these long and involved journeyings" (Preface to the *PI,* p. ix). Basing himself upon these titles to the works and what they imply, Levi finds a gradually descending structural cohesion from a tight, coherent system of coherent truths, to a series of unsystematized comments, to mere inquiries and searchings.

of Wittgenstein's mature view. We have already briefly discussed this issue at the end of Chapter 5; however, the scope of the remarks was limited. Even though our position was therein hinted at, we must now in detail discuss the relation of the *Tractatus as a whole* within the focus of the *PI*.

Representational Language: The PI Perspective

Throughout the history of western philosophy there has existed a widespread attempt to equate linguistic meaning with objective reference or signification. Although the content of the objects of reference has ranged from physical entities to mental images, the basic referential structure remains.[4] Wittgenstein begins the *PI* with a quotation from Augustine's *Confessions*. It is presented as an example of this "meaning is naming" referential theory of language. Augustine states:

> When they (my elders) named some object, and accordingly moved toward something, I saw this and I grasped that the thing was called by the sound they uttered when they meant to point it out. . . . Thus, as I heard words repeatedly used in their proper places in various sentences, I gradually learnt to understand what objects they signified. . . .[5]

Rephrasing the quotation, Wittgenstein explains that "the individual words in language name objects—sentences are combinations of such names.—In this picture of language we find the roots of the following idea: Every word has a meaning. This meaning is correlated with the word. It is the object for which the word stands."[6] This is the view of the

---

4. Cf., Dallas M. High, *Language, Persons, and Belief* (New York: Oxford University Press, 1967), p. 30.

5. Augustine, *Confessions* 1:8. Norman Malcolm in his memoir of Wittgenstein recalls that Wittgenstein once stated that "he decided to begin his *Investigations* with a quotation from the . . . *Confessions*, not because he could not find the conception expressed in that quotation stated as well by other philosophers, but because the conception *must* be important if so great a mind held it." Cf., Malcolm, *Ludwig Wittgenstein: A Memoir*, p. 71.

6. *PI* 1.

Tractatus. According to such a theory, in order for a word to have meaning it *must* name something; that is, it must refer to an object. "You say: the point isn't the word, but its meaning, and you think of the meaning as a thing. . . ."[7] "Once you know *what* the word stands for, you understand it, you know its whole use."[8] The object referred to delimits and perfectly coincides with its linguistic copy, the word. In short, the object is the definition of the word. If I ask, "What is a chair?," someone points to this seat having four legs and a back. If I ask, "What is a book?," someone points to this bound compilation of pages. The end result of this "meaning is naming" theory of language is that *each* and *every* word so as to have meaning must refer to an object, and the very meaning of the word *is* that object. "Sensation," then, becomes objectified into *things* called "the five senses," so as to be meaningful. "Intellection" to be meaningful is objectified into a *thing* called a "universal essence." "Soul," as a principle of life, in order to be meaningful is objectified into a *thing* called a "spiritual substance." In addition, terms such as "length," "number," "infinity" suffer a similar fate.

> The questions "What is length?," "What is meaning," "What is the number one?," etc., produce in us a mental cramp. We feel that we can't point to anything in reply to them and yet ought to point to something. (We are up against one of the great sources of philosophical bewilderment: a substantive makes us look for a thing that corresponds to it.) [9]

In the *PI*, Wittgenstein is extremely critical of the "meaning is naming" theory of language. Is the meaning of "Mr. N. N.," asks Wittgenstein, that very man to whom the name refers? Certainly not. Napoleon has died, there exists nothing to which we can point when we use his name. The name's bearer no longer exists; the name's reference can no longer be ostensibly manifested. Does this mean that we cannot therefore teach someone who Napoleon was because we cannot

---

7. *Ibid.,* 120.
8. *Ibid.,* 264.
9. *The Blue Book,* p. 1.

point ostensibly to the man? Not at all.[10] Names can convey meanings which are not ostensibly designated.

So also, if one asked for the meaning of a "king" in a chess game, the mere pointing to a specific piece on the chessboard is insufficient to convey the information. "When one shews someone the king in chess and says: 'This is the King,' this does not tell him the use of this piece. . . ."[11] And such use is essential to the real meaning of the king. The king's meaning is not merely the carved wood entity; it includes a way of moving the piece and relating it to other pieces—all of which are not given in that first act of ostensible definition. The "meaning is naming" theory of language—the theory of the *Tractatus*—thus has been dealt a critical blow in the *PI*.[12]

Representational Language: The TRACTATUS Perspective

The *Tractatus* deals almost totally with explicating a representational theory of language. Any non-representational, or non-pictorial, use—such as a religious or ethical use—is termed "nonsensical" in the *Tractatus*. This is, in a sense, the death-blow of the *Tractatus*. At the time of the work, Wittgenstein was convinced that it was the final word in its field. He unequivocally states in his preface to the *Tractatus* that "the *truth* of the thoughts that are here set forth seems to me unassailable and definitive. I therefore believe myself to have found, on all essential points, the final solution of the problems."[13]

Gradually, however, Wittgenstein lost confidence in the absolute position of the *Tractatus*. He remarks that he has

---

10. *PI* 40. Cf., for further information on the word-object theory of meaning, William P. Alston, *Philosophy of Language* (Englewood Cliffs, New Jersey: Prentice-Hall, 1964), pp. 12ff. Apart from such complex cases where nominatives have meanings which are not referential, there exist the more obvious cases of "if," "and," "but," "therefore" and other connectives whose meanings are not referential. Perhaps, though, it is an oversimplification to speak of these terms as having meanings which are "obviously" not referential. Bertrand Russell, for example, has attempted to reduce the meanings of these words to physical behavior. Cf., Bertrand Russell, *Inquiry Into Meaning and Truth*, pp. 79ff.
11. *Ibid.*, 31. Cf., 30-33.
12. *Ibid.*, 49.
13. Preface to the *Tractatus*, p. 5.

been "forced to recognize great mistakes in what I wrote in that first book [the *Tractatus*]."[14] As a result of this recognition, the *PI* was born. Wittgenstein's later views grew from those of the *Tractatus* and are understood only in light of them. Wittgenstein states in his preface to the *Investigations:*

> Four years ago I had occasion to re-read my first book (the *Tractatus Logico-Philosophicus*) and to explain its ideas to someone. It suddenly seemed to me that I should publish those old thoughts and the new ones together: that the latter could be seen in the right light only by contrast with and against the background of my old way of thinking.[15]

As Malcolm relates, even though Wittgenstein said disparaging things about the *Tractatus,* "I am sure, however, that he still regarded it as an important work."[16] Wittgenstein was indeed critical of the *Tractatus,* but he never abandoned the ideas therein. He found "great mistakes" in it, but these errors were not ones of commission but ones of omission. As one commentator remarks: "What is 'false' about the *Tractatus* may be mistaking part for the whole."[17] The *Tractatus* deals only with the logic of representational propositions. Its error is to limit sensical linguistic usage to this function. Its error is to confine meaning to naming. Apart from rectifying this too narrow of an approach, the thoughts expressed in the *Investigations* are complementary to those in the *Tractatus.*[18] The non-representational language activities discussed in *PI*

---

14. Preface to the *PI*, p. x.
15. *Ibid.*
16. Malcolm, p. 69.
17. Dennis O'Brien, "The Unity of Wittgenstein's Thought," *International Philosophical Quarterly*, VI (March, 1966), p. 45.
18. In his memoir of Wittgenstein, Malcolm makes a comment which might discredit our interpretation of Wittgenstein's theory. Malcolm remarks that Wittgenstein once told him that "he [Wittgenstein] really thought that in the *Tractatus* he had provided a perfected account of a view that is the *only* alternative to the viewpoint of his later work" (Malcolm, p. 69).

   Alternatives have the connotation of being antithetical positions, mutually exclusive of one another. Given this meaning for alternative, I hesitate to use this term to characterize the relation between Wittgenstein's philosophical periods. It may well be that Wittgenstein

23 are not opposed to pictorial, literal language. In fact, according to the *PI*, language-games are so designated by their use; thus, the utilization of representational propositions characterizes them as a specific "language-game." Depictional language is not antithetical to language-games in general; rather, it complements them by being a language-game unto itself, with its own unique logical structure. As a result, we cannot agree with Toulmin's position concerning the relation of the *PI* to the *Tractatus:*

> In this second phase [the *Investigations*], Wittgenstein apparently implied that ethics and religion have "forms of life" of their own, within which ethical and religious "language-games" become—in their own ways—as verbalizable, as meaningful, and even as true-or-false, as any others. So was he not compelled, by his own later argu-

---

thought them as such, but textual evidence does not justify this belief. As Stenius remarks: "I share the often-expressed feeling that Wittgenstein overshoots the mark when in his later work he criticizes his earlier thought" (Stenius, p. 16).

On the other hand, we must be cautious of interpreting Wittgenstein's writings from the opposite extreme viewpoint. By stating that remarks made in the *PI* are complementary to those in the *Tractatus*, we do *not* mean to associate ourselves with a position like that of Maxwell Charlesworth who somehow understands the *PI* as a mere restatement of the *Tractatus* in new terminology. Charlesworth maintains:

> Perhaps the best way of describing the relation between the two works would be to say that the *Philosophical Investigations* translates the ideas of the *Tractatus* into a new key, presents them in a new context, applies them in a different way. Thus what was said of language in general in the *Tractatus* is translated into terms of particular "language-games" in the *Investigations*. The "limits of language" of the *Tractatus* becomes the limits of particular "language games"; "what cannot be said" becomes the rules, or "paradigms," of specific language games. "Sense" and "nonsense" are no longer conceived univocally, as they seem to be in the *Tractatus*, but they vary from language-game to language-game. [Maxwell T. Charlesworth, *Philosophy and Linguistic Analysis* (Pittsburgh: Duquesne University Press, 1959), p. 104.]

Summing up his position, Charlesworth holds that "what is said of 'language' in the *Tractatus* is said of 'languages' in the *Investigations*" (*Ibid.*, p. 105). This interpretation is textually unsound. What is said of descriptive language in the *Tractatus* is *not* said of language-games in general in the *PI*. Descriptive language has a logic all of its own—the logic of the picture theory—and it is this logic which differentiates it from the languages mentioned in *PI* 22. The limits of descriptive language are indeed different from those of the language-games of the *PI!*

ments, to abandon the dichotomy between the expressible (or factual) and the transcendental (or ethical)?[19]

In response to Toulmin, it must be noted that it is not the case that the "meaning is use" dictum of the *Philosophical Investigations* "will have abandoned entirely the contrast between literal, factual language and transcendental speech." To the contrary, the dictum maintains that there exists a variety of linguistic usages, one of these being the literal use. And, each is differentiable according to its own specific use. There is no attempt to reduce one type of linguistic usage to another. Representational language has its own unique logic of the picture theory; this logic differentiates it from the languages of commands, prayers, jokes, riddles, hypothesis formulation, mathematics, interrogation, etc. To tell a joke, to guess a riddle, to say a prayer, all have as their principal aims something other than to picture a state of affairs. As a result, the terms "truth" and "falsity" have no place in such language activities. Nowhere does Wittgenstein speak of "true" or "false" ethical or religious statements. Truth and falsity pertain only to representational propositions, and the propositions of either ethics or religion are not such. Ethical and religious linguistic usages have a logic different from that of pictorial language, and Wittgenstein acknowledges this to be the case.

Any non-descriptive use of language (such as a religious or ethical use) in *Tractatus* terminology is nonsensical—meaning, it does not represent any state of affairs. Too often philosophers and thinkers have mistakenly understood Wittgenstein's meaning of the term "nonsensical." Some positivists and analysts have insisted that the term means "pure gibberish," implying that nonsensical statements are not worthy of the least iota of consideration. Members of non-analytic philosophical movements, against whom Wittgenstein's thesis of nonsensical language uses is usually directed, have interpreted his remarks in the same manner and have indignantly struck back at a "straw-man" position.

It must be noted that Wittgenstein refers to his own philosophical remarks in the *Tractatus* as nonsense. Certainly,

---

19. Toulmin, p. 70.

this does not mean that he viewed them as not worthy of the least attention. To the contrary, in the preface to the work he relates that "the *truth* of the thoughts that are here set forth seems to me unassailable and definitive. I therefore believe myself to have found, on all essential points, the final solution of the problems."[20] Such words indeed do not indicate that Wittgenstein saw the propositions of the *Tractatus* (at least at the time of its writing) as gibberish. Yet, he calls them nonsense. What does this mean? It means that the statements therein are such that they do not constitute representational propositions. The structures of the statements of the *Tractatus* are such that they do not express states of affairs.

A state of affairs is a concatenation of objects such that this concatenation occupies a specific place in the logical space of representational language; to say that a proposition is non-representational means that there is no place for it in that logical space. What the proposition projects—if anything—is *not* the sense of a state of affairs. In order to represent something in language, it is implied that what is said is picturable. "A proposition states something only insofar as it is a picture."[21] The depictable is the picturable; that which is not a concatenation of objects cannot be pictured, and thus cannot be spoken of representationally. Pictures of reality delineate what is the case, if they are true. As a result, Wittgenstein himself makes it most explicit that his propositions in the *Tractatus* "serve as elucidations,"[22] not representations. They are used not to depict, or picture, a concatenation of objects; they are used "as steps to climb up beyond them. (He [who understands the propositions of the *Tractatus*] must, so to speak, throw away the ladder after he has climbed up it.) He must transcend these propositions, and then he will see the world aright."[23]

The Theory of Showing

The theory of showing [*zeigen*] is extremely important to Wittgenstein's philosophy. In fact, in a letter to Russell, Witt-

---

20. "Preface," *Tractatus*, p. 5.
21. *Tractatus* 4.03.
22. *Ibid.*, 6.54.
23. *Ibid.*

genstein singles out this element as the central point made within the *Tractatus*.

> The main point [of the *Tractatus*] is the theory of what can be expressed by propositions, i.e. by language (and, what comes to the same thing, what can be thought) and what cannot be expressed by propositions, but only shown; which I believe is the cardinal problem of philosophy.[24]

A representational proposition according to the *Tractatus* does two things: it shows the sense of a state of affairs and asserts that the state of affairs is a fact. At 4.022 Wittgenstein states: "A proposition *shows* its sense. A proposition *shows* how things stand *if* it is true. And it *says that* they do so stand." Moreover, Wittgenstein explicitly maintains that what is shown in language can *never* be said.[25] No Russellian hierarchical structures of language-games can be erected within a Wittgensteinian framework so that what is shown in one language-game can be represented within the next-higher one.[26] Clearly, then, what is shown in any language activity becomes totally non-representational. The two are separated

---

24. Wittgenstein, Letter 18: Cassino, 19-8-19. Quoted in Griffin, p. 18. Cf., Griffin, pp. 18-25, for a rather detailed account of this aspect of Wittgenstein's philosophy not only as it is presented in the *Tractatus*, but also as its beginnings appear in the pre-*Tractatus* writings.
25. *Tractatus* 4.1212.
26. I take issue with Matthew Fairbank's statement that Wittgenstein was led "to the realization that it is best to line up our major ideas on distinct levels or 'strata' and think of each level as a 'game.'" ["Wittgenstein and James," *The New Scholasticism*, XL (July, 1966), p. 331.] Fairbank's terminology of "levels" and "strata" would seem to indicate that language-games form a hierarchy, the one above the other. Just as the strata of the earth consist in layers of sedimentary rocks, the one being founded upon another, so also, according to Fairbanks, language would consist in layers of linguistic activities, the one grounded in the other. Whether or not Fairbanks actually interprets Wittgenstein in this manner, is ambiguous in the essay. However, the connotations of the terms "strata" and "levels" lend themselves to an interpretation that the philosophy of language is a second-order language over ordinary language. It is important to see that such is not Wittgenstein's intention. He states: "One might think: if philosophy speaks of the use of the word 'philosophy' there must be a second-order philosophy. But it is not so: it is, rather, like the case of orthography, which deals with the word 'orthography' among others without then being second-order" (*PI* 121).

by an impassable linguistic chasm. What is shown in the proposition becomes the *literally* unspeakable; it is that which cannot be pictured by language since it does not consist in a state of affairs. Any attempt to use language to depict what is not a state of affairs results in nonsense; it would be a statement that literally *says* nothing. But propositions do more than say, they also show.

What effect does the unsayable have upon the showable? Is there a legitimate usage of language such that it literally says nothing, yet shows something. Obviously, the answer is "yes." The very propositions of the *Tractatus* evidence a context wherein nothing literal is said; the propositions of the *Tractatus* do not depict state of affairs. They are "nonsensical," yet they are not purely vacuous utterances having no importance whatsoever. In the preface, he refers to these propositions as correct, as "unassailable and definitive." Clearly, then, the propositions of the *Tractatus* do show something. In a metaphorical way, we can say that the propositions of the *Tractatus* have a sense. Their sense is not to picture, but rather to elucidate and enlighten; their sense is to *show* the meaning of logico-pictorial forms of representational propositions and thus to *show* the limits of literal, factual language. Such a way of speaking of sense, admittedly, is not found in the *Tractatus,* but it certainly is not prohibited by the texts. Wittgenstein unequivocally admits of unspeakables which are only showable. "There are, indeed, things that cannot be put into words. They *make themselves manifest.* They are what is mystical.[27] Being—the existential ground of the world—would definitely come under such a category. Being is itself not a state of affairs.

From these remarks, we can see that Wittgenstein's closing text of the *Tractatus*—"What we cannot speak about we must pass over in silence"—cannot be coherently interpreted within a positivistic framework as some commentators have attempted to do.[28] For the positivist, all communication

---

27. *Tractatus* 6.522.
28. F. H. George, for example, considers Wittgenstein to have been a one-time member of the Vienna Circle. Cf., *Semantics* (London: English Universities Press, 1964), p. 109. Toulmin emphatically denies this. Cf., Toulmin, pp. 60ff.

without residue is reducible to what is literally said. For Wittgenstein, on the other hand, over and above what is said in language, something is shown. Paul Engelmann makes the important remark:

> A whole generation of disciples was able to take Wittgenstein for a positivist because he has something of enormous importance in common with the positivists: he draws the line between what we can speak about and what we must be silent about just as they do. The difference is only that they have nothing to be silent about. Positivism holds—and this is its essence—that what we can speak about is all that matters in life. *Whereas Wittgenstein passionately believes that all that really matters in human life is precisely what, in his view, we must be silent about.*[29]

Toulmin similarly maintains:

> Wittgenstein's opposition to metaphysics (as we shall see) had a great deal in common with Schopenhauer's, and nothing at all with Comte's. For him, the word "metaphysics" was no blanket term of denunciation, to be used cavalierly to sweep aside whatever was not "meaningful" or "factually verifiable," as of no importance. Rather, he used the word in a highly specific sense —to designate the kind of philosophical discussion which "obliterates the distinction between [i.e., confuses] factual and conceptual investigations" (*Zettel*, 458) —and his condemnation of metaphysics extends no further than this.[30]

In a short but extremely dense article entitled "Whereof One Cannot Speak,"[31] Carl H. Hamburg reaches a similar conclusion utilizing a different approach; he points out the *logical* inconsistency which arises if text 7 of the *Tractatus* is interpreted in a Comtean positivist manner. Since for the

---

29. Paul Engelmann, *Letters from Ludwig Wittgenstein With a Memoir* (New York: Horizon Press, 1968), p. 97.
30. Toulmin, p. 70. Cf., Garth Hallett, *Wittgenstein's Definition of Meaning as Use* (New York: Fordham University Press, 1967), pp. 109ff.
31. Carl H. Hamburg, "Whereof One Cannot Speak," *Journal of Philosophy*, L (October 22, 1953), pp. 662-64.

positivist only literal propositions have a sense, then the dictum would assert a "stricture with regard to any language use that fails to be formally or factually communicative."[32] If such were the case, then the dictum would be a *prescription* for literal, factual language usages only. Hamburg states:

> If so interpreted, it means more than the tautology that language, to become communication, must abide by formal and designative rules which define language as communication. Rather does it imply the non-logical prescription that language, if not used for communication, should not be used at all. This maxim is demonstrable only if, besides the premise that "only designative language can contain true or false propositions," another premise is added to the effect that "only true or false propositions are worth making." This second premise, however, is neither implied in the meaning of language nor empirically derived from the observation of actual language behavior.[33]

This second premise of which Hamburg speaks implies a value judgment on the part of the positivists, namely that only factual, literal language is of importance. But, as Hamburg points out, decisions of value-making are not explicable within any kind of propositional form, according to positivist interpretations. "Therefore to utter 'Either use language to make logically consistent and factually designative sense or don't use it at all' can only be offered as a 'proposal' which not testable as either true or false, manifests a non-factual linguistic expression of preference for the value of communicative language or for such values as may be realized by its employment."[34] The dictum cannot be coherently interpreted within a positivist framework—else it becomes an example of that very type of non-factual linguistic usage which positivism asserts cannot be used, a self-defeating position for both Wittgenstein and positivism.

Proposition 7 of the *Tractatus* must be interpreted as a

---

32. *Ibid.*, p. 663.
33. *Ibid.*
34. *Ibid.*, p. 664.

pure tautological statement. The "cannot" and "must" which appear therein refer to the logical impossibility of attempting to depict the non-picturable. Again quoting Hamburg: "The apparently exhortative 'thereof one must be silent' takes a corresponding logical meaning, and thus the dictum amounts to the statement that 'whatever cannot be asserted without contradiction cannot be asserted as [literal] communication.' "[35] The proposition does *not*—and this is *the* important point of our discussion—prescribe or legislate that language cannot be used or should not be used in other non-depictional manners. It does, however, warn of the logical impossibility of using non-representational language in some representational context.

Examples of non-representational usages as enumerated in *PI* 23 all are genuine *de facto* usages, yet these usages are not as pictures of any states of affairs. Does this nullify their validity as uses? Certainly not. Each and every language-game, as we have said above, has its one specific function and thus its own unique structure. Depictional language has its own structure, that of the picture theory. Non-depictional language-games are so determined because either a picture logic is not at all operative within them or such a logic is not primary therein. Sometimes language-games overlap with the representational one; other times not. It is in these later cases that linguistic functions can be coherent within their own operations, yet nonsensical from a literal viewpoint. But, such non-sensicality does not deny their validity as genuine language-games, functioning within a manner entirely different from depiction. All language activities must be seen as legitimate within Wittgenstein's overall philosophical position, assuming that their user knows how the activity in question functions and utilizes it in the proper manner.

We have thus done away with the one extreme interpretation of Wittgenstein's position: that literal, factual language is the only legitimate usage. We must now refute the second extreme interpretation of Wittgenstein's position: that the "meaning is use" dictum means that any grammatical con-

---

35. *Ibid.*, p. 662.

struction is meaningful in accordance with the intent of the user—no holds barred! When Wittgenstein asserts that meaning is use, he is not completely and unreservedly acknowledging as meaningful all existing usages of the language precisely as intended by the user. If Wittgenstein accepted wholesale all statements of ordinary language as legitimate usages, it would be unintelligible to speak of linguistic perplexities or misusages of language, yet the *Investigations* is concerned with just such perplexities. Examine, for example, Wittgenstein's discussions on universals or private languages. The whole trend of the *PI* is directed against linguistic puzzles as these. It is directed against usages of language where something is thought literally to be meant by the language, yet in fact is not. For example, in *PI* 498 Wittgenstein points out that to say "milk me sugar" ends up in linguistic nonsense since this sentence conveys no meaning. Of course, due to the dynamic structure of language, certain meaningless statements as this can become perfectly legitimate uses. For example, to have said six hundred years ago that "the test tube gave birth to the human being" would have been gibberish; no one would have known what was meant. Such a concatenation of words had at that time no specific use. Today, however, with the advancements in science we know that life can be generated in the laboratory, with the result that this sentence has meaning. Why? Because it has a specific use. Perhaps, a few decades from now such a statement will be commonplace. The point is that language is a growing social phenomenon. It is, as Wittgenstein remarks, like an ancient city:

> Our language can be seen as an ancient city: a maze of little streets and squares, of old and new houses, and of houses with additions from various periods; and this surrounded by a multitude of new boroughs with straight regular streets and uniform houses.[36]

Linguistic uses in most cases have no strict rules to follow; the rules are made up and solidified in the actual usages. As Wittgenstein mentions in *Remarks on the Foundations of*

36. *PI* 18.

Mathematics, meanings of words are like rulers of dough.[37]
They can be stretched, contracted, pulled upon, even
kneaded, yet they maintain their consistency as meanings.
"Many words in this sense then don't have a strict meaning.
But this is not a defect. To think it is would be like saying
that the light of my reading lamp is no real light at all because it has no sharp boundary."[38] "One might say that the
concept 'game' is a concept with blurred edges—'But is a
blurred concept a concept at all?'— Is an indistinct photo-
graph a picture of a person at all? Is it even always an ad-
vantage to replace an indistinct picture by a sharp one? Isn't
the indistinct one often exactly what we need?"[39] Yes.

Summarizing our finding, we maintain that there is no
fundamental opposition or contradiction between the ideas
expressed respectively in the *Tractatus* and in the *Investigations.* The *PI* gives the general formula for the structure of
all language-games by its "meaning is use" dictum and the
Tractatus takes a specific language-game (descriptive language) and portrays its use as representational, proceeding
to elucidate its logical structure as picturing. It is this logico-
pictorial structure which differentiates literal usage from
non-literal ones. It is a legitimate language use and so functions within its own context. Its misuse occurs when an individual plays the game, unaware of how it functions, and
begins to utilize it in a manner beyond or in contradiction
to its scope or technique.

Ontological Language

Now, we must determine how our findings are to be related to the language of ontology. First, what is the relation
of the language of representation to that of ontology? From

37. Cf., Ludwig Wittgenstein, *Remarks on the Foundations of Mathe-
    matics,* ed. G. H. von Wright, R. Rhees, and G. E. M. Anscombe,
    trans. G. E. M. Anscombe (Oxford: Basil Blackwell, 1956), pp. 170-71.
    Hereafter this work will be cited as *Remarks.*
38. *The Blue Book,* p. 27.
39. *PI* 71. Cf., 77. "What is true of the particular case is true of words in
    general: there is no precise criterion to separate the meaningful from
    the meaningless. We can only say in a general way that even in the
    most original uses admitted by Wittgenstein, there is a certain minimal
    similarity between the novel use and some customary one" (Hallett,
    p. 109).

Tractatus 6.44, it becomes clear that the subject matter of ontology cannot appear as instantiations of logical objects. As a result, a language of ontology cannot be on Wittgenstein's terms a pictorial language; literally, nothing can be said about Being. It makes no sense to speak of a picture of "that something is," although it does make sense to speak of a picture of "how something is." This does not mean, however, that ontological language is an illegitimate linguistic usage. To the contrary, ontological language can be a legitimate usage, though a non-representational one.

The subject matter of ontology joins the ranks of the mystical; as Wittgenstein remarks at *Tractatus* 6.522: The mystical consists of those "things that cannot be put into words. They *make themselves manifest.*" Ontological statements just cannot be articulated in literal language; ontological notions make themselves manifest. Factual, depictive propositions are impossible conveyances for the import of ontological utterance; there is something poetic—in the sense of non-literal—in ontological statements. In this regard, Wittgenstein would, I believe, concur with the broad orientation of the following quotations by Ayer and Carnap. Whether he would say that aesthetical language has *only* an emotive function, as intimated by Ayer and Carnap, is questionable. Based on texts of *Lectures and Conversations on Aesthetics, Psychology, and Religious Belief* and more especially of the *Investigations*, his position, I conjecture, would be more sophisticated and flexible. There are many language usages; just because one use is non-literal does not mean its intent is to express emotion. Nevertheless, Wittgenstein's position is resemblant to Ayer's and Carnap's in grouping both metaphysical, or ontological, statements and poetic utterances (in the broad sense of aesthetic language) in the category of non-representational functions. Ayer maintains:

> . . . it is fashionable to speak of the metaphysician [and thus the ontologist] as a kind of misplaced poet. As his statements have no literal meaning, they are not subject to any criteria of truth or falsehood: but they may still serve to express, or arouse, emotion, and thus be subject to ethical or aesthetic standards. And it is suggested that

they may have considerable value, as means of moral inspiration, or even as works of art.[40]

Similarly, Rudolf Carnap remarks:

> Many linguistic utterances are analogous to laughing in that they have only an expression of emotion, no representational function. . . . The aim of a lyrical poem in which occur the words "sunshine" and "clouds" is not to inform us of certain meteorological facts, but to express certain feelings of the poet and to excite similar feelings in us. . . . Metaphysical propositions [as well as ontological ones]—like lyrical verses—have only an expressive function, but no representative function. Metaphysical propositions are neither true nor false, because they assert nothing. . . . But they are like laughing, lyrics and music, expressive.[41]

Again, in no way should it be assumed that the above texts are accurate and explicit descriptions of Wittgenstein's thought. We have no way of knowing this. The texts merely manifest the notions prevalent in this regard during the period of Wittgenstein's writings. We can say, however, that for Wittgenstein ontological language usage bears a basic structural kinship to poetic discourse: the prime intent of both is not to represent states of affairs or to assert facts, but to create and present a linguistic experience, an aesthetic experience. And, at *Tractatus* 6.421, he maintains that aesthetics is the same as ethics; neither can be put into words. Both literally say nothing, their sense lies outside the world. Aesthetic language, then, although it uses the words of factual speech, functions in a manner quite different from statements of fact.

---

40. Alfred Jules Ayer, *Language, Truth, and Logic* (New York: Dover, 1936), p. 44.
41. Rudolf Carnap, *The Logical Syntax of Language*, trans. Amethe Smeaton (Peterson, New Jersey: Littlefield, Adams, & Company, 1959), p. 72. Carnap has maintained that the purpose of lyrical poetry is to express certain feelings of the poet. To say this literally would give poetry a certain representational function, which obviously would not be Carnap's intent nor is it that of many contemporary critics. A poem, the latter maintain, *presents* a certain mood, or feeling. Whether this mood coincides with the poet's own is superfluous to the poetic work.

Chapter IX

ONTOLINGUISTICS: A METHODOLOGICAL COMPARISON

> Examine language; what, if you except some few primitive elements (of natural sound), what is it all but metaphors, recognized as such, or no longer recognized.

> —Thomas Carlyle, *Sartor Resartus*

If we compare Heidegger's views on the language of ontology with Wittgenstein's fundamental linguistic thesis, we find some remarkable similarities from our methodological standpoint. For both Heidegger and Wittgenstein representational language deals with objects or things; they both agree that it makes no sense to speak of ontological or metaphysical terms as objects. Consequently, Being is not literally representable; "*that* something is" is not sayable in accordance with the concatenative object-structure of representational language. It is an error to attempt a literal depiction of existence; such an endeavor would be meaningless. The purpose of ontological language is not to represent but to create, something like the poet's language.

The purpose of ontological language is to employ words in contexts which jar the imagination—assuming a representational point of view. If the language of ontology is to do justice to its subject matter, its logical structure must be at variance with that of representational language. If one does not admit this variance and make it known from the start, grave misunderstandings and mistakes will arise. From the logic of representation, ontological language is meaningless jargon, but within its own linguistic structure the latter makes sense—though not a representational one. As a result, for both Heidegger and Wittgenstein the logical structure of ontological language is akin to poetry.

At this point, we must expound upon the logical structure of poetic language in such a way that we will see its similarities—logically speaking—to ontological language. In so doing, we likewise will elucidate why both Heidegger and Wittgenstein on their own principles must call the language of ontology poetical.

The Logical Structure of Poetic Language

The structure of poetic language can be discussed from various viewpoints. One could, for example, analyze it syntactically; in such a study, one would be concerned with the verse as opposed to the prose form of the language and with the resultant structure of the lines of verse into stanzas as opposed to paragraphs. The rhyming scheme of the lines would be disclosed and analyzed, not only within stanzas but also between them. Metrical consideration would also be taken into account; the divisional pattern of uniform rhythmic combinations would be studied. Such procedure, however, is not the one we will utilize.

As opposed to the syntactical structure of poetry, we are concerned with its logical structure. It might seem strange, at first, to speak of a logical structure of poetry, but such terminology is justified. Certain logical patterns and structural guidelines can be discovered within poetic language. The questions which we must discuss, then, are: What are these patterns and guidelines? How do they structure poetic language? How do art works mean? How do they attain significance? Does a poem represent some experience of its creator? Does a poem become significant if it accurately conveys the thoughts of the poet who composed the work?

These are difficult questions, the answers to which are not univocal among either literary critics or philosophers of art. C. L. Stevenson has made clear the difficulties that exist in just attempting to answer the question "What is a Poem?," let alone in explicating its logical structure.[1] He strongly sug-

---

1. Charles L. Stevenson, "On 'What is a Poem?'," *Philosophical Review*, LXVI (July, 1957), pp. 329-62.

gests that the answer to the question does not consist in searching out one and only one characteristic which all poems share
in common but in disclosing a Wittgensteinian family resemblance of traits, a theme we discussed in the introduction. Looking over what has been historically categorized as
poetry, it is this author's opinion that a family-resemblance
concept is likewise applicable in elucidating the logic of
poetic language. This must be kept in mind since throughout
this chapter we will be discussing only two characteristics of
poetic language. These are essential to our discussion, but
not the *only* ones discernible within poetic language. Moreover, the relevance of the literary concepts discussed in this
chapter to the basic theme of this work is paramount; their
importance to schools of literary criticism varies, however.

The concept of the logical structure of poetic language
opens a Pandora's box to questions in aesthetics. The concept is important, indeed basic, to a philosophy of art. Many
books have been written on the subject, and more can be expected. Yet, we introduce this significant issue almost as a
sidelight. This is most misleading. In no way do we want to
detract from the importance, scope, and complexity of the
issues which we will discuss in so superficial of a manner.
Yet, at this point a detailed discussion on aesthetics is out of
the question. The sole purpose of this section is to present
a specific structural approach to poetic discourse—and a respectable one at that—which will act as a frame of reference
from which can be disclosed the similarities between Heidegger's and Wittgenstein's positions on ontological, or metaphysical, language and its relation to that of poetry. Again,
our aim is not to manifest a direct influence of the following
approach in literary criticism upon either thinker. Our intent is solely to present a viewpoint from which their thoughts
can be compared intelligibly.

It is our contention that poetic language does not function
in the same way as literal, representational language. Concurring with Sidney Zink, we maintain:

> Thus the poem is not a representation of a real object;
> the poem is a real object and represents only itself—which
> means, of course, that it represents nothing. The poem

does not refer to, but creates and constitutes, an individual object and experience.[2]

The poem represents nothing; it refers to nothing.[3] Susanne Langer uses the term "presentation" to convey this aim of poetry. Whereas literal factual language re-presents something other than itself, poetic language presents itself. What gives poetry its meaning is not a reference to something else; poetic language stands on its "own feet" and presents itself as its own meaning.[4] As Archibald MacLeish maintains in *Ars Poetica,* "A poem should not mean, but be." Even imitative, or representational, art forms are meaningful in and of themselves; their classifying titles are misleading. It may well be that a specific actual situation was the source of an artist's or poet's creation, but this is extrinsic to the aesthetic character of the work. The questions thus arise: Through what structure does poetry present itself? How does poetry function? An answer, according to some literary critics, is that poetry's aim is to present itself as an evocational perspective.[5] This cannot mean that poetic language is purely emotive. Poetry is certainly not the same as a series of grunts and groans. Somehow poetry is related to representational language in a way that grunts and groans are not.

It is true that poetic language does often convey emotion; however, to limit it to such expression would be erroneous. The poet's language utilizes words which are part of everyday depictional vocabulary. The point is, however, that these words are not used as depictments. The proposi-

---

2. Sidney Zink, "The Poetic Organism," *The Journal of Philosophy*, XLII (August 2, 1945), p. 425. Cf., Lucius Garvin, "The Paradox of Aesthetic Meaning," *Reflections on Art*, ed. Susanne K. Langer (Baltimore: Johns Hopkins Press, 1958), p. 65.
3. Even though the language of poetry is not literal, it is essential that the context of the poem be literally presented. This means that if author A says that his work B is poetical, this must be taken as a literally descriptive statement of the status of work B. Cf., Susanne Langer, *Philosophy in a New Key* (Cambridge, Mass.: Harvard University Press, 1960), p. 140.
4. Cf., Langer, *Philosophy in a New Key,* pp. 79 and 97ff.
5. Lucius Garvin states that "the evocation of feelings, as distinguished from, say, classification or proof, is unquestionably the primary preoccupation of the artistic spirit . . ." (Garvin, p. 65).

tional signs utilized by the poet are those of depictional language but they symbolize in a different manner; that is, they have a sense which functions differently from the representational one.

The poetic usage of language is extremely complex: it utilizes a non-representational form and yet a vocabulary which can be used representationally. It is not intended as a literal representation. Poetry is a mixture of "meaning and nonsense," as Langer remarks.[6] Poetic language just like representational language is generated as well as limited by words which can be used representationally. But, the question remains: How does the representational word within poetic language differ from that of literal, representational language?

One could say that the difference lies in the intent of the poet. The user of literal factual language intends primarily to represent; whereas, the poetic user does not. Such an approach toward distinguishing the two is possible; however, it is also extremely superficial and does *not* in the least explicate the *logico-semantical* structures of either literal or poetic usages, which is our aim. Thus, the above has no bearing upon the solution of our problematic; we must look elsewhere.

Philip Wheelwright approaches the problematic in a different manner. He proposes that the distinction lies within literal language's use of "monosigns" and poetic language's use of "plurisigns." By "plurisigns" Wheelright means words which have several different possible meanings; the term refers to words which are equivocal in meaning. "Monosigns," on the other hand, refer to words which are univocal in meaning. Factual, everyday propositions, according to Wheelwright, aim at precision; for a proposition to give an adequate

---

6. Langer, *Philosophy in a New Key*, p. 87. Cf., Philip Wheelwright, "On the Semantics of Poetry," *Kenyon Review*, II (Summer, 1940), p. 269. Of all the art forms, music seems to contain the least—if any—residue of representational elements. Poetry, however, cannot ever attain such a degree of non-representation, since its medium of conveyance is not sound alone, but sounds which have been incorporated into language as words and which within other contexts can be used descriptively. Cf., Langer, *Philosophy in a New Key*, p. 209.

depiction, its elements must present an exact representation of the fact it describes. Consequently, the constant use of monosigns is the indication of non-poetic discourse, while poetic language thrives upon ambiguity and equivocation in meaning. According to Wheelwright, poetic language utilizes the plurisign with little interest in literal semantics. Whereas each proposition of literal descriptive language points to a specific place in logical space, poetic verse purports a multiplicity of meanings in purposeful ambiguity. Each poetic phrase consists in a multitude of shaded meanings. Thus, Wheelwright concludes:

> A poetic statement differs from a literal statement . . . in their manner of asserting. There are differences of what may be called *assertive weight*. A literal statement asserts heavily; it can do so because its terms are solid. A poetic statement on the other hand, consists as it does in a conjunction or association of pluralisms, has no such solid foundation, and affirms with varying degrees of lightness.[7]

Wheelwright's points do deserve consideration. The shaded, multiple meanings derivative of verse are indeed important marks of poetry. However, poetry's utilization of equivocation is insufficient for distinguishing it from prose. Often in prose equivocation is used extensively. The professional comedian, for example, thrives upon shaded, multi-meaning words to attain comic effects but he is not a poet. Puns are an established element of the comic's language-games, but they are not poetry. Equivocation occurs in both poetic and non-poetic linguistic usages with, at times, equivalent frequency; as a result, equivocation cannot be the distinguishing logico-semantical character of poetry.

Furthermore, Wheelwright's comment that "assertive weight" distinguishes poetic propositions from literal ones— the former asserting lightly, the latter heavily—is unsound. It makes no sense to speak of degrees of assertion. To assert is to do one thing and one thing alone: to state that something is the case. Either one asserts or one does not. There is no middle road. Thus, our problematic still remains: How can

7. Wheelwright, p. 274.

the logico-semantical structure of poetic language differ from that of representational language and yet be similar to it?

We have already determined that what unites poetry to representational language is that both use the same ordinary-language vocabulary. What differentiates them is that in poetry this vocabulary is used in a non-depictional manner. The poem is not a statement of fact. Though its elements are those of factual language, its semantical structure is not depictional. Hart Crane remarks: "As a poet, I may very possibly be more interested in the so-called illogical impingements of the connotations of words . . . than I am interested in the preservation of their logically rigid significations at the cost of limiting my subject matter and perceptions involved in the poem."[8]

Poetry aims at word concatenations such that no denotative sense is obtained; its logico-semantical structures jar literal interpretations. The poet utilizes language in a way which is foreign to literal and representational language uses. Romeo in Shakespeare's *Romeo and Juliet* certainly is not referring to his Juliet as a gaseous body 93 million miles from the earth when he calls: "But, soft! what light through yonder window breaks. It is the east and Juliet is the sun!" By his non-denotational use of language, Shakespeare has concatenated words which together signify nothing literal; he has mixed different kinds of uses to *create* a new one. This mixture, from a representational point of view, abounds in incompatible, inconsistent and incoherent language.

But how can the poet unite these literally incompatible usages? What is the logico-semantical structure by which the non-depictional use of words can be carried out? Metaphor. Command of metaphorical usage is, according to Aristotle, the greatest asset of the poet.[9] Our use of the term "meta-

---

8. Hart Crane, quoted by Wheelwright, pp. 266-67.
9. Aristotle, *Poetics*, 1457ff. As MacLeish points out: "Images in a poem do seem to have some relationship to the emotion a poem contains. . . . These images, however, are produced not only in poetic but also in representational language. How, then, do they differ? Certainly as to intensity and vividness. But is this all—no, the images are not representational ones,—but stretch into metaphor." [Archibald MacLeish, *Poetry and Experience* (Boston: Houghton Mifflin Company, 1961), p. 49.]

phor," however, will be broader than that of Aristotle. In fact, the meaning of metaphor in his technical sense has been disputed.[10] Metaphor, in our context, is tautological with some form of unconventional, non-literal use. Clearly, then, metaphorical language is wider in scope than poetic language. In effect, we are making a distinction regarding metaphorical language similar to the distinction Heidegger has made between *Dichtung* and *Poesie*. Many metaphorical uses can be incorporated into a primarily non-poetical context, but poetical discourse cannot occur except in the broad context of metaphorical language. In any case, metaphorical usage is factually meaningless.

Shakespeare's statement that "Juliet is the sun!" is a literal paradox; but his aim is literally to create linguistic paradoxes with the metaphorical use of language. The poet is a creator. He brings into the realm of language a new expression. Novelty is his goal; without novelty, art degenerates into pure imitation. The poet combines words which have a specific denotative meaning in such a way that their combined denotative meaning (if any) cannot be meant. Indeed, the meanings of poetic language are *presentational*, rather than *representational*. The novel combinations of words and their concatenated meaning are so new that there is no linguistic type of usage in vogue into which they can be analyzed. Poetic propositions cannot be reduced to other propositions as in fact occurs in the analysis of descriptive propositions.

The Poetic Element of Ontological Discourse

Poetry utilizes the same words as ordinary literal language, yet it uses these words metaphorically. Poetic words are so positioned that they stretch and pull representational semantics into new non-literal configurations. Given such a description of the logico-semantical structure of poetry, both the Heideggerian and the Wittgensteinian would agree that

---

10. Cf., Philip Wheelwright, "Semantics and Ontology," *Metaphor and Symbol*, eds. L. C. Knights and Basil Cottle (London: Butterworths Scientific Publications, 1960), pp. 4-6. The entire work should be consulted by anyone interested in the question of metaphorical language.

ontological language (being non-representational in character) is structurally akin to poetical language.

It is characteristic of a representational proposition, Wittgenstein relates, that the latter can be analyzed into other propositions which constitute the meaning of the original proposition.[11] Yet, such analysis does not reveal the meaning of ontological discourse. Why? Because ontological propositions are not representational complexes. They are non-depictive in character and function as primitive signs; they cannot be reduced or analyzed into components since they have no literal semantical components.

Analysis gives literal *representational* meanings to the concatenated objects in the complex; once elucidations for the objects have been given, the now-understood meanings of the analyzed propositions will be *literal* and *representational*. As such, they will not give the meaning of an ontological proposition in that it is metaphorical, and not literal or representational, in character. Ontological propositions, as poetical propositions, cannot be explicated by the same process as representational ones. As Wittgenstein states in gloss 531 of the *Investigations:*

> We speak of understanding a sentence in the sense in which it can be replaced by another which says the same; but also in the sense in which it cannot be replaced by another other. (Any more than one musical theme can be replaced by another.)
>
> In the one case the thought in the sentence is something common to different sentences; in the other, something that is expressed only by these words in these positions. (Understanding a poem.)

How then can one explain or interpret such propositions and any other propositions which because of their metaphorical concatenations of objects are unique, primitive signs? ". . . how can one explain the expression, transmit one's comprehension?" Wittgenstein inquires. "Ask yourself: How does one *lead* anyone to comprehension of a poem or of a theme?

---

11. *Tractatus* 2.0201.

The answer to this tells us how meaning is explained here."[12]
The propositions of ontology and those of poetry both function in the same manner; they are primitive signs. Their primitiveness results from the metaphorical and therefore unique concatenations of ordinary language vocabulary. Their meanings are *shown*, never represented.

This unique metaphorical quality of propositions exists within Heidegger's philosophical writings on ontology. The word in its ordinary representational use is distinct in character from the poetical and the philosophical (which for Heidegger means ontological).

> To speak language is totally different from employing language. Common speech merely employs language. This relation to language is just what constitutes its commonness. But because thought and, in a different way poesie, do not employ terms but speak words, therefore we are compelled, as soon as we set out upon a way of thought, to give specific attention to what the word says.[13]

Ontology concerns itself with Being, which is No-thing to be represented. As a result, the propositions of ontology, like those of poetry, cannot be reduced to other propositions. ". . . we never get to know a mystery by unveiling or analyzing it. . . ."[14] Ontological language is a metaphorical usage. "It is perfectly true that we cannot talk about nothing [Being], as though it were a thing like the rain outside or a mountain or any object whatsoever."[15] Philosophers and poets present and preserve in language the unique; they "take their mediation as the unique. . . ."[16]
Poetical and philosophical thought is non-representational; its linguistic structure "is something which the ordinary understanding will struggle against."[17] From the rep-

---

12. *PI* 533.
13. WT, p. 128 (WD, pp. 87-88).
14. RP, p. 259. (HD, p. 23).
15. IM, p. 21. (EM, p. 19).
16. HD, p. 69. My own translation.
17. RP, p. 260. (HD, p. 24).

resentational viewpoint, such language activities seem to be "violating the fundamental law of ordinary thought, the principle of contradiction, or on the other hand to be playing with empty words, or merely to be making a presumptuous suggestion."[18] "Foolish is my speech" says the philosopher (ontologist) and the poet.[19] Foolish indeed from a representational standpoint. "The poetical projection comes out of nothing in the respect that it does not receive that which it presents out of the familiar. . . ."[20]

The significance of texts like the above should not be underestimated. Heidegger's emphasis upon the presentational non-depictional character of ontological discourse and its resultant kinship to poetic language makes his thought pivotal for contemporary ontological investigations. From a linguistic viewpoint, Heidegger has understood the non-objective logical structure of his writings and has acknowledged it as such. As a result, Rudolf Carnap's original criticism of Heidegger's philosophy which has been taken up again by Ayer is completely unfounded.

Concurring with Carnap, Ayer states:

> In general, the postulation of real non-existent entities results from the superstition . . . that, to every word or phrase that can be the grammatical subject of a sentence, there must somewhere be a real entity corresponding. . . . To this error must be attributed . . . the utterances of a Heidegger, who bases his metaphysics on the assumption that "Nothing" is a name which is used to denote something peculiarly mysterious. . . .[21]

This, however, is an erroneous presentation of Heidegger's position based upon Carnap's original misconception of Heidegger's texts. Nowhere does Heidegger refer to "Nothing" as an entity; it is just the opposite. Nothing (that is Being) is No-thing.[22] ". . . in the word 'Being' in its meaning, we

---

18. *Ibid.* (HD, p. 24).
19. *Ibid.* (HD, p. 24).
20. H, p. 63. My own translation. Cf., Vycinas, pp. 281-82.
21. Ayer, pp. 43-44.
22. Cf., Walsh, pp. 307ff.

pass through word and meaning and aim at Being itself, except that it is not a thing, if by thing we mean something that is in any way essent."[23]

The reason why Ayer and Carnap have misunderstood Heidegger in this matter is that they have interpreted him from a literal point of view, from the point of view of representational language.[24] John Macquarrie makes an interesting comment in this regard:

> Yet analytical philosophers in particular are highly suspicious of any inquiry into Being (especially when this is spelled with a capital letter!) Their nominalism leads them to suppose that anyone engaging in such an inquiry (ontology) has fallen into the error of supposing that because we have a noun "Being" in the language, there must be some thing corresponding to the word, out there in the world.
>
> As a matter of fact, Heidegger has always been quite clear in his mind that Being, however we are to think of it, cannot be considered as a thing, another entity or something that is. . . . He is careful never to formulate the question of the meaning of Being in the form "What is Being?," for to ask this question would be to imply that Being "is" a "what," a thing or substance or entity.[25]

Indeed, if Heidegger thought his ontological language functioned as ordinary representational language, his position would be ludicrous; Heidegger himself admits this. "It is perfectly true that we cannot talk about nothing, as though it were a thing. . . ."[26]

Ayer, continuing in his criticism of Heidegger, asserts:

> The view that the metaphysiciar. [and thus the ontol-

23. IM, p. 74. (EM, p. 67).
24. Cf., *Ibid.*, pp. 19-22, (EM, pp. 17-19), for an excellent statement of Heidegger's defense against criticisms as those proposed by Carnap and Ayer, and the misunderstandings and presuppositions upon which these accusations are based.
25. John Macquarrie, *Martin Heidegger* (Richmond, Virginia: John Knox Press, 1968), pp. 4-5.
26. IM, p. 21. (EM, p. 19).

ogist] is to be reckoned among the poets appears to rest on the assumption that both talk nonsense. But this assumption is false. . . . The difference between the man who uses language scientifically and the man who uses it emotively is not that the one produces sentences which are incapable of arousing emotion, and the other sentences which have no sense, but that the one is primarily concerned with the expression of true propositions, the other with the creation of a work of art. . . . If the author [of a poem] writes nonsense, it is because he considers it more suitable for bringing about the effects for which his writing is designed.

The metaphysician, on the other hand, does not intend to write nonsense. He lapses into it through being deceived by grammar, or through committing errors of reasoning. . . . But it is not the mark of a poet simply to make mistakes of this sort.

. . . what is important to us is to realize that even the utterances of the metaphysician who is attempting to expound a vision are literally senseless. . . .[27]

Ayer maintains that "the metaphysician [and ontologist] . . . does not intend to write nonsense. He lapses into it through being deceived by grammar. . . ." It is here that Heidegger surpasses and overcomes Ayer's blanket statement. By acknowledging the kinship of poetry and ontology, Heidegger has transcended Ayer's claim. By his own analysis of

---

27. Ayer, pp. 44-45. Having denounced metaphysicians in general, Ayer makes a surprising turn-about and concedes that "although the greater part of metaphysics is merely the embodiment of humdrum errors, there remains a number of metaphysical passages which are the work of genuine mystical feeling . . ." (p. 45). On Ayer's own grounds, how does he know of and *objectively* recognize this "genuine mystical feeling"? No criterion can be given. He continues, however, that "the distinction between the kind of metaphysics that is produced by a philosopher who has been duped by grammar, and the kind that is produced by a mystic who is trying to express the inexpressible, is of no great importances . . ." (p. 45). No great importance!—They are of no importance whatsoever! On Ayer's own terms, no linguistic ground can differentiate the one from the other. The "genuine mystic" is, like the metaphysician, "duped by grammar" insofar as he is trying to express the inexpressible. If the mystic knew the logical structure of language, he would be silent.

language, Heidegger realizes that—given the structure of language—Being cannot be represented. Its meaning is rather shown through poetic utterances and as such the propositions of ontology are literal nonsense in the Wittgensteinian sense. Ontological language functions in a manner quite different from literal representational language. Heidegger's opponents have erred by interpreting the former's remarks from a representational viewpoint; their accusations are based upon a misunderstanding of Heidegger's position. So also these criticisms are based upon a mistaken notion concerning the logical structure of language itself. This mistake is to legislate that all linguistic activities in order to be legitimate must be representational in character. Wittgenstein's *PI* is a testament against such an error and Heidegger stands side by side with Wittgenstein on this point. For both thinkers, non-representational language is a legitimate use of language, assuming the user understands its non-representational character—as indeed Heidegger does in his language of Being.

"The Limits of my Language Mean the Limits of my World"

For both Heidegger and Wittgenstein, it is language which demarcates and structures the things of one's world. As Wittgenstein relates at 5.6 in the *Tractatus*, *"the limits of my language* mean the limits of my world." Heidegger concurs: "Only where there is language is there world. . . ."[28] The world around me is the world of my language. Language organizes and delineates my experiences, my surroundings, into a specific form and shape. "Logic pervades the world"; Wittgenstein remarks, "the limits of the world are also its limits. . . . The world is *my* world; this is manifest in the fact that the limits of *language* (the only language that I understand) mean the limits of *my* world."[29] Language and the world are two sides of one and the same reality. The world I know is known inseparably from the language I use. One cannot split the two and discuss them in isolation without some literal misrepresentation. Such a segregation necessitates

28. HEP, p. 276. (HD, p. 35).
29. *Tractatus* 5.61 and 5.62. Cf., Jaakko Hintikka, "On Wittgenstein's 'Solipsism'," *Essays on Wittgenstein's 'Tractatus,'* pp. 157-62.

some metaphorical device, such as logical space, to be intelligible, yet its metaphorical character must be preserved and recognized to avoid even in this context misleading conclusions. "An investigation of the structure of language is at the same time an investigation of the formal aspects of the world. To give the essence of propositions means to give the essence of all description, therefore the essence of the world."[30]

Heidegger likewise maintains that language is the limit of the world. It is language which structures and differentiates things of the world. For, it is only language that creates the very possibility of standing in the overtness of existence, Heidegger remarks. Language is the articulating creation of the world; it demarcates and delineates the world. "If language is the House of Being, we attain, thus, beings when we go permanently through this house. If we go to a spring or if we go through a forest, we already go through the word 'spring,' through the word 'forest' and [this occurs] even if we do not pronounce these words and do not think from a linguistic viewpoint."[31] One cannot structure experience without language subterraneously underpinning that experience.

Things as differentiated entities do not first exist and then language tags them with a name; to the contrary, for Heidegger as for Wittgenstein, words are the differentiating character laid over "raw experience." ". . . words and language are not wrappings in which things are packed for the commerce of those who write and speak. It is in words and language that things first come into being and are."[32] "Naming does not come afterward, providing an already manifest essent with a designation and a hallmark known as a word; it is the other way around: originally an act of violence that discloses being, the word sinks from the height to become a

30. *Ibid.*, 5.4711. Cf., Vycinas, pp. 83-85.
31. H, p. 28. My own translation. Cf., US, p. 166.
32. IM, p. 11. (EM, p. 11). Vycinas remarks: "Things are not prior to words, and words are not the lables [sc., labels] added to already existing things. Our response to the *logos* of Being brings beings into appearance. Words are related to Being, and they are not given to our unrestrained disposition; we are for the disposition of the words of Being" (Vycinas, p. 85).

mere sign, and this sign proceeds to thrust itself before the essent. Pristine speech opens up the being of the essent in the structure of its collectedness."[33] ". . . language first brings the being as a being into overtness."[34]

In one of his most recent essays, Heidegger calls attention to a poem entitled "The Word" by Stefan George. The last line of the poem reads: "Not a thing be there where the word is lacking" [*Kein Ding sei wo das Wort gebricht*]. Indeed this is Heidegger's very own position. Commenting upon this line, Heidegger states: "The poet had learned that first the word lets appear and therefore makes present a thing as the thing which it is. The word tells itself to the poet as that which keeps and preserves a thing in its Being."[35]

This is indeed a pivotal theme of Heidegger's philosophy of language; moreover, it is a theme which he has unceasingly stressed. Let us quote at length a passage from *Hölderlin and the Essence of Poetry:*

> Poetry is the act of establishing by the word and in the word. . . . Being must be opened out, so that the existent may appear. . . . The poet names the gods and names all things in that which they are. This naming does not consist merely in something already known being supplied with a name; it is rather that when the poet speaks the essential word, the existent is by this naming nominated as what it is. So it becomes known *as* existent. Poetry is the establishing of being by means of the word. . . . Being is never an existent. But, because being and essence of things can never be calculated and derived from what is present, they must be freely created, laid down and given. Such a free act of giving is establishment.[36]

In addition, we must not forget that for Heidegger language reveals not only beings but also Being. Man's access to Being is linguistic. When Heidegger speaks of man's pre-predicative encounter with Being, this encounter is *not* pre-

---

33. *Ibid.*, p. 144. (EM, p. 131).
34. H, p. 60. My own translation.
35. WL, p. 64. My own translation. (US, p. 168).
36. HEP, pp. 280-81. (HD, p. 38).

linguistic. The pre-predicatedness of man's encounter with Being is a pre-representational or pre-literal encounter, as occurs within the language of poetry and meditative philosophy. *Yet this encounter is linguistic.* No non-symbolic, non-linguistic mode of cognition is operative within Heidegger's philosophy. Bergsonian intuition has no counterpart within Heideggerian thought.[37] Being as well as beings are made manifest in language. Being as the unique, the undifferentiated, the simple, man encounters in and through language. "Being itself is dependent on the word. . . ."[38] "Poetry is the establishment of Being by means of the word."[39]

As a result, for both Heidegger and Wittgenstein, what can be thought can be put into words and what cannot be put into words cannot be thought. For both thinkers, there are no unutterable thoughts; all thoughts are linguistic in character, for indeed the way of speaking is the way of thinking. The limits of Wittgensteinian language and the limits

---

37. Henri Bergson's thesis, as expressed in *An Introduction to Metaphysics*, is that there are two distinct ways of knowing: analysis and intuition. Analysis employs symbols as points of departure in representing various objects; these symbols, Bergson maintains, always are imperfect in their depiction since they place the knower outside the object, moving about it from one fragmentary viewpoint to another. Intuition, on the other hand, uses no symbols or perspectives; its cognitive process is relative to nothing. It is a kind of intellectual coincidence with the object known whereby one places himself within it and is thereby immediately aware of the object's unique, radical particularity.

Recapitulating, then, it could be said that for Bergson, there are two ways of knowing: analysis which is discursive and symbolic and intuition which is non-discursive and non-symbolic. Intuitive cognition is, as a result, incapable of linguistic articulation insofar as language is always symbolic and discursive. Analytic cognition, on the other hand, is expressible within the symbolic and discursive medium of linguistic expression.

It is here, then, that we see the radical departure of Heidegger's viewpoint from that presented by Bergson. For Bergson, Being would be due to its uniqueness an object of intuition, inexpressible by language. For Heidegger, it is *language* and *primarily* language through which Being appears. The unique is expressible in language, the language of original poetry and the meditative language of philosophy. "Poetry," Heidegger unequivocally states, "is the establishment of Being by means of the word" (HEP, p. 281). (HD, p. 38). "Being itself is dependent on the word . . ." (IM, p. 74). (EM, p. 67).

38. IM, p. 74. (EM, p. 67).

39. HEP, p. 281. (HD, p. 38).

of Heideggerian language are respectively the limits of the two men's worlds.

Turning to another point of comparison, one might say that Heidegger and Wittgenstein both have operative within their philosophies a theory of linguistic showing. For both thinkers, a function of language is to show [*zeigen*] something. Such a position, however, is misleading. This methodological congruence, if indeed we can even call it such, is quite superficial. True, for both thinkers poetic language and their own philosophical propositions *show* something; but what this method of showing entails is quite different in each man's works. It is for this reason, then, that I hesitate to designate this a *methodological* similarity; the real similarity between the two thinkers' theories of showing is the word "showing."

Wittgenstein makes a clear-cut distinction between what is said in language and what is shown therein. What fits into the realm of the sayable is never showable and vice versa. States of affairs are articulated in language and their forms (together with the mystical) are shown in language. Saying and showing are different linguistic activities, each having its own specific "content." For Heidegger, on the other hand, to say *is* to show. Showing is understood in the sense of making something manifest or making it appear, in a phenomenological sense. To articulate something is to disclose it, to bring it into a revealed form. Thus what is said in language is likewise shown. The two terms are not indicative of different kinds of linguistic activities, but terms synonymous for authentic discourse. This is evidently not Wittgenstein's view. Moreover, even if the two thinkers *both* saw as synonymous, or *both* made a radical split between, what is shown and what is said in language, the congruence of thought on this point would still be superficial. There are many ways of showing in language. There is nothing really novel or profound about talking of realities being *shown* linguistically; what is more crucial is the mode of such manifestations. After all, ethics and aesthetics are "one," Wittgenstein remarks; to their unity as non-representational language activities can be added religious and metaphysical languages, plus many more language-games. This unity is a loose one, though, since each of these different language-games *shows* its subject matter in a diverse way. It is precisely these differences which are crucial; since, however, neither Heidegger nor Wittgenstein attempts a detailed discussion in this regard, our range of remarks is confined and their depth limited.

Two points of methodological congruence about the language of both thinkers which *can* be made—now that we look over all our studies—are: both Heidegger and Wittgenstein are concerned with the ordinary, everyday use of language and neither postulates philosophical language as some metalanguage. Heidegger's departure in *Being and Time* is through the everyday activities of Dasein. "We must rather choose," Heidegger states, "such a way of access and such a kind of interpretation that this entity [Dasein] can show itself in itself and from itself. And this means that it is to be shown as it is *proximally and for the most part*—in its average *everydayness*."[40] Even though the language of Heidegger's writings is certainly not everyday speech, the themes of his works are—gossip, care, anxiety, etc.[41] Furthermore, this concern for the commonplace, the ordinary, remains throughout Heidegger's later writings, although this varies from work to work. His examples, nevertheless, remain quite down to earth —a painting of a pair of shoes, a water jug, the activity of hammering, etc.[42]

Wittgenstein's philosophy also is of the everyday. In the *Tractatus,* as we have pointed out, he was not concerned with structuring an ideal language, but with elucidating ordinary everyday language, which is, logically speaking, perfect in its present form. The later philosophy of Wittgenstein follows this same pattern; that it is called "the philosophy of ordinary language" attests to this. His examples and illustrations likewise are taken from the common world of experience: a beetle in a box, a builder and his assistant working, entries recorded in a diary, etc.[43] These are very simple examples set, like Hei-

---

40. BT, pp. 37-38. (SZ, p. 16).
41. Cf., BT, pp. 211, 358, and 228. (SZ, pp. 168, 311, and 184).
42. Cf., PLT, p. 33. (H, p. 22). PLT, p. 167ff. (VA, pp. 164ff). BT, p. 116. (SZ, p. 64).
43. Cf., *PI* 2, 258, 293.

degger's, in a not too simple philosophical framework.

One could almost say that the points which both thinkers make are so fundamental that they are trivial. And, in a sense, this is true. As Wittgenstein observes in the preface to his *Tractatus,* the value of the work consists in showing how little is achieved when the problems with which it deals are solved. The rudimentary character of both men's queries is certainly not a sign of any philosophical naiveté or simple-mindedness. To the contrary, it indicates the very basic, essential level at which they are functioning and suggests the ultimate character of their thoughts. It is for reasons such as these that our studies have been elementary; our comparisons, primary. In this very section, for example, all that we have really shown is that the language of philosophy as understood by both Heidegger and Wittgenstein is really non-representational in structure. So much more could be said by either man about the *kind* of non-representational language which philosophy employs—yet the two thinkers are not concerned with this sort of question. They have left it for those who follow. Both Heidegger and Wittgenstein are philosophical adventurers. Each is exploring a dense intellectual terrain. Each is cutting away brambles from intellectual wilderness, previously untraversed, and creating new paths in philosophy's hinterlands for future philosophical explorers.

CHAPTER X

A POSSIBLE RESOLUTION: CONCLUDING
REMARKS

> The word, even the most contradictory
> word, preserves contact—it is silence
> which isolates.
>
> —Thomas Mann, *The Magic Mountain*

Interest in language is not new, but the increasing *intensity* of concern with which man reflects upon language is new. This interest is tightly woven into the intricate design of our contemporary scene; the fabric of our age is to a large extent language-textured. Our investigations have dealt solely with philosophy's interest in language; we have dealt almost exclusively with Martin Heidegger's and Ludwig Wittgenstein's approaches to language. In so doing, we have attempted to show that both men, although belonging to different philosophical traditions, share in common several definite views, structurally speaking, about language, its cognitive limitations, its relation to the world, and even philosophy in general. The two men's writings are indeed methodologically congruent in many respects; their thoughts are upon many topics structurally complementary rather than contradictory.

Primarily, then, our methodological comparison shows a convergence between two contemporary men of different philosophical traditions. Secondarily, it has suggested a possible approach for genuine communication and mutual learning between all philosophical traditions—the analytical and phenomenological-existential in particular. This, once again, brings to the foreground the question of possible structural similarities between the entire analytic and phenomenolog-

ical-existential movements of contemporary philosophy. No
overall unification or comparison of the movements is intended within this book. Our prime concern is with the
writings of Heidegger and Wittgenstein, and the convergence
of structural techniques found pertains specifically to these
two men's works. However, insofar as the aspects of their
writings herein discussed as convergent reflect and manifest
aspects of the works of other men of a given tradition, then
our methodological remarks pertain to them also.

Mitigated through methodology, the "cold war" which
exists between the two major camps of contemporary philosophy is offered a possible avenue of resolution. A method
for mutual understanding and a means of common recognition are offered herein. A critical mode of alleviating the
state of mere "coexistence" between the two movements is
presented; that isolating silence so pervasively hovering over
today's philosophical scene has been pierced. This does not
mean that analysts must put on the face of existentialism or
existentialists the attitude of analysis. Differences—and significant differences—abound between the movements. Yet in-
terwoven among them are similarities; followers of either
movement are not *a priori* antithetical in philosophical out-
look to their respective counterparts. To maintain such an
absolute gulf is at best to limit philosophy's horizons and at
worst to deny philosophy its past heritage and its future dy-
nasty.

Forms of complementations do indeed exist between philosophers within today's major movements. To make this complementation evident, however, the initial problem is to find
that perspective from which to lay bare these similarities.
Otherwise, purely grammatical barriers would stymie investigations from the very beginning. Gilbert Ryle makes the comment:

> Sometimes thinkers are at loggerheads with one
> another, not because their propositions do conflict, but
> because their authors fancy that they conflict. They
> suppose themselves to be giving . . . rival answers to the
> same questions, when this is not necessarily the case.

They are then talking at cross-purposes with one another. It can be convenient to classify these cross-purposes by saying that the two sides are, at certain points, hinging their arguments upon concepts of different categories. . . .[1]

This indeed was our problem; given the different semantics of the two thinkers, how can one show that their conceptions are less dissimilar than appear at first glance. The key to our problem lay in the proper technique wherein the language (and thus the thoughts) of a philosopher of one tradition can be compared with that of another. It is sincerely believed that our study has found that technique whereby the structural elements of one philosophical position can be compared with those of another, despite the fact these positions belong to different traditions, use different semantical frameworks, and contentfully move in different directions. This technique we have called "methodology," and our actual, successful utilization of it upon Heidegger's and Wittgenstein's writings proves its workability. Our study opens the vistas to possible future methodological comparisons between, for example, W. V. Quine and Maurice Merleau-Ponty or between Bertrand Russell and Paul Ricoeur, to name but a few.

By suggesting such comparisons, we are not intimating any actual, direct influences of these thinkers, one upon the other. The same situation exists between Heidegger and Wittgenstein. Our methodological studies disclose a philosophical space wherein both men dwell, but it says nothing of a direct affectation between the two. Our study has revolved about structural similarities; the possibility of a direct acquaintance by either with the other's writings is simply not

1. Gilbert Ryle, *Dilemmas* (Cambridge: Cambridge University Press, 1954), p. 11. Knut Tranoy, whose views we presented in the introduction of this work, has remarked: ". . . the concepts and terminology of Thomas Aquinas and the medievals are on the whole foreign and neither immediately intelligible nor attractive to us [positivists]. But it has been shown that many of their points can be translated and made accessible to modern readers. If we tried to do this with the continentals, we might be able to see whether their points are points which we also make or would like to have made. . . ." (Tranoy, p. 157).

germane to methodology, although, admittedly, this is an intriguing notion which does invite investigation.

Wittgenstein was to some extent familiar with Heidegger's works and sympathetic toward them. Frank Waismann, in fact, reports of a get-together at Moritz Schlick's home on December 30, 1929, at which Wittgenstein "brushed aside as over-intellectualist the moral philosophy of G. E. Moore and his associates and spoke with genuine respect of Heidegger."[2] Wittgenstein is to have then stated:

> I can well understand what Heidegger means by *Sein* and *Angst*. Man has an impulse to run up against the boundaries of speech . . . which Kierkegaard himself already recognized and characterized very similarly (as running up against the paradoxical).[3]

Toulmin similarly informs us of Wittgenstein's sympathy toward Heidegger's writings:

> During the 1940's, for example, Wittgenstein himself drew a fairly sharp line between the professional, conceptual questions he discussed in his formal seminars and the deeper, more personal topics he used to raise during his "At Homes." The connections between the two aspects of his thought are fully apparent only now, thanks to the letters and memoir of Paul Engelmann. These resolve some residual puzzles within his formal philosophical writings, and help one to understand his sympathy for men like Kierkegaard, Heidegger, and St. Augustine—a sympathy which would have been surprising in the anti-metaphysical, positivistic "L.W." of popular reputation.[4]

Turning to the possibility of Heidegger's actual acquaintance with Wittgenstein's writings, we find less evidence to support such an acquaintance. Only recently in *Heraklit* has

---

2. Frank Waismann, quoted by Toulmin, p. 63.
3. Wittgenstein, quoted by Toulmin, p. 63.
4. Toulmin, p. 60.

Heidegger spoken of Wittgenstein.[5] Prior to that text Heidegger does not mention Wittgenstein; no indication of familiarity exists, to the best of this author's research, in Heidegger's earlier works. However, Heidegger's earlier works and his formal philosophical training do show an acquaintance with Frege's *Philosophy of Arithmetic* and Russell and Whitehead's *Principia Mathematica,* two works which had a profound influence upon Wittgenstein's thought.[6]

Again, such influences or lack thereof are really inconsequential to our studies. It would be mistaken to think that such a direct acquaintance is a presupposition to this work or an inferential goal thereto. Likewise, it would be an empty criticism of this work to assume that we are proposing methodology as the *only* way of relating divergent philosophies or to think we view it as the *best* such way. Neither is our intention. Methodology is offered as a possible—one among many —way of bridging the philosophical gaps which exist among existentialist-phenomenologists, analysts and representatives of other schools of thought.

A value of our method, however, is that it offers the possibility of a complex and in-depth study, unavailable to someone who approaches the texts immediately or at face value. Any commentator, for example, who tackles the two philosophers head on without first specifying a special methodological approach discovers that—although his study may be quite respectable—the accessible themes of comparison are limited both in scope and significance; the themes discovered as coincident within the two thinkers' works would be extrinsic or peripheral to their specific philosophical systems.[7] On the other hand, a commentator who attempts a comparison of notions more central to the systems, without first explicating a specific methodological viewpoint which would take account also of the radical differences between the two

---

5. Cf., Martin Heidegger and Eugene Fink, *Heraklit* (Frankfurt am Main: V. Klostermann, 1970), p. 30.

6. Cf., Borgmann, pp. 139-41.

7. Cf., Karsten Harries, "Wittgenstein and Heidegger: The Relationship of the Philosopher to Language," *Journal of Value Inquiry,* II (Winter, 1968), pp. 281-91.

men's thoughts, ends with a comparison of words, that is
one which superficially looks accurate, but which on closer
analysis shows the two thinkers more diverse in perspective
than anything else.[8] Looking over our preceding nine chapters, we can summarize our major methodological findings by
the following thirteen points, none of which could be ascer-
tained without some form of pre-structured approach to the
texts. The two philosophers maintain:

1. Philosophy is not a science.
2. Philosophy is distinguished from science both in its
   subject matter and its method.
3. The method of philosophy is purely descriptive.
4. Meaning, or significance, is contextually determined.
5. The traditional property theory of meaning, or significance, is stricken from a position of primary philosophical significance.
6. Representational language and the world are relationally structured.
7. The structures of representational language and of
   the world are reciprocally grounded.
8. The structures of language and of the world are operationally determined.
9. The structures of language and of the world are pragmatically determined.
10. The structures of language and of the world are man-
    centered.
11. The language of philosophy is not representational.
12. The language of metaphysics, or ontology, is not rep-
    resentational.
13. The logical structure of the language of metaphysics,
    or ontology, is akin to that of poetry.

We should, at this point, reiterate our remark in the
introduction of this book; namely: All these points of methodological congruence between Heidegger's and Wittgenstein's writings should not be interpreted to mean that an

---

8. Cf., I. Horgby, "The Double Awareness in Heidegger and Wittgenstein," *Inquiry*, II (Winter, 1959), pp. 235-64.

overall methodological similarity can be blanketed over the two men's works. Such would be an oversimplification of the matter at hand. Many aspects of Heidegger's and Wittgenstein's writings are either structurally unrelatable or in plain opposition; the themes which we have discussed and compared were carefully selected.

This selectivity, however, should not be viewed as a lessening of or a disintegration of the potential of our findings. I say this for two reasons:

1. To have believed at the very outset of our investigations that the philosophies of Heidegger and Wittgenstein were *in toto* structurally congruent is too naive. Both men cover a wide variety of topics, and the probability that their viewpoints are in all instances congruent is infinitesimal, if not for all practical purposes nil. If Heidegger's points of view differ on some issues from his fellow existentialists' and Wittgenstein's from his fellow analysts'—how could one expect such an all-encompassing convergence between the two philosophers' views!

2. The elements of convergence which we have discussed cohere into a unity. The elements are not diverse and scattered, but form a cohesion among themselves, interlacing into a definite pattern. Given the remarks on the method of philosophy and its relation to the sciences, the rest of our exposition deals solely with the structures of representational language and of the world, with their relationships, and with resulting comments on the language of ontology.

Despite these encouraging signs we would not wish to create a *false optimism*. For Heidegger, the primary given is the world; language is understood through this given. Wittgenstein—with his own linguistic Copernican revolution—has turned Heidegger upside down. For Wittgenstein, the primary given is language; the world is known through language. Essentially, Heidegger's analysis is of ontology; Wittgenstein's, is of logic. This constitutes the basic opposition between Hei-

degger and Wittgenstein, and no methodological analysis can
reconcile it.

These differences must be both recognized and emphasized
to put our study in a balanced perspective. Methodology concerns itself only with the ways philosophers proceed. It does
not take into consideration their presuppositions, goals, or
philosophical bent. Two philosophers' techniques within a
specific frame of reference can be methodologically congruent,
yet all the other constituent facets of their thoughts different.
Methodological analysis cannot reconcile these differences, it
can only acknowledge them as such. Nevertheless, these differences should not be blown out of proportion, with the
result that our studies be judged as insignificant. Susanne K.
Langer makes the interesting comment:

> Every age [and movement] in the history of philosophy
> has its own preoccupation. Its problems are peculiar to
> it. . . . If we look back on the slow formation and ac-
> cumulation of doctrines which mark that history, we may
> see certain *groupings* of ideas within it, not by subject
> matter, but by a subtler common factor which may be
> called their "technique." It is the mode of handling
> problems, rather than what they are about, that assigns
> them to an age.[9]

If we assume Ms. Langer's point of view, the meaning
and importance of this work is brought to the foreground.
If we, as she suggests, group ideas not by content but by technique and if it is this technique which assigns to them their
proper places in philosophy, then our methodological investigations show Heidegger and Wittgenstein within a common
stream of philosophical discourse. Indeed, then, our study is
significant. Looking at the history of philosophy, methodology creates a different way of examining past inquiry. Within
the present philosophical scene, it provides a fresh mode of
grouping thoughts, a way which assigns a common denomi-
nator to today's predominant thinking. Our study has
shown a point of view from which the writings of two thinkers

---

9. Susanne K. Langer, *Philosophy in a New Key*, p. 3.

from radically different traditions can be compared and found to be on a common ground. Looking to the future, methodology encouragingly extends the possibility of a genuine interchange in areas of philosophy previously isolated and unrelated; it is a potential key to future philosophical studies and a possible avenue toward a richer, fuller philosophical destiny.

SELECTED BIBLIOGRAPHY

*Principal Works of Martin Heidegger
and Ludwig Wittgenstein*

Heidegger, Martin. *Being and Time.* Translated by John Macquarrie and Edward Robinson. New York and Evanston: Harper & Row, Publishers, 1962.

————. *Discourse on Thinking.* Translated by John M. Anderson and E. Hans Freund with an introduction by John M. Anderson. New York: Harper & Row, Publishers, 1966.

————. *Einführung in Die Metaphysik.* Tübingen: Max Niemeyer, 1953.

————. *Erläuterungen zu Hölderlins Dichtung.* Frankfurt am Main: V. Klostermann, 1951.

————. *Essays in Metaphysics: Identity and Difference.* Translated by Kurt F. Leidecker. New York: Philosophical Library, 1960.

————. *Existence and Being.* Introduction by Werner Brock. Chicago: Henry Regnery Company, 1949.

————. *Gelassenheit.* Pfullingen: Neske, 1959.

————. *German Existentialism.* Translated by Dagobert D. Runes. New York: Philosophical Library, 1965.

————*Holzwege.* Frankfurt am Main: V. Klostermann, 1950.

————. *An Introduction to Metaphysics.* Translated by Ralph Manheim. Garden City, New York: Doubleday & Company, Inc., 1961.

————. *Kant and the Problem of Metaphysics.* Translated by James S. Churchill. Bloomington: Indiana University Press, 1962.

————. "Letter on Humanism," *Philosophy in the Twentieth Century,* Vol. III. Edited by William Barrett and Henry D. Aiken. New York: Random House, 1962. 270-302.

————. *On the Way to Language.* Translated by Peter D. Hertz. New York: Harper & Row, 1971.

————. *Platons Lehre von der Wahrheit.* Bern: Francke, 1954.

————. *Poetry, Language, Thought.* Translations and Introduction by Albert Hofstadter. New York: Harper & Row, 1971.

————. "The Problem of a Non-Objectifying Thinking and Speaking in Contemporary Theology," *Philosophy and Religion: Some Contemporary Perspectives,* edited by Jerry H. Gill. Minneapolis, Minn.: Burgess Publishing Company, 1968.

————. *The Question of Being.* Translated with an introduction by William Kluback and Jean T. Wilde. New York: Twayne Publishers Inc., 1958.

————. *Sein und Zeit.* Tübingen: M. Niemeyer, 1949.

————. *Unterwegs zur Sprache.* Pfullingen: Neske, 1959.

————. *Vom Wesen der Wahrheit.* Frankfurt am Main: Vittorio Klostermann, 1943.

————. *Vorträge und Aufsätze.* Pfullingen: Neske, 1954.

————. *Was heisst Denken?* Tübingen: Max Niemeyer, 1954.

————. *Was ist Metaphysik?* Frankfurt am Main: Vittorio Klostermann, 1943.

————. "The Way Back into the Ground of Metaphysics," *Existentialism from Dostoyevsky to Sartre.* Edited by Walter Kaufmann. Cleveland and New York: The World Publishing Company, 1956. 206-21.

————. *What is Philosophy?* Translated with an introduction by William Kluback and Jean T. Wilde. New Haven, Conn.: College & University Press, 1956.

————. *What is a Thing?* Translated by W. B. Barton, Jr. and V. Deutsch. Chicago: Henry Regnery Company, 1967.

————. "Zeit und Sein," in *L'Endurance de la pensée. Pour saluer Jean Beaufret.* Edited by René Char. Paris: Editions Plon, 1968.

Wittgenstein, Ludwig. *The Blue and Brown Books.* New York: Harper & Row, Publishers, 1958.

————. *Lectures & Conversations on Aesthetics, Psychology and Religious Belief.* Edited by Cyril Barrett. Oxford: Basil Blackwell, 1966.

————. *Notebooks 1914-1916.* Edited by G. H. von Wright and G. E. M. Anscombe with an English translation by G. E. M. Anscombe. Oxford: Basil Blackwell, 1961.

————. *On Certainty.* Edited by G. E. M. Anscombe and G. H. von Wright, translated by Denis Paul and G. E. M. Anscombe. Oxford: Basil Blackwell, 1969.

————. *Philosophical Investigations.* Translated by G. E. M. Anscombe. New York: The Macmillan Company, 1953.

————. *Philosophische Bemerkungen.* Edited by Rush Rhees. Oxford: Basil Blackwell, 1965.

————. *Remarks on the Foundations of Mathematics.* Edited by G. H. von Wright, R. Rhees, and G. E. M. Anscombe, and translated by G. E. M. Anscombe. Oxford: Basil Blackwell, 1956.

————. *Tractatus Logico-Philosophicus.* Translated by D. F. Pears & B. F. McGuinness with an introduction by Bertrand Russell. London: Routledge & Kegan Paul Ltd., 1961.

————. *Zettel.* Edited by G. E. M. Anscombe and G. H. von Wright. Translated by G. E. M. Anscombe. Berkeley and Los Angeles: University of California Press, 1967.

Related Materials

Books

Allemann, Beda. *Hölderlin et Heidegger recherche de la relation entre poésie et pensée.* Translated by François Fédier. Paris: Presses universitaires de France, 1959.

Ambrose, Alice. *Essays in Analysis.* London: Allen & Unwin, 1966.

Anscombe, G. E. M. *An Introduction to Wittgenstein's 'Tractatus.'* New York: Harper & Row, Publishers, 1959.

Barrett, William. *What is Existentialism?* New York: Grove Press, Inc., 1964.

Biemel, Walter. *Le concept de monde chez Heidegger.* Louvain: E. Nauwelaerts, 1950.

Black, Max. *A Companion to Wittgenstein's 'Tractatus.'* Ithaca, New York: Cornell University Press, 1964.

———— (ed.). *The Importance of Language.* Englewood Cliffs, New Jersey: Prentice-Hall, Inc., 1962.

————. *Language and Philosophy: Studies in Method.* Ithaca, New York: Cornell University Press, 1949.

Blackham, H. J. *Six Existentialist Thinkers.* New York and Evanston: Harper & Row, Publishers, 1959.

Bochénski, I. M. *The Methods of Contemporary Thought*. Dordrecht, Holland: D. Reidel Publishing Company, 1965.

Bock, Irmgard. *Heideggers Sprachdenken*. Meisenheim am Glan: Anton Hain, 1966.

Bretschneider, Willy. *Sein und Wahrheit; Über die Zusammengehörigkeit von Sein und Wahrheit im Denken Martin Heideggers*. Meisenheim am Glan: A. Hain, 1965.

Buchler, Justus. *The Concept of Method*. New York: Columbia University Press, 1961.

Carnap, Rudolf. *The Logical Structure of the World, Pseudoproblems in Philosophy*. Translated by Rolf A. George. Berkeley and Los Angeles: University of California Press, 1967.

————. *The Logical Syntax of Language*. Translated by Amethe Smeaton. Paterson, New Jersey: Littlefield, Adams, & Co., 1959.

Chapelle, Albert. *L'ontologie phénoménologique de Heidegger*. Paris: Editions Universitaires, 1962.

Chappell, V. C. *Ordinary Language*. Englewood Cliffs, New Jersey: Prentice-Hall, 1964.

Charlesworth, Maxwell John. *Philosophy and Linguistic Analysis*. Pittsburgh, Pa.: Duquesne University, 1959.

Chase, Stuart. *Power of Words*. New York: Harcourt, Brace, and Company, 1954.

Collins, James. *The Existentialists*. Chicago: Henry Regnery Company, 1952.

Collingwood, R. G. *An Essay on Philosophical Method*. Oxford: Clarendon Press, 1933.

Corvez, Maurice. *La Philosophie de Heidegger*. Paris: Presses Universitaires de France, 1961.

Danto, Arthur C. *What Philosophy Is: A Guide to the Elements*. New York: Harper & Row, Publishers, 1968.

Descartes, René. *The Philosophical Works of Descartes*, I. Translated by Elizabeth L. Haldane and G. R. T. Ross. Cambridge: Cambridge University Press, 1967.

Ehrmann, Jacques (ed.). *Structuralism*. Garden City, New York: Doubleday, 1970.

Engelmann, Paul. *Letters from Ludwig Wittgenstein*. Translated by L. Furtmüller. Edited by B. F. McGuinness. New York: Horizon Press, 1968.

Erickson, Stephen A. *Language and Being: An Analytic Phenomenology.* New Haven and London: Yale University Press, 1970.

Fann, K. T. (ed.). *Ludwig Wittgenstein: The Man and His Philosophy.* New York: Dell, 1966.

Farber, Marvin. *Naturalism & Subjectivism.* Springfield, Illinois: Charles C. Thomas, 1959.

—————. *Phenomenology and Existence.* New York: Harper Torchbooks, 1967.

Favrholdt, David. *An Interpretation and Critique of Wittgenstein's 'Tractatus.'* Copenhagen: Munksgaard, 1964.

Feibleman, James. *Inside the Great Mirror.* The Hague: Martinus Hijhoff, 1958.

Findlay, John. *Language, Mind, and Value.* London: G. Allen & Unwin, 1963.

Fodor, Jerry A. and Katz, Jerrold J. (eds.). *The Structure of Language: Readings in the Philosophy of Language.* Englewood Cliffs, New Jersey: Prentice-Hall, Inc., 1964.

Friedlander, Paul. *Plato, An Introduction.* Translated by Hans Meyerhoff. New York and Evanston: Harper & Row, Publishers, 1958.

Gellner, Ernest. *Words and Things.* Boston: Beacon Press, 1960.

Gelven, Michael. *A Commentary on Heidegger's "Being and Time."* New York: Harper & Row, 1970.

Grene, Marjorie. *Martin Heidegger.* London: Bowes & Bowes, 1957.

Griffin, James. *Wittgenstein's Logical Atomism.* London: Oxford University Press, 1964.

Guilead, Reuben. *Etre et liberté; une étude sur le dernier Heidegger.* Louvain: Editions Nauwclaerts, 1965.

Hallett, Garth, S. J. *Wittgenstein's Definition of Meaning as Use.* New York: Fordham University Press, 1967.

Hartnack, Justus. *Wittgenstein and Modern Philosophy.* Translated by Maurice Cranston. New York: Doubleday & Company, 1965.

High, Dallas M. *Language, Persons, and Belief.* New York: Oxford University Press, 1967.

Hinners, Richard C. *Ideology and Analysis.* New York: Desclée De Brouwer, 1966.

Hoernlé, Reinhold Friedrich Alfred. *Studies in Philosophy.* Edited and with a memoir by Daniel S. Robinson. Cambridge: Harvard University Press, 1952.

Hollenbach, Johannes Michael. *Sein und Gewissen*. Baden-Baden: B. Grimm, 1954.

Kielkopf, Charles F. *Strict Finitism: An Examination of Ludwig Wittgenstein's "Remarks on the Foundations of Mathematics,"* The Hague: Mouton, 1970.

King, Magda. *Heidegger's Philosophy: A Guide to His Basic Thought*. New York: The Macmillan Company, 1964.

Knights, L. C. and Cottle, Basil (eds.) *Metaphor and Symbol*. London: Butterworths Scientific Publications, 1960.

Kockelmans, Joseph J. *A First Introduction to Husserl's Phenomenology*. Louvain: Duquesne University Press, 1967.

——. *Martin Heidegger: A First Introduction to His Philosophy*. Pittsburgh, Pa.: Duquesne University Press, 1965.

Kohl, Herbert. *The Age of Complexity*. New York: The New American Library, 1965.

Lane, Michael (ed.). *Structuralism: A Reader*. London: Jonathan Cape, 1970.

Langan, Thomas. *The Meaning of Heidegger, A Critical Study of an Existentialist Phenomenology*. New York and London: Columbia University Press, 1959.

Lévi-Strauss, Claude. *Structural Anthropology*. Translated by Claire Jacobson & Brooke G. Schoepf. Garden City, New York: Doubleday and Company, 1967.

Lewis, H. D. *Elusive Mind*. London: Allen & Unwin, 1969.

Locke, John. *An Essay Concerning Human Understanding*, ed. A. C. Fraser. New York: Dover, 1959.

Mace, C. A. (ed.). *British Philosophy in the Mid-Century*. London: George Allen and Unwin Ltd., 1966.

Macomber, William B. *The Anatomy of Disillusion: Martin Heidegger's Notion of Truth*. Evanston: Northwestern University Press, 1967.

Macquarrie, John. *Martin Heidegger*. London: Lutterworth Press, 1968.

——. *Twentieth-Century Religious Thought*. New York and Evanston: Harper & Row, Publishers, 1963.

Malcolm, Norman. *Ludwig Wittgenstein: A Memoir*. London: Oxford University Press, 1958.

Maslow, Alexander. *A Study in Wittgenstein's 'Tractatus.'* Berkeley and Los Angeles: University of California Press, 1961.

Mauro, Tullio de. *Ludwig Wittgenstein: His Place in the Development of Semantics.* Dordrecht, Holland: D. Reidel Publishing Company, 1967.

Molina, Fernando. *Existentialism as Philosophy.* Englewood Cliffs, New Jersey: Prentice-Hall, Inc., 1962.

Müller-Lauter, Wolfgang. *Möglichkeit und Wirklichkeit bei Martin Heidegger.* Berlin: De Gruyter, 1960.

Murdoch, Iris. *Sartre.* New Haven: Yale University Press, 1953.

Naess, Arne. *Four Modern Philosophers.* Chicago: University of Chicago Press, 1968.

Newell, R. W. *The Concept of Philosophy.* London: Methuen & Co. Ltd., 1967.

Ogden, C. K. and Richards, I. A. *The Meaning of Meaning.* New York: Harcourt Brace & World, Inc., 1923.

Pears, David. *Ludwig Wittgenstein.* New York: The Viking Press, 1969.

Piaget, Jean. *Structuralism.* Translated and edited by Chaninah Maschler. New York: Harper Torchbooks, 1971.

Pitcher, George. *The Philosophy of Wittgenstein.* Englewood Cliffs, New Jersey: Prentice-Hall, Inc., 1964.

Plochmann, George Kimball and Lawson, Jack B. *Terms in Their Propositional Contexts in Wittgenstein's 'Tractatus': An Index.* Carbondale: Southern Illinois University Press, 1962.

Pole, David. *The Later Philosophy of Wittgenstein.* London: The Athlone Press, 1958.

Rhees, Rush. *Discussions of Wittgenstein.* New York: Schocken Books, 1970.

Richardson, William J. *Heidegger, Through Phenomenology to Thought.* The Hague: Martinus Nijhoff, 1963.

Ruggiero, Guido de. *Existentialism.* New York: Social Science Publishers, 1948.

Russell, Bertrand. *An Outline of Philosophy.* London: George Allen & Unwin Ltd., 1927.

Sallis, John (ed.). *Heidegger and the Path of Thinking.* Pittsburgh, Pa.: Duquesne University Press, 1970.

Schmitt, Richard. *Martin Heidegger on Being Human.* New York: Random House, 1969.

Seidel, George Joseph. *Martin Heidegger and the Pre-Socratics: An Introduction to His Thought.* Lincoln: University of Nebraska Press, 1964.

Specht, Ernst Konrad. *Sprache und Sein.* Berlin: de Gruyter, 1967.

Stenius, Erik. *Wittgenstein's 'Tractatus': A Critical Exposition of its Main Lines of Thought.* Oxford: Basil Blackwell, 1964.

Thévenaz, Pierre. *What is Phenomenology?* Edited with an introduction by James M. Edie. Translated by James M. Edie, Charles Courtney, Paul Brockelman. Chicago: Quadrangle Books, Inc., 1962.

Tymieniecka, Anna-Teresa. *Phenomenology and Science, European Thought.* New York: The Noonday Press, 1962.

Urban, Wilbur M. *Language and Reality.* New York: Macmillan Company, 1951.

Urmson, James O. *Philosophical Analysis; Its Development Between the Two Wars.* Oxford: Clarendon Press, 1956.

Versényi, Laszlo. *Heidegger, Being and Truth.* New Haven: Yale University Press, 1965.

Vycinas, Vincent. *Earth and Gods: An Introduction to the Philosophy of Martin Heidegger.* The Hague: Martinus Nijhoff, 1961.

Waelhens, Alphonse de. *Chemins et impasses de l'ontologie Heideggerienne; à propos des Holzwege.* Louvain: E. Nauwelaerts, 1953.

—————. *La philosophie de Martin Heidegger.* Louvain: Institut supérieur de philosophie, 1942.

—————. *Phénoménologie et vérité; essai sur l'évolution de l'idée de vérité chez Husserl et Heidegger.* Paris: Presses universitaires de France, 1953.

Wahl, Jean A. *Mots, mythes, et réalité dans la philosophie de Heidegger.* Paris: Centre de Documentation Universitaire, 1961.

—————. *Vers la fin de l'ontologie; étude sur l'introduction dans la metaphysique par Heidegger.* Paris: Société d'édition d'enseignement supérieur, 1956.

Warnock, Geoffrey James. *English Philosophy Since 1900.* London: Oxford University Press, 1958.

Warnock, Mary. *Existentialist Ethics.* London: Macmillan Company, 1967.

Winch, Peter (ed.). *Studies in the Philosophy of Wittgenstein.* London: Routledge & Kegan Paul, 1969.

Wisdom, John. *Discovery and Paradox.* New York: Philosophical Library, 1965.

Wyschogrod, Michael. *Kierkegaard and Heidegger, The Ontologie of Existence.* London: Routledge and Kegan Paul, Ltd., 1954.

Articles and Chapters

Adkins, Arthur. "Heidegger and Language," *Philosophy,* XXXVII (July, 1962) , 229-37.

Albritton, Rogers. "On Wittgenstein's Use of the Term 'Criterion,'" *Wittgenstein, The Philosophical Investigations.* Edited by George Pitcher. Garden City, N.Y.: Doubleday, 1966. 231-50.

Alderman, Harold G. "Heidegger's Critique of Science," *The Personalist,* L (Fall, 1969) , 549-58.

————. "Heidegger: Necessity and Structure of the Question of Being," *Philosophy Today,* XIV (Summer, 1970) , 141-47.

————. "Heidegger: Technology as Phenomenon," *The Personalist,* LI (Fall, 1970) , 535-45.

Aldrich, Virgil C. "Art and the Human Form," *Journal of Aesthetics and Art Criticism,* XXIX (Spring, 1971) , 295-302.

Allaire, Edwin B. " 'Tractatus' 6. 3751," *Essays on Wittgenstein's 'Tractatus.'* Edited by Irving M. Copi and Robert W. Beard. New York: The Macmillan Company, 1966. 189-94.

————. "The 'Tractatus': Nominalistic or Realistic?" *Essays in Ontology,* I. The Hague: Martinus Nijhoff, 1963. 148-65.

Allers, Rudolf. "Heidegger on the Principle of Sufficient Reason," *Philosophy and Phenomenological Research,* XX (1960) , 365-73.

————. "The Meaning of Heidegger," *The New Scholasticism,* XXXVI (October, 1962) , 445-74.

Anderson, James F. "Bergson, Aquinas, and Heidegger on the Notion of Nothingness," *Proceedings of the American Catholic Philosophical Association,* XLI. Edited by George F. McLean and Valerie Voorhies. Washington, D.C.: The Catholic University of America, 1967. 143-48.

Anscombe, G. E. M. "Misinformation: What Wittgenstein Really Said," *Tablet,* CCIII (April 17, 1954) , 373.

————. "Mr. Copi on Objects, Properties, and Relations in the *Tractatus*," *Essays on Wittgenstein's 'Tractatus.'* Edited by Irving M. Copi and Robert W. Beard. New York: The Macmillan Company, 1966. 187-88.

Asborne, H. "Wittgenstein on Aesthetics," *British Journal on Aesthetics*, VI (October, 1966), 385-90.

Ayer, A. J. "The Genesis of Metaphysics," *Analysis*, I (May, 1934), 55-58.

Ballard, Edward G. "On the Pattern of Phenomenological Method," *Southern Journal of Philosophy*, VIII (Winter, 1970), 421-31.

Barrett, Cyril, Margaret Paton, and Harry Blocker. "Symposium, Wittgenstein and Problems of Objectivity in Aesthetics," *British Journal of Aesthetics*, VII (April, 1967), 158-74.

Bartky, S. L. "Heidegger's Philosophy of Art," *British Journal of Aesthetics*, IX (October, 1969), 353-71.

Beard, Robert W. "On the Independence of States of Affairs," *Australasian Journal of Philosophy*, XLVII (May, 1969), 65-68.

Behl, L. "Wittgenstein and Heidegger," *Duns Scotus Philosophical Association Convention Report*, XXVII (1963), 70-115.

Bergmann, Gustav. "The Glory and the Misery of Ludwig Wittgenstein," *Essays on Wittgenstein's 'Tractatus.'* Edited by Irving M. Copi and Robert W. Beard. New York: The Macmillan Company, 1966. 343-58.

Bernstein, Richard J. "Wittgenstein's Three Languages," *Essays on Wittgenstein's 'Tractatus.'* Edited by Irving M. Copi and Robert W. Beard. New York: The Macmillan Company, 1966. 231-48.

Bespaloff, R. "Lettre sur Heidegger à M. Daniel Halévy," *Revue Philosophique*, CXVI (November, 1933), 321-39.

Black, Max. "Dewey's Philosophy of Language," *Journal of Philosophy*, LIX (September 13, 1962), 505-22.

————. "Some Problems Connected with Language," *Essays on Wittgenstein's 'Tractatus.'* Edited by Irving M. Copi and Robert W. Beard. New York: The Macmillan Company, 1966. 95-114.

Bogen, James. "Was Wittgenstein a Psychologist?" *Inquiry*, VII (Winter, 1964), 374-78.

Borgmann, Albert. "Heidegger and Symbolic Logic," *Heidegger and the Quest for Truth*. Edited with an Introduction by Manfred S. Frings. Chicago: Quadrangle Books, 1968. 139-62.

————. "Language in Heidegger's Philosophy," *The Journal of Existentialism*, VII (Winter, 1966), 161-80.

————. "Philosophy and the Concern for Man," *Philosophy Today*, X (Winter, 1966), 236-46.

————. "The Transformation of Heidegger's Thought," *The Personalist*, XLVII (October, 1966), 484-99.

Bossart, William H. "Heidegger's Theory of Art," *The Journal of Aesthetics and Art Criticism*, XXVII (Fall, 1968), 57-66.

Bouwsma, O. K. "The Blue Book," *The Journal of Philosophy*, LVIII (March 16, 1961), 141-61.

Breton, S. "Ontology and Ontologies: The Contemporary Situation," *International Philosophical Quaterly*, III (Summer, 1963), 339-69.

Bridgman, Percy. "The Nature of Some of our Physical Concepts," *British Journal of the Philosophy of Science*, I (February, 1951), 257-72.

————. "Operational Analysis," *Philosophy of Science*, V (April, 1938), 114-31.

————. "Philosophical Implications of Physics," *American Academy of Arts and Sciences Proceedings*, III (January, 1950), 1-6.

Brunner, August. "Das Ding dingt Welt," *Stimmen der Zeit*, CLVI (April, 1955), 69-72.

————. "Die Rückkehr ins Sein," *Stimmen der Zeit*, CLIV September, 1954), 401-13.

————. "Holzwege," *Stimmen der Zeit*, CXLVI (June 1950), 226-28.

Brunton, J. A. "The Absolute Existence of Unthinking Things," *Philosophy*, XLV (October, 1970), 267-80.

Campbell, R. "Sur l'Introduction à la Métaphysique de Heidegger," *Etudes Germaniques*, XV (Janvier-Mars, 1960), 29-43.

Caracciolo, Albert. "Evento e linguaggio in un recente scritto di Martin Heidegger," *Giornale Critico della Filosofia Italiana*, XL (1961), 222-46.

Carnap, Rudolf. "Empiricism, Semantics, and Ontology," *Semantics and the Philosophy of Language.* Edited by Leonard Linsky. Urbana: University of Illinois Press, 1952. 208-30.

————. "Uberwindung der Metaphysik durch logische Analyse der Sprache," *Erkenntnis,* II (1932).

Cavell, Stanley. "The Availability of Wittgenstein's Later Philosophy," *Wittgenstein, The Philosophical Investigations.* Edited by George Pitcher. Garden City, New York: Doubleday & Company, Inc., 1966. 151-85.

Chihara, Charles S. "Mathematical Discovery and Concept Formation," *The Philosophical Review,* LXXXII (January, 1963), 17-34.

Chihara, Charles S. and Fodor, J. A. "Operationalism and Ordinary Language: A Critique of Wittgenstein," *Wittgenstein, The Philosophical Investigations.* Edited by George Pitcher. Garden City, New York: Doubleday & Company, Inc., 1966. 384-419.

Chiodi, Pietro. "Essere e linguaggio in Heidegger e nel 'Tractatus' di Wittgenstein," *Rivista di Filosofia,* XLVI (1955), 170-91.

Coleman, Francis J. "A Critical Examination of Wittgenstein's Aesthetics," *Philosophy,* V (October, 1968), 257-66.

Copi, Irving M. "Objects, Properties, and Relations in the 'Tractatus,'" *Essays on Wittgenstein's 'Tractatus.'* Edited by Irving M. Copi and Robert W. Beard. New York: The Macmillan Company, 1966. 167-86.

Coreth, E. "Auf der Spur der entflohenen Götter?" *Wort und Wahrheit,* IX (February, 1954), 107-16.

————. "Für und wider Heidegger," *Wort und Wahrheit,* VIII (September, 1953), 694-96.

Cowan, Joseph L. "Wittgenstein's Philosophy of Logic," *The Philosophical Review,* LXX (July, 1961), 362-72.

Daitz, E. "The Picture Theory of Meaning," *Essays in Conceptual Analysis.* Edited by Anthony Flew. London: Macmillan & Co. Ltd., 1956. 53-74.

Daly, C. B. "New Light on Wittgenstein," *Philosophical Studies,* X (1960), 5-49 and XI (1961), 28-62.

Delman, Ilham. "Wittgenstein, Philosophy and Logic," *Analysis,* XXXI (December, 1970), 33-42.

Demske, James M. "Heidegger's Quadrate and Revelation of Being," *Philosophy Today,* VII (Winter, 1963), 245-57.

DeWaelhens, Alphonse. "Reflections on the Development of Heidegger: Apropos of a Recent Book," *International Philosophical Quarterly*, V (September, 1965), 475-502.

Dondeyne, A. "La différence ontologique chez M. Heidegger," *Revue Philosophique de Louvain*, LVI (February and May, 1958), 35-62, 251-93.

Douglas, George H. "Heidegger's Notion of Poetic Truth," *The Personalist*, XLVII (October, 1966), 500-08.

Erickson, Stephen A. "Worlds and World Views," *Man and World*, II (May, 1969), 228-47.

Evans, Ellis. "About 'aRb'," *Essays on Wittgenstein's 'Tractatus.'* Edited by Irving M. Copi and Robert W. Beard. New York: The Macmillan Company, 1966. 195-200.

————. "'Tractatus' 3.1432," *Essays on Wittgenstein's 'Tractatus.'* Edited by Irving M. Copi and Robert W. Beard. New York: The Macmillan Company, 1966. 133-36.

Fabro, Cornelio. "The Problem of Being and the Destiny of Man," *International Philosophical Quarterly*, I (September, 1961), 407-36.

Fairbanks, Matthew. "Wittgenstein and James," *The New Scholasticism*, XL (July, 1966), 331-40.

Farber, Marvin. "Phenomenological Tendency," *Journal of Philosophy*, LIX (August 2, 1962), 429-39.

Farrell, B. A. "An Appraisal of Therapeutic Positivism," *Mind*, LV (January, 1946), 279-89.

Feyerabend, Paul. "Wittgenstein's *Philosophical Investigations,*" *Wittgenstein, The Philosophical Investigations*. Edited by George Pitcher. Garden City, New York: Doubleday & Company, Inc., 1966. 104-50.

Fontaine-De Visscher L. "La pensée du langage chez Heidegger," *Revue Philosophique de Louvan*, LXIV (1966), 224-62.

Forest, A. "L'Existence selon Bergson," *Archives de Philosophie*, XVII (Paris, 1947).

Garulli, Enrico. "L'Unité idéale de la pensée heideggérienne, d'après un essai de Gianni Vattimo," *Revue de Metaphysique et de Morale*, LXXII (Janvier-Mars, 1967), 116-25.

Garvin, Lucius. "The Paradox of Aesthetic Meaning," *Reflections on Art*. Edited by Susanne K. Langer. Baltimore: The Johns Hopkins Press, 1958. 62-70.

Gerber, Rudolph. "Focal Points in Recent Heidegger Scholar-
      ship," *The New Scholasticism*, XLII (Fall, 1968), 561-
      77.
————. "Thinking and Thanking Being," *The Modern
      Schoolman*, XLIV (March, 1967), 205-22.
Gill, Jerry H. "Wittgenstein and the Function of Philosophy,"
      Metaphilosophy, II (April, 1971), 137-49.
————. "Wittgenstein's Concept of Truth," *International
      Philosophical Quarterly*, VI (March, 1966), 45-70.
Glicksman, Marjorie. "A Note on the Philosophy of Heidegger,"
      Journal of Philosophy, XXXV (February 17, 1938), 93-
      103.
Goff, Robert Allen. "Wittgenstein's Tools and Heidegger's Im-
      plements," *Man and World*, I (August, 1968), 447-62.
Gray, J. Glenn. "Heidegger 'Evaluates' Nietzsche," *Journal of
      the History of Ideas*, XIV (April, 1953), 304-09.
————. "Heidegger's 'Being.'" *Journal of Philosophy*, XLIX
      (June 5, 1952), 415-24.
————. "Poets and Thinkers: Their Kindred Roles in the
      Philosophy of Martin Heidegger," *On Understanding
      Violence Philosophically*. New York: Harper R Row,
      1970.
Gregory, T. S. "Mere Words? Wittgenstein and the Care of Lan-
      guage," *Tablet*, CCIII (April 10, 1954), 343-45.
Grene, Marjorie. "Heidegger: Philosopher and Prophet," *Twen-
      tieth Century*, CLXIV (December, 1958), 545-55.
Gruender, D. "Wittgenstein on Explanation and Description,"
      Journal of Philosophy, LIX (September 13, 1962), 523-
      30.
Gründer, Karlfried. "Heidegger's Critique of Science in its His-
      torical Background," *Philosophy Today*, VII (Spring,
      1963), 15-32.
Hahn, Hans. "Conventionalism," *Logic and Philosophy*. Edited
      by Gary Iseminger. New York: Appleton, Century-
      Crofts, 1969. 45-51.
Hall, R. L. "Heidegger and the Space of Art," *Journal of Ex-
      istentialism*, VIII (Fall, 1967), 91-108.
Hallie, P. P. "Wittgenstein's Grammatical-Empirical Distinc-
      tion," *Journal of Philosophy*, LX (September 26,
      1963), 565-78.
Hamburg, Carl H. "Whereof One Cannot Speak," *Journal of
      Philosophy*, L (October 22, 1953), 662-64.

Hamrick, William S. "Heidegger and the Objectivity of Aesthetic Truth," *Journal of Value Inquiry*, V (Spring, 1971), 120-30.

Hannay, Alastair. "Was Wittgenstein a Psychologist?" *Inquiry*, VII (Winter, 1964), 379-86.

Harries, Karsten. "Heidegger and Hölderlin: The Limits of Language," *Personalist*, XLIV (1963), 5-23.

————. "Wittgenstein and Heidegger: The Relationship of the Philosopher to Language," *Journal of Value Inquiry*, II (Winter, 1968), 281-91.

Hinners, Richard C. "Being and God in Heidegger's Philosophy," *Proceedings of the American Catholic Philosophical Association*, XXXI. Edited by Charles A. Hart. Washington, D.C.: The Catholic University of America, 1957. 157-62.

Horgby, Ingvar. "The Double Awareness in Heidegger and Wittgenstein," *Inquiry*, II (Winter, 1959), 235-64.

Hunter, J. F. M. "Forms of Life in Wittgenstein's *Philosophical Investigations*," *American Philosophical Quarterly*, V (October, 1968), 233-43.

Hyppolite, Jean. "Du bergsonisme à l'existentialisme," *Mercure de France*, CCCVI (July, 1949), 403-16.

————. "Un texte de Heidegger: note en manière d'introduction," *Mercure de France*, CCCXVII (March, 1953), 385-91.

Ihde, Don. "Language and Two Phenomenologies," *Southern Journal of Philosophy*, VIII (Winter, 1970), 399-408.

Jakobson, Roman. "Les lois phoniques du langage enfantin et leur place dans la phonologie générale," *Principles de Phonologie*, par N. S. Troubetzkoy. Traduits par J. Cantineau. Paris: Editions Klincksieck, 1964. 367-80.

James, William. "Preface to 'Meaning of Truth,'" *Pragmatism and Four Essays from 'The Meaning of Truth.'* Cleveland: World Publishing Co., 1955. 195-203.

Janik, A. "Schopenhauer and the Early Wittgenstein," *Philosophical Studies*, XV (1966), 76-95.

Kenny, Anthony. "Aquinas and Wittgenstein," *Downside Review*, LXXVII (Fall, 1959), 217-35.

Keyt, David. "Wittgenstein's Notion of an Object," *Essays on Wittgenstein's 'Tractatus.'* Edited by Irving M. Copi and Robert W. Beard. New York: The Macmillan Company, 1966. 289-304.

————. "Wittgenstein's Picture Theory of Language," *Essays on Wittgenstein's 'Tractatus.'* Edited by Irving M. Copi and Robert W. Beard. New York: The Macmillan Company, 1966. 377-92.

Khatchadourian, Haig. "Metaphor," *British Journal of Aesthetics,* VIII, No. 3 (July, 1968), 227-43.

King, Magda. "Heidegger Reinterpreted: On L. Versényi's 'Heidegger, Being, and Truth,'" *International Philosophical Quarterly,* VI September, 1966), 483-92.

Klenk, G. F. "Das sein und die dichter; zu Heideggers Hölderlinauslegung," *Stimmen der Zeit,* CXLVIII (September, 1951), 419-28.

Kockelmans, Joseph J. "Heidegger on Time and Being," *Southern Journal of Philosophy,* VIII (Winter, 1970), 319-40.

Kuntz, Paul G. "Order in Language, Phenomena, and Reality: Notes on Linguistic Analysis, Phenomenology, and Metaphysics," *Monist,* XLIX (January, 1965), 107-36.

Langan, Thomas D. "Heidegger in France," *The Modern Schoolman,* XXXIII (January, 1956), 114-18.

————. "Is Heidegger a Nihilist?" *Thomist,* XXI (July, 1958), 302-319.

————. "Transcendence in the Philosophy of Heidegger," *The New Scholasticism,* XXXII (January, 1958), 45-60.

Levi, Albert W. "Wittgenstein as Dialectician," *The Journal of Philosophy,* LXI (February 13, 1964), 127-38.

Levin, David Michael. "More Aspects to the Concept of Aesthetic Aspects," *Journal of Philosophy,* LXV (August, 1968), 483-89.

Levinas, E. "Martin Heidegger et l'ontologie," *Revue Philosophique,* CXIII (May, 1932), 395-431.

Levison, A. B. "Wittgenstein and Logical Necessity," *Inquiry,* VII (Winter, 1964), 367-73.

Lindstrom, P. "On Relations Between Structures," *Theoria,* XXXII (1966), 172-85.

Lingis, A. F. "On the Essence of Technique," *Heidegger and the Quest for Truth.* Edited with an Introduction by Manfred S. Frings. Chicago: Quadrangle Books, 1968. 126-38.

Linsky, Leonard. "Wittgenstein on Language and Some Problems of Philosophy," *The Journal of Philosophy,* LIV (May 9, 1957), 285-92.

Mace, C. A. "Metaphysics and Emotive Language," *Analysis*, II (October, 1934), 6-10.

—————. "On the Directedness of Aesthetic Response," *British Journal of Aesthetics*, VIII (April, 1968), 155-60.

—————. "Representation and Expression," *Analysis*, I (March, 1934), 33-38.

Magnus, Bernd. "Heidegger and the Truth of Being," *International Philosophical Quarterly*, IV (May, 1964), 245-64.

Malcolm, Norman. "Wittgenstein's 'Philosophische Bemerkungen,'" *The Philosophical Review*, LXXVI (April, 1967), 220-29.

Mandelbaum, Maurice. "Family Resemblances and Generalization Concerning the Arts," *American Philosophical Quarterly*, II (1965), 219-28.

McCormick, Peter. "Heidegger's Meditation on the Word," *Philosophical Studies* (Ireland), XVIII (1969), 76-99.

—————. "Interpreting the Later Heidegger," *Philosophical Studies* (Ireland), XIX (1970), 83-101.

McGuinness, B. F. "Philosophy of Science in the *Tractatus*," *Revue Internationale de Philosophie*, XXIII (1969), 155-66.

Miller, J. "Wittgenstein's *Weltanschauung*," *Philosophical Studies*, XIII (1964), 127-40.

Moeller, Joseph. "Nietzsche and Metaphysics," *Philosophy Today*, VIII (Summer, 1964), 118-32.

Moore, G. E. "Wittgenstein's Lectures in 1930-33," *Mind*, LXIII (Jan., 1954), 1-15; LXIII (July, 1954), 289-316; and LXIV (Jan., 1955), 1-27.

Morot-Sir, Edouard. "What Bergson Means to us Today," *The Bergsonian Heritage*. Edited by T. Hanna. New York: Columbia University Press, 1962.

Morrison, James C. "Heidegger's Criticism of Wittgenstein's Conception of Truth," *Man and World*, II (November, 1969), 551-73.

Moser, Simon. "Toward a Metaphysics of Technology," *Philosophy Today*, XV (Summer, 1971), 129-56.

Munson, Thomas N. "Heidegger's Recent Thought on Language," *Philosophy and Phenomenological Research*, XXI (March, 1961), 361-72.

McGuinness, B. F. "Pictures and Forms in Wittgenstein's *Tractatus*," *Filosofia e Simbolismo, Archivio di Filosofia*. Edited by E. Castelli. Nos. 2-3 (Rome, 1956), 207-28.

Nagel, Ernest. "Impressions and Appraisals of Analytic Philosophy in Europe," *The Journal of Philosophy*, XXXII (January 2, 1936), 5-23.

————. "Logic Without Ontology," *Readings in Philosophical Analysis*. Edited by Herbert Feigl and Wilfrid Sellars. New York: Appleton-Century-Crofts, Inc., 1949. 191-210.

————. "Operational Analysis as an Instrument for the Critique of Linguistic Signs," *The Journal of Philosophy*, XXXIX (March 26, 1942), 177-89.

Nielsen, H. A. "Wittgenstein on Language," *Philosophical Studies*, VIII (1958), 115-21.

O'Brien, Dennis. "The Unity of Wittgenstein's Thought," *International Philosophical Quarterly*, VI (March, 1966), 45-70.

Pap, Arthur. "Laws of Logic," *Logic and Philosophy*. Edited by Gary Iseminger. New York: Appleton-Century-Crofts, Inc., 1969. 52-59.

Pears, D. F. "Universals," *Logic and Language*. Edited with an Introduction by Anthony Flew. New York: Doubleday & Company, 1965. 267-80.

Piguet, J.-Claude. "Les oeuvres récentes de Martin Heidegger," *Revue de Théologie et de Philosophie*, VIII (1958), 283-90.

Pöggeler, Otto. "Heidegger Today," *Southern Journal of Philosophy*, VIII (Winter, 1970), 273-308.

Poole, Roger C. "Structuralism and Phenomenology: A Literary Approach," *Journal of the British Society for Phenomenology*, II (March, 1971), 3-16.

Proctor, George L. "Scientific Laws and Scientific Objects in the 'Tractatus,'" *Essays on Wittgenstein's 'Tractatus.'* Edited by Irving M. Copi and Robert W. Beard. New York: The Macmillan Company, 1966. 201-16.

Prufer, Thomas. "Martin Heidegger: Dasein and the Ontological Status of the Speaker of Philosophical Discourse," *Twentieth-Century Thinkers*. Edited with an Introduction by John K. Ryan. Staten Island, New York: Abba House, 1964. 159-74.

Quinton, A. M. "Excerpt from 'Contemporary British Philosophy,'" *Wittgenstein, The Philosophical Investigations*. Edited by George Pitcher. Garden City, New York: Doubleday & Company, Inc., 1966. 1-21.

Ramsey, Frank P. "Review of 'Tractatus,'" *Essays on Wittgenstein's 'Tractatus.'* Edited by Irving M. Copi and Robert W. Beard. New York: The Macmillan Company, 1966. 9-24.

Rhees, Rush. "The *Tractatus* Seeds of Some Misunderstandings," *The Philosophical Review,* LXXII (April, 1963), 213-20.

Richardson, William J. "Heidegger and Aristotle," *The Heythrop Journal,* V (January, 1964), 58-64.

————. "Heidegger and Plato," *The Heythrop Journal,* IV (July, 1963), 273-79.

————. "Heidegger and the Origin of Language," *International Philosophical Quarterly,* II (Summer, 1962), 404-16.

————. "Heidegger and the Problem of Thought," *Revue Philosophique de Louvain,* LX (February, 1962), 58-78.

————. "Heidegger's Critique of Science," *The New Scholasticism,* XLII (Autumn, 1968), 511-36.

Ricoeur, Paul. "Structure-Word-Event," *Philosophy Today,* XII (Summer, 1968), 114-29.

Rohatyn, Dennis Anthony. "A Note on Heidegger and Wittgenstein," *Philosophy Today,* XV (Spring, 1971), 69-71.

Ryle, Gilbert. "Martin Heidegger: *Sein und Zeit,*" *Journal of The British Society of Phenomenology,* I (October, 1970), 3-13.

————. "Review of *Sein und Zeit,*" *Mind,* XXXVIII (1929), 355-70.

————. "Systematically Misleading Expressions," *Logic and Language.* Edited with Introductions by Anthony Flew. New York: Doubleday & Co., 1965. 13-39.

Sellars, Wilfrid. "Naming and Saying," *Essays on Wittgenstein's 'Tractatus.'* Edited by Irving M. Copi and Robert W. Beard, New York: The Macmillan Company, 1966. 249-70.

Schmitt, Richard. "Heidegger's Analysis of 'Tool,'" *The Monist,* XL (January, 1965), 70-86.

————. "Phenomenology and Metaphysics," *The Journal of Philosophy,* LIX (August 2, 1962), 421-28.

Schweppenhäuser, Hermann. "Studien über die Heideggersche Sprachtheorie," *Archiv für Philosophie,* VII (1957), 279-324 und VIII (1958), 116-44.

Schwyzer, H. R. G. "Wittgenstein's Picture-Theory of Language," *Essays on Wittgenstein's 'Tractatus.'* Edited by Irving M. Copi and Robert W. Beard. New York: The Macmillan Company, 1966. 271-288.

Shwayder, David S. "Gegenstände and Other Matters," *Inquiry,* VII (Winter, 1964), 387-413.

Smiley, P. "Importance of Wittgenstein," *Tablet,* CCIII (January 30, 1954), 116.

Smith, F. Joseph. "Heidegger's Kant Interpretation," *Philosophy Today,* XI (Winter, 1967), 257-64.

Sokolowski, Robert. "Ludwig Wittgenstein: Philosophy as Linguistic Analysis," *Twentieth-Century Thinkers.* Edited with an Introduction by John K. Ryan. Staten Island, New York: Abba House, 1964. 175-204.

Spiegelberg, Herbert. "The Puzzle of Wittgenstein's *Phänomenologie* (1929-?) ," *American Philosophical Quarterly,* V (October, 1968), 244-56.

Stebbing, Lizzie S. "Logical Positivism and Analysis," *Proceedings of the British Academy,* XIX (1933), 53-87.

Steiner, George. "The Retreat from the Word," *Kenyon Review,* XXIII (Spring, 1961), 187-216.

Stock, George J. "The Being of the Work of Art in Heidegger," *Philosophy Today,* XIII (Fall, 1969), 159-73.

Strasser, Stephen. "The Concept of Dread in the Philosophy of Heidegger," *The Modern Schoolman,* XXXV (November, 1957), 1-20.

Strawson, P. F. "Review of Wittgenstein's 'Philosophical Investigations,' " *Wittgenstein, The Philosophical Investigations.* Edited by George Pitcher. Garden City, New York: Doubleday & Company, Inc., 1966. 22-64.

Stroud, Barry. "Wittgenstein and Logical Necessity," *The Review of Metaphysics,* LXXIV (October, 1965), 504-18.

Struthl, Karsten J. "Language Games and Forms of Life," *Journal of Critical Analysis,* II (July, 1970), 25-30.

Suszko, Roman. "Ontology in the 'Tractatus' of Ludwig Wittgenstein," *Notre Dame Journal of Formal Logic,* IX (January, 1968), 7-33.

Thomson, Judith Jarvis. "Professor Stenius on the 'Tractatus,' " *Essays on Wittgenstein's 'Tractatus.'* Edited by Irving M. Copi and Robert W. Beard. New York: The Macmillan Company, 1966. 217-230.

Toulmin, Stephen. "Ludwig Wittgenstein," *Encounter,* XXXII (January, 1969), 58-71.

Tranoy, Knut E. "Contemporary Philosophy—Analytic and Continental," *Philosophy Today,* VIII (Fall, 1964), 155-68.

Trethowan, I. "Importance of Wittgenstein, A Reply," *Tablet,* CCIII (February 6, 1954), 140.

Turnbull, Robert G. "Linguistic Analysis, Phenomenology and the Problem of Philosophy: An Essay in Metaphilosophy," *The Monist,* XLIX (January, 1965), 44-69.

Vail, Loy M. "Heidegger's Conception of Philosophy," *The New Scholasticism,* XLII (Fall, 1968), 470-96.

Van de Water, Lambert. "The Work of Art, Man, and Being: A Heideggerian Theme," *International Philosophy Quarterly,* IX (June, 1969), 214-35.

Versényi, Laszlo. "The Quarrel Between Philosophy and Poetry," *Philosophical Forum* (Boston), II (Winter, 1970), 200-12.

Von Wright, Georg Henrik. "The Wittgenstein Papers," *Philosophical Review,* LXXVIII (October, 1969), 483-503.

Wald, Henri. "Structure, Structural, Structuralism," *Diogenes,* LXVI (Summer, 1969), 15-24.

Walsh, John H. "Heidegger's Understanding of No-Thingness," *Cross-Currents,* XIII (Summer, 1963), 305-23.

Weissman, David. "Ontology in the *Tractatus,*" *Philosophy and Phenomenological Research,* XXVII (June, 1967), 475-501.

Weitz, Morris. "The Role of Theory in Aesthetics," *Journal of Aesthetics and Art Criticism,* XV (1956), 27-35.

Werkmeister, W. H. "Heidegger and the Poets," *The Personalist,* LII (Winter, 1971), 5-22.

White, David A. "Revealment: A Meeting of Extremes in Aesthetics," *Journal of Aesthetics and Art Criticism,* XXVIII (Summer, 1970), 515-20.

———. "World and Earth in Heidegger's Aesthetics," *Philosophy Today,* XII (Winter, 1968), 282-86.

Wienpahl, Paul. "Wittgenstein and the Naming Relation," *Inquiry,* VII (Winter, 1964), 329-47.

Wild, John. "English Version of Martin Heidegger's *Being and Time,*" *Review of Metaphysics,* XVI (December, 1962), 296-315. "Discussion," XVI (June, 1963), 780-85 and XVII (December, 1963), 296-300.

————. "The Exploration of the Life-World," *Proceedings and Addresses of the American Philosophical Association*, XXXIV (October, 1961), 116.

————. "Is There a World of Ordinary Language?" *Philosophical Review*. LXVII (October, 1958), 460-76.

————. "The Philosophy of Martin Heidegger," *The Journal of Philosophy*, LX (October 24, 1963), 664-77.

Will, Frederic. "Heidegger and the Gods of Poetry," *The Personalist*, XLIII (1962), 157-67.

Williams, C. J. "The Marriage of Aquinas and Wittgenstein," *Downside Review*, LXXVIII (Summer, 1960), 203-12.

Wilson, Fred. "The World and Reality in the *Tractatus*," *The Southern Journal of Philosophy*, V (Winter, 1967), 253-60.

Wolgast, Elizabeth H. "Wittgenstein and Criteria," *Inquiry*, VII (Winter, 1964), 348-66.

Wolter, Allan B., O.F.M. "The Unspeakable Philosophy of the Late Wittgenstein," *Proceedings of the American Catholic Philosophical Association*, XXXIV. Edited by Leo A. Foley. Washington, D.C.: The Catholic University of America, 1960. 168-93.

Zemach, Eddy. "Wittgenstein's Philosophy of the Mystical," *The Review of Metaphysics*, XVIII (September, 1964), 38-57.

Zink, Sidney. "The Poetic Organism," *Journal of Philosophy*, XLII (August 2, 1945), 421-33.

INDEX